AF714875

Criminal Law in Italy

Criminal Law in Italy

Third Edition

Astolfo Di Amato

Contributing Author
Federica Fucito

This book was originally published as a monograph in the International Encyclopaedia of Laws/Criminal Law.

General Editors: Roger Blanpain, Frank Hendrickx
Volume Editors: Frank Verbruggen, Vanessa Franssen

Wolters Kluwer

Published by:
Kluwer Law International B.V.
PO Box 316
2400 AH Alphen aan den Rijn
The Netherlands
Website: www.wklawbusiness.com

Sold and distributed in North, Central and South America by:
Wolters Kluwer Legal & Regulatory U.S.
7201 McKinney Circle
Frederick, MD 21704
United States of America
Email: customer.service@wolterskluwer.com

Sold and distributed in all other countries by:
Turpin Distribution Services Ltd.
Stratton Business Park
Pegasus Drive, Biggleswade
Bedfordshire SG18 8TQ
United Kingdom
Email: kluwerlaw@turpin-distribution.com

DISCLAIMER: The material in this volume is in the nature of general comment only. It is not offered as advice on any particular matter and should not be taken as such. The editor and the contributing authors expressly disclaim all liability to any person with regard to anything done or omitted to be done, and with respect to the consequences of anything done or omitted to be done wholly or partly in reliance upon the whole or any part of the contents of this volume. No reader should act or refrain from acting on the basis of any matter contained in this volume without first obtaining professional advice regarding the particular facts and circumstances at issue. Any and all opinions expressed herein are those of the particular author and are not necessarily those of the editor or publisher of this volume.

ISBN 978-90-411-6944-0

This title is available on www.kluwerlawonline.com

© 2016, Kluwer Law International BV, The Netherlands

All rights reserved. No part of this publication may be reproduced, stored in a retrieval system, or transmitted in any form or by any means, electronic, mechanical, photocopying, recording, or otherwise, without the prior written permission of the publisher.

Permission to use this content must be obtained from the copyright owner. Please apply to: Permissions Department, Wolters Kluwer Legal & Regulatory U.S., 76 Ninth Avenue, 7th Floor, New York, NY 10011-5201, USA. Website: www.wklawbusiness.com

The Authors

Professor Avvocato Astolfo Di Amato is the founder and senior partner of Astolfo Di Amato & Associati – Avvocati. He began his career as a Judge (1965–1984); and was elected directly by his fellow magistrates to serve as a member of the Superior Council of the Magistracy (*Consiglio Superiore della Magistratura*) (1978–1982). Professor Di Amato recently retired as a full Professor of Corporate and Business Law at the University of Naples (1985–2012), where he also taught International Trade Law (2004–2012) and Telecommunications and Media Law (2000–2012). Previously, he was a professor of Business Crime Law at LUISS University in Rome (1972–1985).

Professor Di Amato served on both the Ministry of Justice's Committee for the Reform of the Italian Law on Business Crimes (1991) and the Ministry's Committee for the Reform of the Italian Law on Tax Crimes (1993). He was also a member of the Ministry of European Policies Committee on Culture (Theatre and Movies).

A prolific writer, Professor Di Amato has authored twenty-nine books and over 200 articles on the topics of business law and criminal law. He also serves as Director of *Trattato di Diritto Penale dell'Impresa* (Treatise on the Law on Business Crime); Director of the Law Reviews *Diritto ed Economia dei Mezzi di Comunicazione* (Law and Economics of Communications and Media) (2002 to date) and *Diritto dell'Impresa* (Business Law) (1988 to date).

Contributing Author

Avv. Federica Fucito is a partner of Astolfo Di Amato & Associati. She received her law degree from the University of Naples and a Masters in European and Transnational Law from the University of Trento (2004). Avv. Fucito was responsible for *Rassegna di Diritto Comunitario* of the law review *Diritto & Guistizia* (Law and Justice) and also a collaborator with the law review *Rivista di Diritto delle Relazioni Industriali* (The Review of Industrial Relations Law). She is also a collaborator with the newspaper, *Il Denaro*, and a member of the Editorial Committee of *Rivista di Diritto ed Economia dello Sport* (The Review of Sports Law and

Economics). Avv. Fucito is a contributor to the *Trattato di Diritto Penale dell'Impresa* (Treaty on Business Crime Law) and an academic collaborator in commercial law at the University of Salerno. Her practice areas include business crimes and investigations, corporate and commercial, European law, environmental, litigation and dispute resolution.

Table of Contents

List of Abbreviations

Art.	Article
Arts	Articles
Cass.	Court of Cassation
Cass. Pen. Mass. Ann.	*Cassazione Penale Massimario Annotato*
CCP	Code of Criminal Procedure
CAT	Convention against Torture and Other Cruel Inhuman or Degrading Treatment or Punishment
CED	Convention for the Protection of All Persons from Enforced Disappearance
CEDAW	Convention on the Elimination of All Forms of Discrimination against Women
CFSP	Common Foreign and Security Policy
CISA	Convention Implementing the Schengen Agreement Mutual Assistance in Judicial Matters
CPD	Convention on the Rights of Persons with Disabilities
CRC	Convention on the Rights of the Child
CST	Civil Service Tribunal
ECHR	European Convention on Human Rights
ECSC	European Coal and Steel Community
EURATOM	European Atomic Energy Community
Foro it.	*Foro Italiano*
Giur. Cost.	*Giurisprudenza Costituzionale*
Giur. It.	*Giurisprudenza Italiana*
Giust. Pen.	*Giustizia Penale*
ICCPR	International Covenant on Civil and Political Rights
CERD	International Convention on the Elimination of All Forms of Racial Discrimination

List of Abbreviations

CESCR	International Covenant on Economic, Social and Cultural Rights
JHA	Justice and Home Affairs
NGO	Non-Governmental Organization
Nuov. Dig. It	*Nuovissimo Digesto Italiano*
OECD	Organisation for Economic Co-operation and Development
PC	Penal Code
Mass. Pen.	*Massimario Penale*
Mass. Dec. Pen.	*Massimario Decisioni Penali*
para.	Paragraph
paras	Paragraphs
PJCC	Police and Judicial Cooperation in Criminal Matters
Riv. Pen.	*Rivista Penale*
TEC	Treaty establishing the European Community
TEU	Treaty on European Union
TFEU	Treaty on the Functioning of the European Union
VOM	victim-offender mediation

1–2

General Introduction

§1. The General Background of the Country

I. Geography and Climate

1. Italy (officially the Italian Republic), is a country located in Southern Europe and a peninsula extending into the Mediterranean Sea (i.e., the Ligurian, Tyrrhenian, Ionian and the Adriatic Seas), covering a total of 301,333 square kilometres and having a wide variety of geographical, climatic, and cultural environments. The country's sole land border consists of the Alpine arc stretching from the Varo River (at Nice) and the Vrata Pass (at Fiume). Italy borders France to the west, Switzerland and Austria to the north, and Slovenia to the east. In addition to its continental territory, Italy includes a number of islands, including Sicily and Sardinia and many minor archipelagos. However, the country's territory does not encompass all the areas within its physical reach (e.g., Malta, Corsica, Istria, the Republic of San Marino and Vatican City).

The Italian territory is predominantly high altitude area with 39.7% hilly terrain and 38.7% mountainous, while only 21.6% is plain land.

Italy is frequently viewed as being separated into three parts: northern Italy (Piedmont, Valle d'Aosta, Lombardy, Trentino-Alto Adige, the Veneto, Friuli-Venezia Giulia, Liguria and Emilia Romagna); central Italy (Tuscany, Umbria, Latium, the Marches, the Abruzzi, Molise and Sardinia); and southern Italy (Campania, Puglia, Basilicata, Calabria and Sicily).

The country is divided into twenty administrative regions – five of which have special autonomous status which enables them to enact legislation on certain specific local matters (Valle d'Aosta, Trentino-Alto Adige, Friuli-Venezia Giulia, Sicily and Sardinia). Italy is further divided into 110 provinces and 8,047 municipalities. The regions vary significantly with respect to surface area, density of population, economic activities, and resources, as well as customs, traditions and dialects.

2. The climate varies greatly throughout Italy. In the north, there is an alpine climate, with a high average rainfall and temperatures ranging broadly throughout the day. The Padana Plain has a sub-continental climate (cold winters, hot summers, mist and fog), while the centre and south have hot summers and mild winters. As a result of the barrier created by the Apennine chain, there is significantly more rainfall on the Tyrrhenian side than on the Adriatic coast. Italy's islands enjoy a Mediterranean climate and significant natural beauty.

II. Population

3. As of January 2015, Italy's population exceeded 60.7 million, with over 70% living in cities and towns and the remainder living in rural areas. The population is concentrated in northern Italy, on the west coast around Rome and Naples, and in the Po Valley. Rome is the largest of Italy's cities (approximately 2.7 million inhabitants).[1]

The number of foreigners living in Italy has increased substantially over the past twenty years to around 5.3 million. There are now approximately eight foreigners for every 100 Italian nationals. The majority of foreigners live in northern and central Italy (6.4%–7.2% foreigners), as compared to the south, where the number is dramatically less (1.6%).[2]

III. Economy

4. Based on nominal Gross Domestic Product (GDP) calculations, Italy was ranked as the ninth largest economy in the world in 2013, behind the United States (US), China, Japan, Germany, France, the United Kingdom (UK) Brazil and Russia,[3] and the fourth largest in Europe. According to the World Trade Organization (WTO), in 2012, Italy was the world's ninth largest exporter of manufactured goods.[4] The primary Italian stock exchange, *Borsa Italiana*, is based in Milan.

5. Italy's economy remains split into two parts: the developed industrial north, dominated by private companies, and the less developed agriculture-based south. There is also a significant 'underground' component of the economy that is not included in the official data, but which the Ministry of Finance has considered as approximately one-sixth of the official GDP and responsible for significant tax evasion. There is a current push within the government to bring this sector into the mainstream economy.

The country must import the vast majority of the raw materials needed by industry and more than 81% of its energy requirements.[5]

At times, Italy's economic performance has been lacklustre as compared to its European Union (EU) partners, including at the present moment, as the global economic and the European sovereign-debt crisis has profoundly impacted the country. Since 2007, Italy's public debt has continued to increase and its structural political obstacles have made the country susceptible to intense scrutiny from the financial markets. In late 2011 and in 2012, a series of austerity measures were enacted with the objective of balancing the budget and reducing the debt. The measures included

---

1. ISTAT – Resident Population as of 1 Jan. 2015, http://www.istat.it/it/popolazione (Accessed 4 Jun. 2015).
2. ISTAT – Resident Foreign Population as of 1 Jan. 2015, http://www.istat.it/it/popolazione (Accessed 4 Jun. 2015).
3. Intl. Monetary Fund, *World Economic Outlook Database*. www.imf.org (Accessed 15 Jun. 2013).
4. World Trade Org. *International Trade Statistics*, www.wto.org (Accessed 15 Jun. 2013).
5. *Eurostat – Energy Dependence Table*, http://epp.eurostat.ec.europa.eu/tgm/table.do?tab=table&init=1&language= en&pcode=tsdcc310&plugin=1 (Accessed 15 Jun. 2013).

reforms of the public administration and pension systems, as well as a 1% increase in value added tax. Unfortunately, these measures did little to alleviate the situation: economic growth continues to stagnate and unemployment – particularly among youth – continues to rise. According to the OECD and others, Italy's struggles will continue in the near future.

Italy joined the Euro from its introduction in 1999.

6. A substantial base of small and medium-size companies is Italy's primary economic strength, while the country has fewer multinational corporations than other economies of comparable size. In recent years, the government has made efforts to overhaul the country's company laws and enact measures to encourage mergers and corporate growth. Among these laws was Legislative Decree No. 231 of 8 June 2001, which introduced into Italian law the principle of administrative liability of corporate bodies for crimes committed by persons working within the organization.

7. Italy is well known for its work in the fields of fashion (Versace, Armani, Valentino, Prada, Luxottica), the food industry (Barilla, Martini & Rossi), luxury vehicles (Ferrari, Maserati, Lamborghini) and yachts (Ferretti, Azimut). The country also has significant exports in firearms, motor vehicles, chemicals, petrochemicals and electric goods, and aerospace and defence technology. As competition from China and other Asian economies increases due to the reduced labour costs of these countries, Italy is responding by focusing on technology and its cultural tradition of high quality products.

Tourism also contributes significantly to the Italian economy.

IV. Political System and Administrative Structure

8. Italy is a democratic republic[6] and a member of the G8, the EU (a founding member – having signed the Treaty of Rome in 1957), the Council of Europe, the Western EU, and the Central European Initiative.

A. The Founding Principles of the Italian Constitution

9. Italy's Constitution came into effect in 1948 and provides for a bicameral Parliament (*Parlamento*),[7] an independent Judiciary[8] and an Executive branch. The Parliament consists of the Chamber of Deputies (*Camera dei Deputati*) and the Senate (*Senato della Repubblica*),[9] while the Executive branch is comprised of a Council of Ministers (cabinet) (*Consiglio dei Ministri*), led by the Prime Minister

6. Constitution Art. 1.
7. Constitution Art. 55.
8. Constitution Art. 104.
9. Constitution Art. 55.

(*Presidente del Consiglio dei Ministri*).[10] In order to preside, a government must have the consent of both chambers.[11]

A unique aspect of Italy's Parliament is that the upper chamber, the Senate has almost the same level of power as the Chamber of Deputies, the lower chamber. Apart from the budget, either House may introduce any law, however both chambers must approve the law in the same form.[12] This might however change in the future (*infra*, paragraph 16).

Under Article 3 of the Constitution, the Republic recognizes and guarantees inalienable human rights and equal social dignity to its citizens, without discrimination with regards to gender, race, language, religion, political opinion, personal or social conditions. While the Republic is one and indivisible, it nevertheless recognizes and promotes local autonomies.[13] The State and Catholic Church are independent and have their own laws, and their relations are regulated by the Lateran Pacts[14] and successive treaties.

Italian law conforms to the rules of generally recognized international law.[15]

B. *Political System*

10. In addition to its bicameral Parliament, Italy is led by a Prime Minister and a President. The President of the Republic is the head of State and represents national unity,[16] while the Prime Minister is the head of government.

1. The President of the Republic

11. The President of the Republic is elected by an electoral college consisting of the Parliament in joint session and fifty-eight regional delegates, with one delegate from Valle d'Aosta and three delegates from the other regions. The term of the position of President is seven years.[17] The election takes place by secret ballot and requires a two-thirds majority; after a third ballot, an absolute majority is sufficient.[18] Any citizen over the age of 50 can be elected President of the Republic.[19] If the head of State is unable to perform his duties, the President of the Senate acts

10. Constitution Art. 92.
11. BBC News, *Q&A: Italian Elections*, http://www.bbc.co.uk/news/world-europe-21327856 (Accessed June 2015).
12. *Ibid.*
13. Constitution Art. 4.
14. Constitution Art. 7.
15. Constitution Art. 10.
16. Constitution Art. 87.
17. Constitution Arts 83 and 85. In April 2013, the electoral college consisted of 1,007 voting members: four senators for life, 58 regional delegates and 945 members of the Parliament. http://www.internazionale.it/news/da-sapere/2013/04/17/come-si-elegge-il-presidente-della-repubblica/ (Accessed June 2015).
18. Constitution Art. 83.
19. Constitution Art. 84.

in his place.[20] The President's duties include: calling for new parliamentary elections, promulgating laws, commanding the armed forces, presiding over the Supreme Defence Council, declaring a state of war deliberated by the Houses of Parliament, presiding over the Supreme Council of the Magistracy, granting clemency and commuting sentences, appointing the Prime Minister and, upon the recommendation of this latter, the other ministers.[21] No act of the President of the Republic is valid in the absence of the counter-signature of the proposing ministers, who assume responsibility for it.[22]

2. The Prime Minister

12. The Prime Minister is appointed and then presents himself before the Parliament in order to obtain its vote of confidence. Each legislature lasts five years,[23] unless the Houses are prematurely dissolved (prerogative of the President of the Republic). In post-war history, this has occurred in 1972, 1976, 1979, 1983, 1994, 1996, 2008 and 2012. The electoral system is proportional, with majority orientation.

3. The Parliament

13. The Parliament is composed of 630 deputies and 315 senators.[24] The President also can appoint '*senators for life*' (*senatore a vita*) '*for outstanding patriotic merits in the social, scientific, artistic or literary field*'. In addition, former Presidents of the Republic are ex officio senators for life. The Constitution limits the number of senators for life to five, excluding former presidents.[25] These senators have the same rights as their elected colleagues; however, the mandate of senators for life is indefinite.

The Parliament has legislative power, and the President of the Republic promulgates laws within one month of their being passed.[26] The Parliament delegates the issuance of decrees to the government, and these have the value of regular laws. In extraordinarily urgent cases, the government, on its own initiative, adopts decree laws that become immediately effective but which must be converted into law within sixty days by the Chamber and Senate. If not timely converted, the decree law expires.

The current Parliament was voted in with the elections of 23 and 24 February 2013.

---

20. Constitution Art. 86.
21. Constitution Art. 87.
22. Constitution Art. 89.
23. Constitution Art. 60.
24. Constitution Arts 56 and 57.
25. Constitution Art. 59.
26. Constitution Art. 73.

14. In recent years, Italy's political system has been in a state of upheaval. In April 2008, Silvio Berlusconi was elected Prime Minister during early parliamentary elections, which were held following the collapse of Prime Minister Romano Prodi's centre-left coalition government, after it lost confidence vote in the Italian Senate. In November 2011, Berlusconi resigned after a dramatic increase in Italy's cost of borrowing and pressure from the other Eurozone leaders for Italy to have more credible leadership. To fill the vacancy, economist and former European Commissioner, Mario Monti was appointed by President Giorgio Napolitano and charged with creating a technocratic government.[27] A little over one year later, in December 2012, Berlusconi's coalition withdrew their support for the Monti government, and he announced that he intended to run again for Prime Minister. Without this support, the government lacked the backing to go forward, thus Monti resigned, President Napolitano dissolved Parliament and new elections were set for February 2013.

15. For the 2013 elections, the majority of the various political parties grouped into one of three coalitions: the Centre-Right Coalition, led by Silvio Berlusconi; the 'Italy, The Common Good' coalition led by Democratic Party Secretary Pier Luigi Bersani; and the 'With Monti for Italy' headed by Mario Monti. The election resulted in a three-way split between the Centre-Left, Centre-Right, and the 'Five Star Movement', an independent party headed by comedian-turned-politician Beppe Grillo, which ended up taking 25.5% in the Chamber of Deputies – making it the largest single party – and 23.8% in the Senate.[28,29]

For two months after the February elections, the parties could not agree on the formation of the new government. The matter was further complicated by the need for Parliament to elect a new President of the Republic. Following the rejecting of several candidates, the incumbent President, 87-year-old Giorgio Napolitano, was persuaded to postpone retirement and stand again. Eventually a Centre-Left and Centre-Right coalition was formed, and Napolitano appointed Enrico Letta of the Democratic Party to form a new government.[30] However, the government headed by Letta only lasted until February 2014, when it was replaced by a new government headed by Matteo Renzi, due to internal strife in the Democratic Party. This situation seemed undemocratic because the new government was formed only on the basis of agreements reached in the Parliament and the people could not express themselves on the new alliances.

27. BBC News, *Has Mario Monti Done a Good Job?* http://www.bbc.co.uk/news/business-20766952 (Accessed 21 Jun. 2013).
28. BBC News, *Q&A: Italian Elections*, http://www.bbc.co.uk/news/world-europe-21327856 (Accessed June 2015).
29. *Ibid.* Under the existing Italian electoral system, for the Chamber of Deputies, the coalition or grouping which wins the most votes is guaranteed at least 340 of the Chamber's 630 seats, while for the Senate the winning majority is determined by regional results, with the winning coalition receiving 55% of the seats for in their respective region.
30. *Ibid.*

16. A new election law was enacted (Law No. 52/2015, informally named Italicum) to prevent situations such as the February 2013 election, which failed to produce a clear winner and resulted in a two-month political deadlock. This law, which will enter into force only in 2016, regards only the Deputy Chamber. The new electoral law includes a majority premium for the list that obtains 40% of the vote and, in the event that no list obtains this percentage, provides a runoff between the two lists that have obtained the most votes. Proposals are also being put forward to change the current requirement that all laws must be approved by both the Chamber of Deputies and the Senate, and to reform the current configuration of Parliament so that the Chamber of Deputies (lower House) would remain the main political chamber, while the Senate would become an assembly of the Italian regions.

Table 1 Composition of the Italian Parliament after the 2013 Elections

	Senate	
Coalition	*Party*	*Seats*
Italy Common Good *(Italia. Bene Comune)*	The Democratic Party (*Partito Democratico*)	111
	Left Ecology Freedom (*Sinistra Ecologia Libertà*)	7
	South Tyrolean People's Party (*Südtiroler Volkspartei)*	2
	Trentino Tyrolean Autonomous Party	1
	Union for *Trentino* (Unione per Trentino)	1
	The Megaphone (*Il Megafono*)	1
Subtotal		123
Centre-Right Coalition	People of Freedom (*Il Popolo della Libertà*)	98
	Northern League (*Lega Nord)*	18
	Great South (*Grande Sud*)	1
Subtotal		117
	Five Star Movement (*Movimento 5 Stelle Grillo*)	54
	With Monti for Italy (*Con Monti per Italia*)	19
	Associative Movement of Italians Abroad *Movimento Associativo Italiani*	1
	Aosta Valley List *Valle d'Aosta*	1
Total		**315**
Senators for Life		3

	Chamber of Deputies	
Coalition	*Party*	*Seats*
Italy Common Good (*Italia. Bene Comune*)	The Democratic Party (*Partito Democratico*)	297
	Left Ecology Freedom (*Sinistra Ecologia Libertà*)	37
	Union of the Centre (*Unione di Centro*),	6
	South Tyrolean People's Party (*Südtiroler Volkspartei*)	5
Subtotal		345 (54.8%)
Centre-Right Coalition	People of Freedom (*Il Popolo della Libertà*)	98
	Northern League (*Lega Nord*)	18
	Brothers of Italy	9
Subtotal		125 (19.8%)
	Five Star Movement (*Movimento 5 Stelle Grillo*)	109 (17.3%)
With Monti for Italy (*Con Monti per Italia*)	Civic Choice	37
	Union of the Centre (*Unione di Centro*),	8
	With Monti for Italy (*Con Monti per Italia*)	2
Subtotal		47 (7.6%)
	Associative Movement of Italians Abroad (*Movimento Associativo Italiani*)	2
	South American Union of Italian Emigrants (*Unione Sudamericana Emigranti Italia*)	1
	Aosta Valley List *Valle d'Aosta*	1
Total		**630**

4. The Government

17. The government is the expression of the Parliamentary majority, i.e., the coalition of parties that have obtained the greatest number of seats in Parliament.

The President of the Republic formally appoints the Prime Minister who proposes ministers.[31] The ministers are individually responsible for the acts of their ministries and jointly responsible for those deliberated by the Council of Ministers.[32] The Prime Minister and the other ministers take an oath before the President of the Republic before undertaking their duties.[33] The government must have the confidence of both Houses and each House gives or revokes its consent through motions, which are argued and then submitted to roll call vote.[34] The government can introduce its legislative bills to the Parliament. The Prime Minister can issue directives on specific matters or decrees. Each minister has the power to sign ministerial decrees within the context of his or her specific authority.

Figure 1 Summary of Italian Political and Judicial System

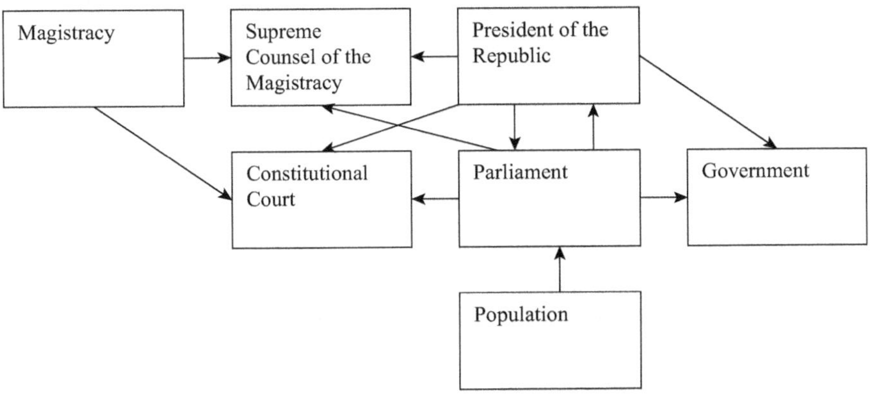

C. *Judicial System*

1. Overview

18. The Italian judicial system originates from Roman law as modified by the Napoleonic Code and subsequent statutes. The principles of the system are set forth in Articles 101–113 of the Constitution. The system is regulated by Royal Decree 12 of 30 January 1941, better known as the Law on the Judiciary (*Ordinamento Giudiziario*). However, over time, this text has undergone numerous changes.

Two provisions particularly important to the judicial system are Royal Decree No. 511 of 31 May 1946, which guarantees the independence and impartiality of judges,[35] and Law No. 195 of 24 March 1958, which regulates the Superior Council of the Magistracy (*Consiglio Superiore della Magistratura*).

31. Constitution Art. 92.
32. Constitution Art. 95.
33. Constitution Art. 93.
34. Constitution Art. 94.
35. Constitution Art. 104.

19. The Superior Council of the Magistracy is a self-governing body and finds its basis in Article 104 of the Constitution. The Council issues orders for the appointment, assignment, transfer and promotion of magistrates (judges and public prosecutors) and has responsibility for disciplinary actions. The Council is comprised of the President of the Republic (acting as its chairman), the first President of the Court of Cassation, and the Court of Cassation's public prosecutor (all these being members by right). In addition, there are twenty-four elected members holding office for four years: two-thirds are ordinary magistrates (elected by the Magistracy) and one-third are full professors in law and lawyers with fifteen years of practice (so-called lay members elected by Parliament in joint session).[36]

20. In Italy, judges and prosecutors are not elected, but stipend public officers are selected through national public competitions.[37] A Masters of Law degree is required and once selected, judges must go through a period of training as *uditori giudiziari* – under the tutelage of experienced judges – before serving on the bench.

21. In terms of structure, the Italian justice system is based on the principle of a 'three tier justice system', thus allowing the appeal of cases decided at first instance. A further appeal may be made to the Court of Cassation; however, at this final stage, the Court only considers the legality of the proceedings conducted in the lower courts and respect of substantial rules.

22. The administration of justice is divided between ordinary and special judicial functions. The ordinary judicial function is exercised by ordinary judges and is concerned with those areas of law not reserved to the jurisdiction of special courts or judges.

The Italian judicial system was reformed by Legislative Decree No. 51 of 19 February 1998 (Legislative Decree No. 51/98).[38] Among other things, Legislative Decree 51/98 established the new single judge of first instance. As a result, the Ordinary Court exercises its functions, both in civil and criminal law, sitting as a single judge or as a collegiate body (three-judge panel), depending on the matter.

Moreover, Legislative Decree No. 51/98 essentially abolished the position of *Pretore* (a magistrate with limited jurisdiction in criminal and civil matters), transferring the latter's civil and criminal jurisdiction to the Ordinary Courts (*tribunali*), with the exception of those matters which are the jurisdiction of justices of the peace.

23. Of utmost importance is the distinction between extraordinary judges (created after the fact that must be judged), special judges (those external to the court system), and ordinary judges (those who are part of the court system). The Italian Constitution allows the institution of specialized judges (e.g., the Juvenile Court), while it forbids the creation of extraordinary judges. The institution of special

36. Constitution Art. 104.
37. Constitution Art. 106.
38. Legislative Decree No. 51 of 19 Feb. 1998, in effect as of 2 Jun. 1999.

judges is generally forbidden as well, except for the Military Court for crimes carried out by armed forces personnel, while charges against the President of the Republic related to high treason and attempt against the Constitution are within the competence of the Constitutional Court (Articles 103 and 134 of the Italian Constitution).

24. Generally, special jurisdiction is divided into four areas: administrative, military, accounting and taxation. Administrative jurisdiction is exercised by the Regional Administrative Courts (*Tribunali Amministrativi Regionali – TAR*) and the Council of State (*Consiglio di Stato*). Public accountancy matters are the jurisdiction of the State Auditors' Department (*Corte dei Conti*), while the Provincial Fiscal Commissions (*Commissioni Tributarie Provinciali*) and District Fiscal Commissions (*Commissioni Tributarie Distrettuali*) have jurisdiction over tax matters. Military jurisdiction is exercised by the Military Courts (*Tribunali Militari*), Military Appeal Courts (*Corti Militari di Appello*) and the Military Surveillance Courts (*Tribunali Militari di Sorveglianza*) for military offences committed by members of the Armed Forces.

25. Within the Italian court systems, there are also specialized courts for minors (i.e., *Tribunale per i Minorenni*). This is a specialized judicial body and functions as a Court of First Instance for all criminal, civil and administrative matters concerning minors under the age of 18. The Juvenile Court was established in 1934, and each court is comprised of two professional judges (one qualified for the Court of Appeal – who acts as the chairman – and one judge qualified for the Ordinary Court) and two lay judges (one male and one female), who are expert in human sciences. There are twenty-nine Juvenile Courts set up under each of the twenty-six appeal courts and three detached appeal court divisions. The Court's geographical area of jurisdiction is the same as that for the Courts of Appeal or as that section of the Court of Appeal where the Juvenile Court is based.

The Juvenile Court has jurisdiction in civil, criminal and administrative matters for proceedings regarding:

- offences committed within the district by minors under 18;
- the application of rehabilitative measures on minors under 18 resident in the court's district; and
- the exercise of parental powers, of the protection of the court, financial administration, assistance, affiliation, and adoption, as before in relation to minors resident in the Court of Appeal district.

The competence of the Juvenile Court ceases when the juvenile reaches the age of 18. Juveniles are transferred into the adult system when they reach majority.

Decisions of the Juvenile Court may be appealed in the juvenile division of the Court of Appeal.

26. There are also other special courts – the Regional Court of Water (*Tribunale Regionale delle Acque Pubbliche*) and High Court of Water (*Tribunale Superiore delle Acque Pubbliche*) – exercising jurisdiction over public water matters.

27. Italy is divided into local territorial jurisdictional areas, with the magistrates based and working from court offices within the various jurisdictions. The division of the country is fixed by law by Royal Decree No. 12 of 30 January 1941, as modified by Legislative Decree No. 51 of 19 February 1998 and Law No. 234 of 22 July 1999. The geographical area of jurisdiction of the Ordinary Courts is called a *circondario* (jurisdictional area), the Court of Appeal's area of jurisdiction is called a *distretto* (district), while the Court of Cassation has jurisdiction over the entire Republic.

Ordinary Courts have jurisdiction in both civil and criminal matters within their *circondario.* Following the enactment of Legislative Decree 51/98, the Ordinary Court became the sole Court of First Instance except for those matters which are the jurisdiction of the Justices of the Peace (the Justice of the Peace being the Court of First Instance in these cases). The Ordinary Court may adjudicate with a single judge or as a collegiate court (with three judges sitting). The decisions of the Ordinary Court and the Justice of the Peace may be challenged on appeal to the Court of Appeal for reasons based on the merits and before the Court of Cassation on grounds related either purely to the law (relating to legal legitimacy) or to jurisdictional powers (jurisdictional grounds).

The Ordinary Court also exercises the functions of a tutelary court together with other specific functions laid down by the law. There are 140 Ordinary Courts following the reduction made by Legislative Decree No. 155/2012 and by Legislative Decree No. 14/2014 (this second Decree was adopted to correct the results of the reduction made with the previous one).

In summary, ordinary civil and criminal matters are heard by the following:

- Justices of the Peace (*Giudice di Pace*).
- Tribunal (*Tribunale Ordinario*).
- Surveillance Courts (i.e., Courts responsible for the Enforcement of Sentences) (*Tribunale di Sorveglianza*).
- Juvenile Courts (*Tribunale per i Minorenni*).
- Courts of Assizes (*Corte di Assise*).
- Courts of Appeal (*Corte di Appello*).
- Courts of Appeal of Assizes (*Corte d'Assise d'Appello*).
- The Court of Cassation (*Corte di Cassazione*) – the highest Court of Appeal.

2. The Criminal Courts

28. The Italian criminal courts are essentially divided into three levels. The first instant courts include the Justices of the Peace, the Tribunal, and the Court of Assizes, each dealing with different types of offences. Whereas the Justice of the Peace is always a single judge court, the Court of Assizes is a collective organ, and the Tribunal can be a mono judge or panel.

29. The Court of Assizes handles more serious offences at first instance. It consists of two professional judges (*giudice togati*): a president (a judge qualified for the Court of Appeal) and a panel judge (*giudice a latere*) who is one qualified for an Ordinary Court. The panel also includes six lay judges (*giudici popolari*). The lay judges are ordinary citizens who are called upon to assist in the adjudication. And, although their role is similar to that of a juror under the Anglo-Saxon model, when exercising their duties, these lay judges are considered public officials, and they cannot be excused or sequestered. To appoint lay judges, names are extracted at random from the local lists specifically drawn up for the purpose. The lay judges must: (1) possess Italian citizenship, (2) be between the ages of 30 and 65, (3) enjoy full political and civil rights, (4) be of good moral conduct, (5) possess at least a junior high/middle school (*scuola media*) certificate (for the Court of Assizes) or a high school (*scuola superiore*) certificate (for the Court of Assizes of Appeal). Ineligible persons include serving judges and officials of the judicial system, members of the armed forces and the police, ministers of religion, and members of religious orders or congregations of any kind. Jurors are not permitted in the other courts, i.e., the Justice of the Peace courts, the Tribunals and the Court of Cassation.

3. Justices of the Peace

30. Justices of the Peace hear small claims and cases of lesser importance. The position of Justice of the Peace was introduced into the Italian judicial system on 1 May 1995, replacing the office of Conciliation Judge, the latter office then ceasing to exist. The civil jurisdiction of the Justice of the Peace is much broader than its predecessor. On 1 January 2002, criminal jurisdiction was given to the Justice of the Peace, thus giving the office competence to deal with minor criminal matters not requiring a complex investigation.

Justices of the Peace are honorary magistrates given judicial powers on a temporary basis. Justices are required to comply with the duties imposed on judges and magistrates generally and are subject to disciplinary responsibility. The term of office is four years. Justices must be under the age of 75.

4. The Court of Appeal

31. The Court of Appeal represents the second level of the juridical system, hearing decisions of the Tribunal and the Justice of the Peace courts. The Court of Assizes of Appeal handles appeals of decisions of the Court of Assizes. Appeal panels are made up of three judges; The Court is usually located in the region capital and has territorial jurisdiction within its own district, normally corresponding to that region.

The Court of Appeal of Assizes has the same composition of judges as the Court of Assizes (two professional judges (*giudice togati)* and six lay judges (*giudici popolari*)). However, the president of the panel must be qualified as a member of the Court of Cassation, and the panel judge (*giudice a latere*) must be qualified as a member of the Court of Appeal.

In appeals to the Court of Appeal of Assizes, all evidence is reviewed; thus, it is essentially a new trial. Also, like the Court of Assizes, all decisions by the Court of Appeal of Assizes and the reasoning on which the decision is based must be published in writing.

5. The Court of Cassation

32. The Court of Cassation is one of Italy's Supreme Courts and, as the main court of last resort, it is entrusted with ensuring the precise observance and uniform interpretation of the law. It is a collegiate body dealing with ordinary jurisdiction. Thus, the Court cannot judge on the merit of the sentence. Questions relating to conflict of jurisdiction, competence and powers within the Magistracy are also referred to it for adjudication. It hears appeals both in civil and criminal matters against decisions reached by lower courts, but only on points of law (assessment of legitimacy). The Court of Cassation ensures that the court dealing with the merits of the case has correctly applied and interpreted the law in reaching its decision. However, the Court of Cassation does not rule on the constitutionality of laws as that function belongs to Italy's second Supreme Court, the Constitutional Court.

The Court of Cassazione is divided into different divisions, based on the type of case (i.e., seven criminal, four civil, one for tax disputes and one for labour disputes). Typically, only one section (with five judges) examines and decides a case; in cases of particular importance, it sits in United Session (with nine judges).

The Court has one main president, and a president for each section. Its offices are in Rome, and the Court has jurisdiction over the entire territory of the Italian Republic.

33. The Court of Cassation has competence to consider both if the correct procedures were used and if the criminal provisions were correctly applied. One of the most significant functions of the Court is providing a uniform and homogeneous interpretation of the law. However, it is important to note that this does not signify that the Court's decisions can be used as a precedent for other cases as Italy is a civil law country. As such, when interpreting a law, the presiding judge must decide on the objective meaning of the law in questions. Nevertheless, the Court of Cassation decisions do carry weight in future decisions because if the Court has treated a law in a consistent manner, any rulings to the contrary are at risk of being overturned on appeal.

6. The Constitutional Court

34. Like the Court of Cassation, the Constitutional Court (*Corte Costituzionale della Repubblica Italiana*) is considered to be a Supreme Court, and its decisions cannot be appealed. The Constitutional Court is composed of fifteen judges: one-third appointed by the President of the Republic, one-third elected by Parliament, and one-third elected by the ordinary and administrative courts. The judges of the Constitutional Courts are chosen from among judges, including those retired, of the ordinary and administrative higher courts, full university professors of law and lawyers with at least twenty years of practice.[39]

35. The Constitutional Court has jurisdiction over: (1) controversies on the constitutional legitimacy of laws and enactments having the force of law issued by the State and the regions; (2) conflicts arising from allocation of powers of the State and those allocated to State and regions, and between regions; and (3) accusations made against the President of the Republic, according to the provisions of the Constitution.[40]

When the Court declares the constitutional illegitimacy of a law or enactment having the force of law, the law ceases to have effect from the day following the publication of the decision.[41]

Figure 2 Summary of the Italian Criminal Courts

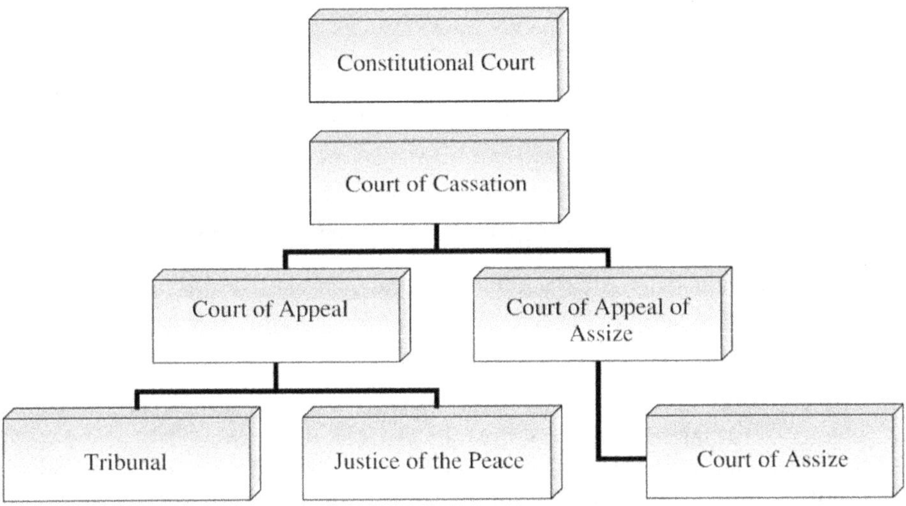

§2. Criminal Law, Criminal Justice and Criminal Science

I. Definition of Criminal Law

A. Criminal Law

36. The criminal (or penal) law of Italy is the public law that deals with offences, with penalties, and all the procedures connected with charging, trying, sentencing and imprisoning defendants convicted of offences. Violations of criminal law are prosecuted by the State, as compared to civil law, wherein breaches may be

39. Constitution Art. 135.
40. Constitution Art. 134.
41. Constitution Art. 136.

enforced by private parties. Sanctions for criminal violations include loss of liberty, government supervision, and/or forfeiture of assets, depending on the offence and its severity.

Italian criminal law is divided into substantive and procedural laws.

B. Substantive Criminal Law

37. Substantive criminal law is the rules or principles related to the conditions which must exist in order to define an act or omission as a criminal offence. It creates, defines and regulates the crime and sets out the sanctions which may be applied in the event of a particular criminal offence.

The Italian Penal Code (PC) is the primary source of the substantive criminal law.

C. Criminal Procedure

38. Procedural law is those methods and mechanics for enforcing rights, and includes rules relating to the investigation, prosecution and adjudication of criminal offences.

39. Procedural law is found in the Italian Code of Criminal Procedure (CCP). The existing Code was approved in 1988 and supersedes the former Code, which dated back to 1930.

The current CCP contains the main criminal procedure provisions as well as special procedures for certain offences.

The CCP is divided into eleven books:

- Book 1 focuses on the judge, defendant, public prosecutor, judicial police, civilly liable persons, injured party, civil parties and defence counsel.
- Book 2 regulates the acts of the trial and contains the most important provisions regarding the procedural terms and nullity or invalidity of acts.
- Book 3 covers investigation and collection of evidence.
- Book 4 addresses precautionary measures directed against the person or property.
- Book 5 regulates pre-trial investigations and the preliminary hearing.
- Book 6 covers special procedures, i.e., the alternative procedures aimed at shortening or expediting the court proceedings under special circumstances, such as those cases where evidence is easily assimilated or the defendant may request a lighter sentence.
- Book 7 addresses the trial: the preliminary phase, the trial hearing and the decision, including the sentence.
- Book 8 regulates lower court proceedings.
- Book 9 covers appeals.
- Book 10 deals with the enforcement/execution of the sentence.
- Book 11 covers judicial relationships with foreign authorities (e.g., extradition, international rogatory letters, and the effects of foreign sentences).

D. Criminal Offences

40. Criminal law relates to criminal offences and illegal acts or omissions for which offenders can be punished by the State.

II. Overview of the Criminal Justice System

A. The Police

41. Italy has various police forces, each having a specific status and structure. The two most prominent forces are the State police and the *Arma dei Carabinieri* (Carabinieri). The State police force is a part of the Ministry of the Interior, while the Carabinieri is a component of the military (thus having a military structure and military regulations) and reports to the Ministry of Defence. Additionally, there are other forces governing specific areas such as the excise police (*Guardia di Finanza*), the municipal police, the penitentiary police, and the State forest corps (*Corpo forestale dello Stato*). Each force has a pyramid like structure, led by a head (in case of the State police) or commander (in the case of the Carabinieri), and lower-level ranks divided by province.

The Prefect is the highest internal administrative organ and has a presence in every Italian region. The entity is charged with enforcing the orders of the central government and has authority over the province and municipal entities. Among other duties, the regional Prefects are responsible for investigating offences.

42. The CCP sets forth the functions of the judicial or investigating police (Articles 55–59 CCP). Judicial police (*ufficiali di polizia giudiziaria*) are officers appointed from the various police forces to carry out criminal investigation functions (*funzioni di polizia giudiziaria*), i.e., investigating crimes and identifying the alleged offenders (Articles 55 and 57 CCP). If there is no local police force, nor a Carabinieri Command Office, nor the Excise Police Force, those functions normally carried out by the judicial police may be exercised by the mayor of the municipality (Article 57(1)(c) CCP).

The judicial police work directly under the direction of the judicial authority as required under Article 109 of the Constitution.[42] The goal of this provision is for the judiciary to remain autonomous from the executive power. If the judicial police were fully subordinated to the Ministry of Justice, this independence would be at risk.

43. Each Public Prosecutor's Office (*Procuratore della Repubblica*) has a special police unit and officers can be promoted or removed from duty with the acquiescence of the Chief Prosecutor. The Central Operating Service (*Servizio Centrale Operativo*) coordinates all police criminal investigation activities under the authority of the Chief of Police and the Ministry of the Interior.

---

42. Constitution Art. 109.

In addition, there are specialized judicial police corps which investigate certain types of offences, in particular organized crime. These include the DIA or Antimafia Investigative Directorate (*Direzione Investigativa Antimafia*) and specialized sections within the State police, the Carabinieri, and the excise police.

B. The Prosecution Service

44. The Public Prosecutor's Office is responsible for all prosecutorial activities. The prosecutors are part of the Judiciary and therefore, any administrative decisions regarding them are made by the Superior Council of the Magistracy (*Consiglio Superiore della Magistratura*). As professional magistrates, prosecutors are guaranteed independence by the Italian Constitution and are subject to the same norms which apply to other judges.[43] In order to assure independence and to comply with the principle of mandatory prosecution,[44] in executing their public prosecution function, the judiciary must remain separate and free from executive power.

45. According to the Italian Constitution, prosecution is mandatory, and thus public prosecutors are bound to prosecute all perpetrators of offences that come to their attention and have no leeway in evaluating criminal policy. Under the law, only the adjudicating judge has the power to determine if the offender will be punished, and if so, how adjudication will be carried out. Once the adjudicating judge decides to pursue a case, there is no judicial authority which can challenge the decision. However, as a result of mandatory prosecution, the Italian criminal law system has become inundated with cases, and it has become difficult for prosecutors to process all offences which come to their attention. This situation has created a form of discretionary power in that, although the prosecutors must consider every case, they do have control over the order and speed in which the cases are addressed. There have been suggestions that mandatory prosecution be abolished in favour of discretionary prosecution. However, this proposal has been rejected as it could go against the principle of equality of citizens before the law and the discretion could be misused.

46. The public prosecutors' activities are monitored by the Minister of Justice[45] and their functions are assigned by the relevant head of the office.[46] The public prosecutor is charged with enforcing compliance with the law; protecting the rights of the State, legal persons and persons lacking legal capacity; and requesting in cases of emergency, the orders he or she considers necessary. Suppressing crime, applying security measures, and enforcing final orders and judgments are also duties of the public prosecutor.

Legal scholars have asserted that the professional homogeneity between the public prosecutor and the adjudicating judge creates an imbalance between prosecution

---

43. Constitution Art. 107.
44. Constitution Art. 112.
45. Article 69 of the Judicial Regulations, Royal Decree 12 of 1941 and following modifications.
46. Article 70 of the Judicial Regulations, Royal Decree 12 of 1941 and following modifications.

and defence. In order to remedy this imbalance, it has been suggested that the two careers be separated, however this proposal has not yet gained acceptance as the two solutions for separating the public prosecutor and the ordinary magistrates are unacceptable. Under the first solution, the public prosecutor would be subordinate to the executive power. However, this solution would be counter to the principle that prosecution is compulsory and against the equality of citizens before the law. The second solution would be to create a completely independent and autonomous accusatorial organ, however with this option there is the risk of creating an overly powerful super police force.

47. The Public Prosecution Service is divided among the first-instance courts, the Juvenile Court, the Court of Appeal and the Court of Cassation. The public prosecutors at the first-instance courts are accusatorial organs that perform before the first-instance judges. In the Court of Appeal, the Public Prosecutor's Office (*Procuratore Generale presso la Corte di Appello*) does not carry out preliminary investigation, but only acts as the public prosecutor before the second-instance judges. The Prosecutor General's Office at the Court of Cassation acts as an accusatory organ.

Additionally, the Prosecution Service has special offices for the National Antimafia Public Prosecutor and the District Antimafia Public Prosecutor. The public prosecutor's offices are autonomous and distinct from the judicial body where they exercise their functions.

Each office is comprised of a head (chief prosecutor) and numerous prosecutors, who work according to a hierarchy, except during court hearings at which time they act in complete autonomy. As a result, the prosecutors can only be substituted under certain circumstances set forth by law, but not merely the dissent of the chief prosecutor. The decisions of the public prosecutors may only be contested by judges. There is no form of control from political, public or private entities. Prosecutors do not have the power to autonomously close or plea bargain a case; they may only make suggestions to the judge, who makes the final decision.

C. *Investigating Magistrates and Investigating Jurisdictions*

48. The investigation and criminal procedure begin when the prosecutor is notified of an offence. There are two parts to the investigation: (1) the preliminary investigation (*indagini preliminari*), which precedes trial and is driven by the public prosecutor (Articles 326 and 327 CCP), and (2) the probatory hearing (Articles 392 et seq. CCP).

49. Preliminary investigations commence when a public prosecutor is informed (in sufficient detail) of the commission of a criminal offence (i.e., receives a *notitia criminis*). Under Article 330 CCP, the public prosecutor and the judicial police may act on notification by others or they may act *sua sponte*.

Once the preliminary investigation starts, a time limit is set, running from the date on which the offender is specifically identified. Generally, preliminary investigations last six months; however, the term can be extended up to eighteen months unless, a serious offence is involved, in which case the term can be extended up to two years (Article 407, paragraphs 1 and 2 CCP).

The public prosecutor leads the preliminary investigation and theoretically, the evidence collected cannot be used since evidence is to be collected at trial. However, according to the CCP, there are certain exceptions to this rule.

Investigative methods that cannot be duplicated (e.g., inspection reports, confiscation, search, unrepeatable technical controls, phone interceptions) may be used as evidence. The CCP also provides for a probatory hearing (*incidente probatorio*). This probatory hearing is made upon request of the parties and allows for the gathering of evidence which is at risk of being lost or altered (see *infra* paragraphs 451 et seq.).

50. The preliminary investigation may be supervised by a judge for preliminary investigations (*giudice per le indagini preliminari* or GIP), who oversees the activities of the public prosecutor and guarantees the rights of the person being investigated (Article 328 CCP). The GIP may adopt, upon request of the public prosecutor, measures restricting the personal freedom of the accused during the preliminary investigation. If this proves necessary during the investigation, the GIP decides whether evidence should be admitted, and presides over the proceedings.

D. *Trial Jurisdictions*

1. The Justice of the Peace

51. The Justice of the Peace is a Trial Court of First Instance and has the jurisdiction to try criminal cases of minor importance as provided for by Legislative Decree No. 274 of 28 August 2000. The public prosecutor carries out the prosecution at the Justice of the Peace level.

2. The Court of Assizes

52. The Court of Assizes has jurisdiction over offences having a maximum penalty of twenty-four years incarceration or life imprisonment, and other serious offences, such as murder, criminal association and human trafficking. The *Pubblico Ministero presso la Corte d'Assise* (the Public Prosecutor at the Court of Assizes) carries out the prosecution at the Court of Assizes (Article 5 CCP).

Decisions are made jointly by the professional/stipendiary judges (i.e., the president and panel judge (*giudice a latere*) and the six lay judges (*giudici popolari*) during a closed-door meeting (*Camera di Consiglio*). All decisions by the Court of Assizes and the reasoning on which the decision is based must be published in writing.

3. The Tribunal

53. The Tribunal (*Tribunale*) has jurisdiction over all other offences. Generally, at the Tribunal, the public prosecutor carries out the prosecution, except for those offences related to organized crime, ransom kidnapping, drug trafficking and related offences, in which case the Antimafia Public Prosecutor is responsible.

4. Appeals

54. The Court of Appeal (*Corte d'Appello*) hears appeals against decisions of the Tribunal and the Tribunal itself hears appeals against decisions of the Justices of the Peace (*Giudice di Pace*). The Court of Assizes appeals are handled by the Court of Assizes of Appeal. At the appeal stage, prosecution is conducted by the Public Prosecutor's Office at the Court of Appeal (*Procuratore Generale presso la Corte di Appello*).

5. The Court of Cassation

55. The jurisdiction of the Court of Cassation is set forth *supra*, paragraphs 32–33. Prosecution is conducted by the Prosecutor General.

E. Prison System and After-Care

1. The Department of Prison Administration

56. Prior to 1922, the Italian prison system was subordinated to the Ministry of Interior. Subsequently, supervision of the criminal justice system was passed to the Ministry of Justice.

The Department of Prison Administration (*Il Dipartimento dell'Amministrazione Penitenziaria*)[47] runs the Italian prison system. Seated in and subordinated to the Ministry of Justice, the Department is typically led by a judge from the Court of Cassation. The Department is divided into regional districts and comprised of officials, support staff, the correctional police corps and the social service staff.

2. The Surveillance Magistracy

57. Two key components of the prison system are the surveillance judge (*Giudizio di Sorveglianza*) and the Surveillance Court (*Tribunale di Sorveglianza*), which are the two offices or bodies through which the Surveillance Magistracy

---

47. *Giustizia Dipartimento Amministrazione Penitenziaria* ('Ministry of Justice, Department of Prison Administration'), http://www.giustizia.it/giustizia/it/mg_12_3.wp (Accessed June 2015).

works. However, in order to better guarantee the rights of the detainees, they are not directly part of the Prison Administration.

The Surveillance Magistracy was introduced in 1975 by Law No. 354 of 26 July 1975 and has the duty of supervising the enforcement of sentences. Specifically, the Magistracy is responsible for controlling that the law is respected in the execution of the sentence, considers the application of substitute sanctions (*infra*, paragraphs 357 et seq.) and alternative measures (*infra*, paragraph 359) as well as the application and enforcement of security measures (*infra*, paragraph 391). The Magistracy also considers matters concerning leave permits, leave permits for good conduct, permission to work outside the correctional institution and conditional release (*infra*, paragraph 634). Jurisdiction of the Magistracy has broadened substantially to reflect the current efforts to emphasize the rehabilitative role of sanctions required under Article 27 of the Constitution.

58. The surveillance judge is a mono judge, while the Surveillance Court acts as a collegiate body. The Surveillance Court operates both as a Court of First Instance and as a Court of Appeal in relation to decisions of the surveillance judge. The Court's geographical jurisdiction is the same as the districts of the Courts of Appeal. Members of the Surveillance Court are drawn from surveillance judges working in the district or in the jurisdictional area of a separate Court of Appeal division together with professionals with expertise in psychology, social services, education, psychiatry and clinical criminology.

59. Sentences are executable only upon final judgment. At that time, the public prosecutor issues an order of execution and transmits it to the judicial police.

3. Penal Institutions

60. In Italy, the penal institution system for adults is divided into three parts:

(a) preventive detention institutions;
(b) institutions for the execution of sentences; and
(c) institutions for the execution of security measures.

The institutions for the execution of sentences are subdivided into arrest centres and detention centres, while the institutions for the execution of security measures are subdivided into treatment and custody centres, judicial psychiatric hospitals, prison farms and work homes. However, frequently these divisions are only theoretical, as in practice the system does not actually select the penal institution according to the category of offender. This failure to implement the selection criteria is primarily due to financial constraints, and unfortunately, as a result there is a mixing of the prison population and the opportunity for more dangerous convicts to exert a strong negative influence on the other prisoners.

61. Generally, prisoners are placed in the institution in the territory in which he or she lives. Transfers can be granted for serious security concerns, unfavourable conditions within an individual institution (e.g., overcrowding), or reasons relating to justice or the prisoner's health, studies or family. In these cases, the detainee is to be transferred to an institution in close proximity to their residence.

62. Prison overcrowding was a serious problem in Italy, with the country's prisons being the third most overcrowded in Europe after Serbia and Greece, with 147 inmates for every 100 beds in 2011. The situation has improved considerably in recent years since there are now only 110 inmates for every 100 beds. This is due to Law No. 199 of 26 November 2010 (Provisions on the implementation at home of a prison sentence not exceeding one year), which introduced a measure alternative to detention in prison, applicable for persons sentenced to a term – even residual – not exceeding one year. This will enable them to serve their sentences in their homes, or at '*other public place or private nursing, care and hospitality*'.

In January 2013, the European Court of Human Rights ordered Italy to correct the 'degrading and inhumane' conditions in the country's prisons and to pay EUR 100,000 in damages to seven inmates for violations of Article 3 of the European Convention on Human Rights (ECHR). In terms of inmates awaiting trial, Italy is third behind Ukraine and Turkey.[48]

63. For minors, Italy has approximately twenty penal institutes. Juveniles serving a sentence of detention and those awaiting trial are kept in these institutions. Young adults serving a sentence for offences committed while minors are also kept in these institutions.

4. The Probation Service

64. In Italy, the Directorate General for the Execution of Sentences in the Community (*la Direzione Generale dell'Esecuzione Penale Esterna;*[49] hereinafter the 'Probation Service')[50] is the primary provider of the country's probation services. Although it had been operating previously for a number of years, the adult system was introduced formally with Title III of Law No. 354 of 26 July 1975. The Italian juvenile probation service system was developed at the time the juvenile courts were created in 1934 (see *supra,* paragraph 25).

Originally, the probation service centres were referred to as Probation Service Centres for Adults (*Centri di Servizi Sociale per Adulti*); however, the name was changed to Local Offices for the Execution of Sentences in the Community (*Uffici*

48. *Torreggiani and Others v. Italy* (Nos 43517/09, 46882/09, 55400/09, 57875/09, 61535/09, 35315/10 and 37818/10), judgment of 8 Jan. 2013, http://hudoc.echr.coe.int/sites/eng/pages/search.aspx?i=001-115860#{'itemid':[' 001-115860']} (Accessed 15 Jun. 2013). The Court gave Italy one year to resolve its problem of prison overcrowding and to implement a procedure for providing redress to victims after finding the petitioners' rights under Art. 3 (prohibition of torture and inhumane or degrading treatment) of the European Convention on Human Rights because they were being given only 3 square metres of personal space. On 27 Jun. 2013, the Grand Chamber rejected Italy's appeal against the January provisional sentence.

49. www.giustizia.it/giustizia/it/mg_12_3_6.wp (Accessed June 2015).

50. In Italy, the terms 'social services' or 'UEPE' are often used to refer to the 'probation service'.

Locali di Esecuzione Penale Esterna) in 2005 with the enactment of Law No. 154 of 27 July 2005.

The entity is a state service and part of the prison administration. The Service becomes involved after the final sentence has been passed (i.e., in the enforcement phase). In cases of incarceration, the Probation Service acts as a liaison between the offender, the institution and the community (e.g., the families, social services). The Service is also involved in the enforcement of alternative measures.

F. The Bar

65. Under the Constitution, the right to defence is an inviolable right at every stage of the criminal proceedings, and indigent suspects must be provided with counsel during all phases of the criminal procedure.[51]

66. The role of defence counsel is set forth in the CCP. Under Article 96 CCP, a person who has been indicted or is under investigation may name up to two defence attorneys. In the event two lawyers are not named, the Court appoints counsel from a list of qualified attorneys prepared by the local bar association (*Consiglio all'Ordine degli Avvocati*).

67. To qualify as an attorney (*Avvocato*) in Italy, the lawyer must graduate with either a three-year or five-year degree in jurisprudence, complete an eighteen-month training period within a law firm and pass the written and oral bar exams. Upon passing the exams, the lawyer becomes part of the bar association, at which time he can practise any type of civil, penal or administrative law in the lower and appellate courts. In order to practise before the Court of Cassation, a lawyer must have worked before the magistrates' courts for five years and pass a specific exam or attend the '*Scuola Superiore dell'Avvocatura*'[52] after eight years of practising.

68. With respect to indigence, Law No. 217 of 30 July 1990 provides that upon written request, those earning less than a certain threshold (Italian Liras (ITL) 10 million or Euro (EUR) 5,164.57 in 1990 and adjusted annually according to the official inflation indices) are entitled to defence counsel of their choice at State expense. As of 2015, the threshold was EUR 11,369.24.[53]

---

51. Constitution Art. 24.
52. That is, a law school aimed exclusively at obtaining the authorization to practise before the Court of Cassation.
53. www.giustizia.it/giustizia/it/mg_3_7_7.wp?tab=d (Accessed June 2015). If the person is living with a spouse or other family members, for purposes of determining the granting of the benefit, the level of income is the sum of the incomes of all members of the family. For criminal matters, the income limit is raised EUR 1,032.91 for each of the family members living with the accused. Moreover, only personal income is considered in the calculation when the subject is accused of a personal crime (i.e., against family members) or in proceedings where the interests of the applicant are in conflict with those other family members living with him.

G. *Statistical Overview*

69. The rate of imprisonment per 100,000 persons in Italy is equal to 103.8, as compared to an average of 128 in Europe and 145 in the world.

Over the past eleven years, the amount of the prison population has increased by 25.8%. However, as of 31 December 2013, 62,536 people were being held in Italian prisons, a reduction of 4.8% compared to 2012. The present number of inmates is far higher than the set capacity of 47,709 places.

Most of the prisoners who entered prison in 2013 (59,330) are awaiting trial, while only 14% have a final conviction. A total of 16% of those detained are released within a week. The so-called phenomenon of 'revolving door' (referring to offenders who are repeatedly subject to short detentions but continue to commit new offences upon their release) relates almost exclusively to those accused who are released within a week, with 98% of repeat offenders.

Among those detained, drug violations are the most common type of crime (24,273), followed by property crimes, with 18,064 being held on robbery charges and 13,531 for theft.

Other relevant statistics include:

- 95.7% of the prisoners held in Italy are male, a consistent percentage over time.
- Since 2000, the percentage of foreign prisoners has grown from 29% in 2000 to 34.9% in 2013. Among those detainees who are entering prison from a state of freedom, foreigners account for 43%. Most of the foreign detainees come from Africa (46.3%), in particular from Morocco and Tunisia, or from Europe (41.6%).
- 45.6% of the detainees had no previous incarcerations, 41.8% have had from one to four previous incarcerations and the remaining 12.6% more than five.
- 64% of inmates were born in Italy, with 32% in the southern part of the country and in particular the region of Campania region, which is the most common place of birth for both male and female detainees.
- 54.4% of the inmates are under 40 years old. Less than 20% are older than 50 years and 5% older than 60.[54]

54. *Anno 2013: I detenuti nelle carceri italiane* (Year 2013: Inmates in Italian Prisons), Statistical Report by *Ministero della Giustizia Dipartimento Amministrazione Penitenziaria* (Ministry of Justice, Department of Prison Administration), http://www.istat.it/it/archivio/153369 (Accessed in June 2015).

1. Criminal Actions by Trial Level

70.

Table 2 Criminal Actions by Level: 2012[55]*

Level	*Movement*	*Perpetrator*	*Filed*	*Closed*	*Pending at the End of the Year*
First Instance					
	Public Prosecutor				
		Known	1,588,379	1,588,482	1,711,244
		Unknown	1,541,024	1,590,710	921,163
	GIP and GUP				
		Known	921,697	876,408	779,225
		Unknown	1,159,388	1,214,812	624,878
	Single Judge		373,322	328,764	487,355
	Justice of the Peace				
		Trial	95,801	89,649	143,518
		GIP known and unknown	158,193	155,204	34,997
	Panel of Judges		13,645	12,951	22,470
	Court of Assizes		278	293	341
Second-Instance					
	Court of Appeal		104,216	92,949	246,740
	Court of Appeal of Assizes		634	603	658

55. *Annuario statistico italiano 2014* (Italian Statistical Yearbook 2012) Ch. 6: Justice, ISTAT, http://www3.istat.it/dati/catalogo/20121218_00/PDF/Cap6.pdf http://www3.istat.it/dati/catalogo/20121218_00/PDF/Cap6.pdf (Accessed in June 2015).

Level	Movement	Perpetrator	Filed	Closed	Pending at the End of the Year
	Single Judge (appeals from Justice of the Peace)		5,053	4,886	5,274
Court of Cassation					
	Court of Cassation		52,342	51,614	31,289

* Not Including Minors.

2. Reported Offences and Persons

71. By far, the most common crime in Italy is theft, making up almost one-half of all reported offences. Other offences significantly effecting Italy include swindling, personal injury, robbery and drug trafficking.

3. Reported Offences

72. In the first half of the twentieth century, the crime rate in Italy remained relatively constant, however in the second half, there was a dramatic increase, particularly with regards to theft. In fact, although between 1954 and 1974, the reported number of offences per 100,000 inhabitants doubled, the level of reported number of thefts increased almost five-fold. However, the ISTAT statistics also show that in the beginning of the twenty-first century, the level of thefts is remaining somewhat constant, while in recent history the total number of offences per 100,000 inhabitants continues to increase.

*Table 3 Reported Offences: 1926–2004, Per 100,000 Inhabitants**

Year	Total Number of Offences	Number of Theft Offences
1926	1,706.2	499.3
1934	1,270.4	492.3
1954	1,658.9	520.9
1974	3,279.1	2,441.4
1994	4,884.9	2,931.0
2004	5,077.8	2,591.5

*ISTAT, *Italy in Figures 2007*, http://www3.istat.it/dati/catalogo/20070517_00/Italy2007Ing.pdf (Accessed 15 June 2013).

Table 4 Offences Reported by Police by Type – Year 2012[56]

Type of Offence	*Number*
Murder	528
Attempted murder	1,327
Personal injury	69,527
Sexual violence	4,689
Aiding and abetting prostitution	1,306
Theft	1,520,623
Robbery	42,631
Extortion	6,478
Fraud and Informatics Fraud	116,767
Receiving stolen goods	25,080
Drug-related offences	33,852
Total	**2,818,834**

4. Convictions

73. In the period 2000–2002, there was a substantial decrease in the number of convicted people. In 2004, the number of convictions began to rise again. Since then, the percentage of females convicted has decreased steadily, while the percentage of foreign people convicted has risen considerably over the past ten years.

Table 5 Convictions by Type of Offence and Gender – Year 2013[57]

	Male	*Female*
Voluntary homicide	797	34
Negligent homicide	1,726	331
Personal Injury	7,961	1,246
Theft	22,886	6,909
Robbery	5,911	499
Drug-related offences (e.g., production, sale, purchase)	21,438	1,825

56. *Annuario statistico italiano 2015* (Italian Statistical Yearbook 2015) Ch. 6: Justice, ISTAT, http://www.istat.it/it/files/2015/12/Asi-2015.pdf (Accessed 15 Feb. 2016).

57. *Annuario statistico italiano 2015* (Italian Statistical Yearbook 2015) Ch. 6: Justice, ISTAT, http://www.istat.it/it/files/2015/12/Asi-2015.pdf (Accessed 15 Feb. 2016).

	Male	Female
Driving under the influence of alcohol	41,833	4,304
Total	**267,307**	**50,886**

Table 6 Convictions by Type of Offence and Age – Year 2013[58]

	Less Than 16	*16–17*	*18–24*	*25–34*	*35–44*	*45–54*	*55–64*	*Over 65*
Voluntary homicide	6	21	222	256	182	84	41	19
Negligent homicide	-	6	329	482	462	403	240	135
Personal injury	22	94	1.466	2.281	2.419	1.555	971	399
Theft	353	785	8.616	8.961	6.244	3.151	1.232	453
Robbery	116	346	2.127	2.072	1.194	425	114	16
Drug-related offences (e.g., production, sale, purchase)	61	370	7.266	8.773	4.604	1.715	413	61
Driving under the influence of alcohol	-	22	9.214	16.831	11.289	5.623	2.305	853
Total	768	**2.486**	**57.800**	**92.209**	**80.539**	**49.687**	**25.100**	**9.604**

Table 7 Convictions by Type of Offence and Prior Offences – Year 2013[59]

	With Prior Offence	*Without Prior Offence*	*Total*
Voluntary homicide	465	366	**831**
Negligent homicide	409	1.648	**2.057**
Personal injury	4.046	5.161	**9.207**
Theft	13.971	15.824	**29.795**

58. *Ibid.*
59. *Ibid.*

	With Prior Offence	*Without Prior Offence*	*Total*
Robbery	3.758	2.652	**6.410**
Drug-related offences (e.g., production, sale, purchase)	12.077	11.186	**23.263**
Driving under the influence of alcohol	14.066	32.071	**46.137**
Total	**149.231**	**168.962**	**318.193**

III. Trends within Criminal Justice

74. In recent years, there have been numerous reform proposals relating to the substantive and procedural criminal laws. The basis for these reform projects is the need to adapt the PC to a historic, social and institutional situation which is greatly different from that when the PC was first enforced, while attempting to create a coherent and complete criminal procedure system based on experience of the Code in force and characterized by equality between the parties and full respect for cross-debate.

Enforcement of many of these reform projects is impossible; thus, they will become mere topics for scholarly debate.

75. The main reform made to date was with regards to the Constitution. Article 111 of the Italian Constitution was amended in November 1999. As a result of the amendment, the new text establishes that the trial is carried out by cross-examining all the parties involved on an equal basis (thus giving the defendant the right to question his accuser). Accordingly, no one can be convicted solely on the basis of statements made during the preliminary phase by persons who refuse to confirm the statement during trial. Thus, the Italian criminal law system can be considered to have reacquired the accusatory character assigned to it in the original version of the 1988 Code, while still guaranteeing the provisions of the Constitution.

76. Furthermore, with specific regards to the Italian PC, it is necessary to point out that for approximately twenty years, there has been a series of scholarly and practical commissions working with the Minister of Justice seeking to put in point the reform of the Criminal Law.

The issues relating to the reform which are under debate are essentially two:

(1) The first regards whether or not there is the necessity to rewrite the general parts of the criminal law. Above all with regards to the subjective elements of the crime and to a new and more expansive formulation of the concept of criminal intent.

(2) The second regards the opportunity to insert in the PC, the more significant offences which are today contained in special laws and regard, above all, business crimes.

77. Nevertheless, this does not mean that during this time period, the PC has remained unchanged. There have been numerous modifications regarding both the General Part and the Special Part. Of particular note are: (1) the reforms concerning the statute of limitations, which has brought a general reduction of terms; and (2) the introduction of specific offences regarding organized crime.

78. With regards to the CCP, although it was relatively recently reformed, the works were not aimed at changing completely the Code, but just at making certain adjustments to render more effective the principle of parity between the accuser/prosecution and the defence.

§3. Historical Background

79. The current PC (also known as the 'Rocco Code') dates back to 1930 and although its origins can be traced back to Roman and Middle-Age canon law, its general principles were strongly influenced by the Napoleonic Code of 1810 and the Code of William of 1870.

During the French Enlightenment, general principles were developed with respect to criminal law. Namely, principles relating to clarity of the law, no punishment without trial, proportionality between crime and punishment, definitions of crime and punishment based on a system of written laws and fixed penalties, and the elimination of secret accusations. These principles were affirmed in the 1791 and 1795 French PCs and then in the Napoleonic Code of 1810.

80. Late in the nineteenth century, Italy was reunified and Victor Emmanuel II of the House of Savoy was proclaimed King. In 1889, the then Minister of Justice, Zanardelli promulgated a general PC for the new Kingdom.

In 1919, a commission was established and chaired by Italian criminologist and socialist, Enrico Ferri in order to consider revisions of the Zanardelli PC. This project – known as the Ferri Project or the Project of PC – was completed in 1921, but was rejected as it was considered too radical by the Mussolini regime.

In 1925, jurist Arturo Rocco – a professor of Penal Law and Procedure – chaired another commission which resulted in the Italian PC, or Rocco Code. The PC and the accompanying CCP became effective in 1930. Because the Rocco Code was approved during the Fascist Period, the original version of the PC was quite severe and gave the State a highly repressive role. With the downfall of the Fascist movement, changes began to be made to the PC in order to conform to the principles of the Italian Constitution; however, the general structure remains unchanged, and the PC is still in force in Italy. The related CCP was in force until its amendment in 1988.

In 1944, the death penalty was abolished with the exception of the cases provided for by the war laws.[60] (This exception was abolished in 1994 – see *infra*, paragraph 326). Although, the death penalty had been banned by the Zanardelli Code, it had been reintroduced in 1926. Also during this year, legislation was passed reintroducing general extenuating circumstances and legal excuses in cases of legitimate reactions to arbitrary acts by public officials.[61]

During the following years, a decriminalization process began to take place. The process began in 1967[62] and included, among others, the changes in 1975[63] and 1981.[64] In late 1999, the decriminalization process was concluded.[65]

There have been other significant changes to the PC in recent years, particularly with respect to mafia-type associations;[66] offences against the public administration;[67] money laundering and the laundering of criminal proceeds;[68] usury offences;[69] abuse of official duties;[70] and sexual violence.[71]

Recently, the Italian Legislator has implemented a new process of decriminalization. More specifically Legislative Decrees Nos 7 and 8 of 15 January 2016, entered into force from 6 February 2016, have introduced significant changes to the Italian criminal justice system by repealing[72] various minor offences, depenalizing[73] other offences and introducing a new set of torts[74] punished by pecuniary sanctions.

81. With respect to the Italian CCP, the previous CCP reflected the authoritarianism of the political regime of the time, having great emphasis on the inquisition and limiting significantly the role of defence counsel during this phase. With the fall of Mussolini and the Fascist regime, the government began to reform the CCP, which was finally accomplished in 1955. The goal of the revisions was to place into effect the principles of the new Constitution. Over 200 articles of the PC were

60. Legislative Decree No. 22 of 22 Jan. 1948.
61. Legislative Decree No. 288 of 16 Sep. 1944.
62. Law No. 317 of 3 May 1967.
63. Law No. 706 of 24 Dec. 1975.
64. Law No. 689 of 24 Nov. 1981.
65. Law No. 205 of 25 Jun. 1999.
66. Law No. 646 of 13 Sep. 1982.
67. Law No. 86 of 26 Apr. 1990; Law No. 190 of 12 Nov. 2012.
68. Law No. 328 of 9 Aug. 1993.
69. Law No. 108 of 7 Mar. 1996.
70. Law No. 234 of 16 Jul. 1997.
71. Law No. 66 of 15 Feb. 1996.
72. According to Art. 1 of Legislative Decrees No. 7, 20161 the following offences have been repealed: (i) forgery of private agreement (Art. 485 PC); (ii) forgery of signed blank sheet (Art. 486 PC); (iii) insulting behaviour (Art. 594 PC); (vi) misappropriation of common properties (Art. 627 PC); (v) appropriation of lost objects, lost treasure and objects received by mistake or by fortuitous event (Art. 647 PC).
73. Among them have been decriminalized, or reclassified as administrative offences the following offences: (i) non-payment of social security deductions for amounts below EUR 10,000.00 (Art. 2, para. 1 Legislative Decree 462/1983); (ii) indecent behaviour (Art. 527 PC); (iii) obscene publications and performances (excluding the case provided for by Art. 528, para. 3 PC); (vi) refusal to supply services during a riot (Art. 652 PC); (v) exploiting popular credulity (Art. 661 PC); (vi) abusive theatre or film performances (Art. 668 PC).
74. The new provisions introduce innovative measures, such as the torts punished by civil fines (inspired to the punitive damages in common law).

amended in order to better guarantee the right to defence. Subsequently, the Court of Cassation further modified the Code so as better protect defendants' civil rights during criminal proceedings.

In 1962–1963, the government established the Carnelutti Project, which had the task of insuring the Code properly expressed Italian democracy. Moves were made during the 1970s to enact a new Criminal Procedure Code; however, the rise of terrorism within Italy resulted in a more protectionist criminal law system. The present CCP was enacted with Presidential Decree No. 447 of 22 September 1988, according to Proxy Law No. 81 of 16 February 1987 and came into force on 24 October 1988.

The current Code shifts the basis of Italian procedural law from an inquisitorial to an accusatorial model. Trial hearings have become a central means of obtaining evidence and the process streamlined by emphasizing alternative or special procedures such as abbreviated trial (*giudizio abbreviato*) (*infra*, paragraph 496); plea bargaining (*patteggiamento*) (*infra*, paragraphs 497 et seq.); proceeding by decree (*decreto penale di condanna*) (*infra*, paragraphs 502 et seq.); immediate trial (*giudizio immediato*) (*infra*, paragraph 507); and abbreviated trial (*giudizio diretissimo*) (*infra*, paragraphs 509–510).

82. During the 1990s, the criminal justice system established by the 1988 CCP experienced numerous changes as a result of the 1992 interventions by the Constitutional Court and legislature. The interventions, which stemmed from the increase in organized crime, emphasized the importance of pre-trial statements. In Decision No. 24 of 1992, the Constitutional Court declared Article 195, paragraph 4 CCP inconsistent with the Constitution because under this provision judicial police were prohibited from testifying on declarations made to them by witnesses. The Court also declared Article 500, paragraph 3 CCP unconstitutional because it did not allow for the inclusion in the court-hearing file (i.e., the file on which the court bases its decision) of the declarations made previously by the witnesses to the public prosecutor, if the statements are contested at trial. (Constitutional Court Decision No. 255 of 1992).

In 1997, Law No. 267 of 7 September 1997 amended Article 513 CCP prohibiting the insertion in the court-hearing file of the statements made by the co-defendants to the public prosecution. However, by Decision No. 361 of 1998, the Constitutional Court declared that the reformulated part of Article 513 CCP was unconstitutional as it did not foresee the inclusion of the previous statements made by the defendant, if the accused refused or omitted to repeat them in court.

Numerous legal scholars have asserted that these interventions by the Constitutional Court denied the court hearings their central role, which is an open contradiction of the accusatorial system. As a result, the Code lost its original clearly accusatorial character, but without taking on another specific profile, since the Court lacked the power to bring about a return to a coherent and organic inquisitorial type of criminal law system.

To resolve the resulting ambiguity regarding criminal law procedures, it was proposed that the principles inspiring the accusatorial process be included in the Fundamental Law of the Republic in order to prevent the Constitutional Court from prohibiting any further changes aimed at returning the Code in force to its original version.

83. One of the most significant changes in the judicial system was the result of Law Decree No. 51 of 19 February 1998, which created a mono-judge system by unifying the various first-instance judges and eliminating the figure of the lower court judge by merging it with that of the Tribunal. As a result of this law, it was necessary to make certain modifications to the CCP. Additionally, the basis for incompatibility of judges has been broadened; the competence of the various adjudicating bodies has been modified; and the list of offences to be judged by a single body rather than by a panel of judges has been expanded.

§4. Sources of Criminal Law

84. The sources of criminal law are both international and national.

I. International Sources

85. As a member of various international and supranational organizations, such as the United Nations, the Council of Europe, and the EU, Italy also has an increasing number of international obligations in the field of criminal law.

The main international sources of criminal law are the European Convention for the Protection of Human Rights and Fundamental Freedoms (ECHR),[75] the International Covenant on Civil and Political Rights (ICCPR)[76] (adopted and opened for signature, ratification, and accession by General Assembly Resolution of 16 December 1966, entered into force on 23 March 1976) and several other international conventions such as:

(1) the Convention against Torture and Other Cruel Inhuman or Degrading Treatment or Punishment (CAT) ratified by Italy on 12 January 1989;
(2) the Convention for the Protection of All Persons from Enforced Disappearance (CED) signed by Italy on 3 July 2007;
(3) the Convention on the Elimination of All Forms of Discrimination against Women (CEDAW) ratified by Italy on 10 June 1985;
(4) the International Convention on the Elimination of All Forms of Racial Discrimination (CERD) ratified by Italy on 5 January 1976;
(5) the International Covenant on Economic, Social and Cultural Rights (CESCR) ratified by Italy on 15 September 1978;
(6) the Convention on the Rights of Persons with Disabilities (CPD) signed by Italy on 30 March 2007;
(7) the Convention on the Rights of the Child (CRC) ratified by Italy on 5 September 1991.

---

75. The ECHR was ratified by Italy by means of Law No. 848 of 8 Aug. 1955.
76. The ICCPR was ratified by Italy on 15 Sep. 78.

II. EU Law and Domestic Criminal Law

A. EU Law

86. Article 117(l) of the Constitution specifies the Italian State has exclusive legislative powers over criminal law matters. However, the Italian Constitutional Court has held that EU Law prevails over conflicting domestic provisions: when there are conflicting domestic provisions, the Italian courts must set aside these provisions and directly apply EU Law.[77] Accordingly, when an Italian criminal provision conflicts with EU Law, it cannot be applied, and no crime arises.

In addition, practice has shown the possibility of applying a combination of EU and Italian criminal law, resulting in the creation of new offences: this occurs when EU Law prescribes the applicability of domestic criminal provisions (aimed at protecting specific domestic interests) in order to protect interests pertaining to the EU (the so-called technique of assimilation).

87. Although the Member States have not transferred legislative powers to the EU in the sector of criminal law and the EU cannot issue new offences, the EU still has considerable impact on the laws of the Member States, including Italy. The impact on Italian criminal law has become even more evident since the Lisbon Treaty entered into force.[78]

As widely known, the Lisbon Treaty amended the Treaty on European Union (TEU or 'Maastricht Treaty')[79] and the Treaty establishing the European Community (TEC or Rome Treaty).[80] Under the Lisbon Treaty, the TEC has been renamed the Treaty on the Functioning of the European Union (TFEU).

Prior to the Lisbon Treaty, the EU was comprised by the three-pillar structure, with each pillar covering certain policy areas. The structure, which was introduced by the Treaty of Maastricht, consisted of: (1) the European Communities,[81] (2) Common Foreign and Security,[82] and (3) Police and Judicial Cooperation in Criminal Matters (PJCC).[83]

77. Constitutional Court Decision No. 170 of 8 Jun. 1984.
78. Treaty of Lisbon amending the Treaty on European Union and the Treaty establishing the European Community, signed at Lisbon, 13 Dec. 2007 and entered into force on 1 Dec. 2009.
79. The Treaty of Maastricht (formally, the Treaty on European Union (TEU)) was signed on 7 Feb. 1992 and entered into force on 1 Nov. 1993.
80. The Treaty on the Functioning of the European Union (The Treaty of Rome) was signed on 25 Mar. 1957 and entered into force on 1 Jan. 1958.
81. Comprised of the EC, the European Coal and Steel Community (ECSC, until its expiry in 2002), and the European Atomic Energy Community (EURATOM), this pillar was the only one with and was responsible for handling economic, social and environmental policies.
82. The Common Foreign and Security Policy (CFSP) pillar was responsible for addressing foreign policy and military matters. This pillar was originally known as Justice and Home Affairs (JHA).
83. Police and Judicial Cooperation in Criminal Matters (PJCC) was responsible for coordinating crime efforts between the Member States.

88. Among the objectives of creating the EU is to provide citizens with a high level of safety within an area of freedom, security and justice by developing common action among the Member States in the fields of police and judicial cooperation in criminal matters and by preventing and combating racism and xenophobia:

> *[The EU aims to achieve this] objective by preventing and combating crime, organised or otherwise, and in particular terrorism, trafficking in persons and offences against children, illicit drug trafficking and illicit arms trafficking, corruption and fraud, through (...) closer cooperation between [countries and] approximation, where necessary, of rules on criminal matters in the Member States, in accordance with the provisions of Article 31(e).* (former Article 29 of the TEU).

The original text of Article 31(1)(e) TEU read:

> *Common action on judicial cooperation in criminal matters shall include: (...) progressively adopting measures establishing minimum rules relating to the constituent elements of criminal acts and to penalties in the fields of organised crime, terrorism and illicit drug trafficking.*

However, under the Lisbon Treaty, this provision has been replaced by Article 83, paragraph 1 TFEU, which states:

> *On the basis of developments in crime, the Council may adopt a decision identifying other areas of crime that meet the criteria specified in this paragraph. It shall act unanimously after obtaining the consent of the European Parliament.*

89. Previously, under Article 34 of the TEU,[84] the EU could be involved in criminal policy in one of three ways: (1) common positions; (2) framework decisions for the purpose of approximation of the laws and regulations of the Member States; and (3) decisions for any other purpose consistent with the objectives of this title, excluding any approximation of the laws and regulations of the Member States.

After the Lisbon Treaty entered into force, harmonization now is achieved through directives rather than framework decisions. Despite the change in format

84. Former Art. 34(2) TEU read as follows: The Council may: (a) adopt common positions defining the approach of the Union to a particular matter; (b) adopt framework decisions for the purpose of approximation of the laws and regulations of the Member States. Framework decisions shall be binding upon the Member States as to the result to be achieved but shall leave to the national authorities the choice of form and methods. They shall not entail direct effect; (c) adopt decisions for any other purpose consistent with the objectives of this title, excluding any approximation of the laws and regulations of the Member States. These decisions shall be binding and shall not entail direct effect; the Council, acting by a qualified majority, shall adopt measures necessary to implement those decisions at the level of the Union; and (d) establish conventions which it shall recommend to the Member States for adoption in accordance with their respective constitutional requirements. Member States shall begin the procedures applicable within a time limit to be set by the Council.

from decisions to directives, in practice there is little change. While the EU may continue to introduce models of conduct for all of the Member States, the applicable punishments will continue to vary from State to State.

B. The Court of Justice of the European Union

90. Italian law is increasingly influenced by decisions of the Court of Justice of the EU, the judicial institution of the EU, and of the European Atomic Energy Community (EURATOM). The Court is actually comprised of three courts: the Court of Justice, the General Court and the Civil Service Tribunal (CST). The primary task of these courts is to examine the legality of EU measures and ensure the uniform interpretation and application of EU law.

91. The first tribunal, the Court of Justice[85] consists of twenty-seven judges and eight advocates general, which are appointed by common accord of the governments of the EU Member States. They are appointed for a renewable six-year term. The judges elect from amongst themselves the president of the Court who serves for a three-year renewable term.

The Court may sit as a full court, in a Grand Chamber, or in panels of three to five judges. When the Court considers a matter to be of exceptional importance or involves particular issues set forth in the Statute of the Court, the matter is heard by the full court. Matters are considered by a Grand Chamber of thirteen judges when requested by a Member State or institution which is a party to a proceeding, and in particularly complex or important cases. Other matters are heard by the panels (or chambers) of three to five judges.

The Court of Justice has jurisdiction over issues relating to:

(1) *References for preliminary rulings* (i.e., to clarify a point concerning the interpretation of or review the validity of EU law). Only a national court may ask for a preliminary ruling; however, all the parties to the proceedings before that court, the Member States and the institutions of the EU may take part in the Court's proceedings. The Court of Justice's ruling is issued as a reasoned judgment or order, which is binding on the national court which raised the issue, but also other courts considering the same problem.
(2) *Actions for failure to fulfil obligations, so-called infringements proceedings.* These proceedings are usually brought by the Commission; however, they may also be requested by a Member State. The purpose of these actions is to determine whether a Member State has fulfilled its obligations under EU law. If the Court determines that the Member State has not fulfilled its obligation, the State must cure the default without delay. If, after a further action is brought by the Commission, the Member State does not fulfil its obligations and the judgments, the Court may impose a financial sanction.

85. http://curia.europa.eu/jcms/jcms/Jo2_7024/. (Accessed June 2015).

(3) *Actions for annulment.* In these proceedings, the applicant is requesting the annulment of a measure (i.e., regulation, directive, or decision) adopted by an EU institution, body, office or agency. The Court of Justice has exclusive jurisdiction over actions brought by a Member State against the European Parliament and/or against the Council (apart from Council measures in respect of State aid, dumping, and implementing powers) or brought by one EU institution against another. The General Court has jurisdiction, at first instance, in all other actions of this type and particularly in actions brought by individuals.
(4) *Actions for failure to act.* When an EU institution, body or agency has failed to act despite calls to act, an action may be brought to the Court to determine if the failure is unlawful. If so, the institution involved must put an end to the failure by adopting or undertaking the appropriate steps. Jurisdiction for these types of actions is shared between the Court of Justice and the General Court according to the same criteria as for actions for annulment.
(5) *Appeals.* Reviews of judgments and orders of the General Court may be brought before the Court of Justice on appeal. If the Court finds the appeal admissible and well founded, it will set aside the General Court's judgment. If the proceedings permit, the Court may render its own decision; otherwise, the case is remanded to the General Court which is bound by the Court of Justice's decision.
(6) *Reviews.* The Court may review decisions of the General Court on appeals against decisions of the EU CST, in exceptional circumstances, as provided in the Protocol on the Statute of the Court of Justice of the EU.[86]

92. The General Court is comprised of at least one judge from each Member State, who is appointed for a renewable term of six years. The judges are appointed by the common agreement of the Members States. The General Court does not have permanent Advocate's General as does the Court of Justice; however, in exceptional circumstances, a judge may fulfil the role of an Advocate.

The General Court hears matter in panels (or chambers) of one, three, or five judges, with the overwhelming majority of the matters heard by a panel of three judges. Judges perform their duties in a totally impartial and independent manner. When a case is particularly complex or important, the Court may sit in a Grand Chamber of thirteen judges.

With respect to jurisdiction, the General Court may consider actions:

(1) directly brought by natural or legal persons against: (a) the acts of an EU institution, body, office, or agency (which are addressed to the person or are of direct and individual concern to them), (b) regulatory acts (which concern the person directly and which do not entail implementing measures), or (3) failure to act on the part of an EU institution, body, office, or agency;
(2) brought by a Member States against the Commission;

86. http://curia.europa.eu/jcms/jcms/Jo2_7033/. (Accessed June 2015).

(3) brought by a Member States against the Council relating to acts adopted in the field of State aid, 'dumping' and acts by which it exercises implementing powers;
(4) seeking compensation for damage caused by the institutions of the EU or their staff;
(5) based on contracts made by the EU which expressly give jurisdiction to the General Court;
(6) relating to Community trade marks; and
(7) brought against decisions of the Community Plant Variety Office or of the European Chemicals Agency.

The General Court may also hear appeals, limited to points of law, against the decisions of the EU CST. Decisions rendered by the General Court may be appealed (but limited to points of law) to the Court of Justice within two months of issuance.

93. The third court is the CST,[87] a specialized forum which considers at first instance – pursuant to Article 270 TFEU – disputes between the EU and the people working for EU institutions. It may not hear matters between national administrations and their employees. Examples of disputes heard by the CST include typical labour issues (pay, career progress, recruitment, disciplinary measures, etc.), as well as social security system matters (sickness, old age, invalidity, accidents at work, family allowances, etc.).

The CST is comprised of seven judges, appointed for a six-year renewable term. The CST judges are appointed by the Council, which strives to create a balanced court with a geographical basis as broad as possible in order to consider the Member States and their legal systems.

Typically, the CST sits in panels (chambers) of three judges, although in cases determined by the Tribunal's Rules of Procedure, it may sit as a mono judge or a panel of five judges. Matters which are particularly complex or involve important questions of law, may be hear by the full court.

Decisions rendered by the CST may be appealed (but limited to points of law) to the Court of Justice within two months of issuance.

C. The European Court of Human Rights

94. The other judicial forum with jurisdiction to hear matters is the European Court of Human Rights, which was established in 1959. The Court rules on individual or State applications alleging violations of the civil and political rights set out in the ECHR. As of 1998, it is a full-time court, and individuals can apply to it directly. Since the Court was created, nearly half of its judgments have concerned Italy or one of three other Member States (Turkey, Russia and Poland).[88]

---

87. http://curia.europa.eu/jcms/jcms/T5_5230/.
88. *The European Court of Human Rights in Facts and Figures* (2010), 6, www.echr.coe.int (Accessed June 2015).

Applications to the European Court of Human Rights may be made by individuals (including any person, group of individuals, company or Non-Governmental Organization (NGO)) or by one State by another. To date, the majority of applications have been brought by individuals. The Court may not take up cases *sua sponte*.[89]

95. The Court composition is determined by the number of parties to the ECHR, i.e., forty-seven at present. The judges are elected for a non-renewable nine-year-term by the Parliamentary Assembly of the Council of Europe from lists of three candidates proposed by each State.

The Court sits in one of four formations: single or mono judges; panels of three or seven judges; or a Grand Chamber of seventeen judges. Single judges are responsible for examining manifestly in admissible applications, while three-judge panels may rule by a unanimous vote on the admissibility and merits of cases that are already covered by well-established case law of the Court. Seven-judge panels rule by majority vote on the admissibility and merits of other cases, and the Grand Chamber considers cases referred to it either after relinquishment of jurisdiction by a Chamber or when a request. Judges may not hear matters as a solo judge when the matter involves their own country. However, national judges may sit on a three-judge panel and are always included as part of a seven-judge chamber or Grand Chamber.

96. Judgments issued by the European Court of Human Rights are binding on the Member State involved. If a violation is found, the State concerned must make efforts to make certain that the violations do not occur again in the future. In some situations, it is necessary for the State to amend its national legislation to make it in line with the ECHR. With that purpose Law No. 12 of 9 January 2006, containing the 'Provisions on enforcement of judgments of the European Court of Human Rights', introduced the letter *a-bis*) in Article 5, paragraph 3 of Law No. 400/1988, according to which the Prime Minister '*promotes the fulfillment of governmental obligations resulting from decisions of the European Court of Human Rights issued against the Italian state*'.

In addition, the execution of the rendered judgments is monitored by the Committee of Ministers of the Council of Europe, particularly to ensure that the violating State pays any damages awards issued by the Court.

97. Chamber judgments may be appealed within three months of delivery by requesting referral to the Grand Chamber. Such requests are examined by a panel of judges who determine if the referral is appropriate. If so, the matter is referred and the Grand Chamber reviews the case anew.

Grand Chamber judgments and inadmissibility decisions are final and may not be appealed.

89. *European Court of Human Rights: the ECHR in 50 questions* (Provisional Edition – December 2010), www.echr.coe.int. (Accessed June 2015).

98. In 2014, the European Court of Human Rights dealt with a total of 9,769 applications involving Italy, with 9,625 being declared inadmissible or struck out. Of the remaining 144 applications, the court delivered 44 judgments, with 39 of the judgments finding at least one violation of the ECHR.[90]

III. The Council of Europe

99. The Council of Europe was founded in 1949 and operates by means of multilateral European conventions, resolutions and recommendations containing guidelines on legal standards (including criminal policy), human rights, democratic development, the rule of law and cultural cooperation. At present, the Council has forty-seven Member States. In particular, the Council of Europe has the following tasks:

(1) Harmonizing as much as possible the criminal laws of different countries through conventions or directives in order to fulfil common fundamental principles and limiting the power of a State in order to protect fundamental human rights or to extend such protection for those interests which deserve an higher protection.
In this sense, it is important to recall the ECHR of 4 November 1950. The ECHR creates not only obligations for the State but also rights which are enforceable by individuals. In addition to Article 5, which guarantees the right to freedom of persons and Article 6, which contain special guarantees protecting the parties who are involved in criminal proceedings, a considerable number of other provisions of the Convention and of the Protocols to the Convention are likely to relate to substantive criminal law as well as to criminal procedure. Article 2 concerns justifying circumstances for homicide and voluntary bodily injury; Article 3 prohibits the use of torture and all inhuman or degrading treatment of convicted persons and in obtaining proof or information from suspects; Article 7 forbids inflicting a punishment stronger than that which was applicable at the moment the infraction was committed; searches and seizures of property are authorized to the extent to which they comply with the conditions defined by Article 8, paragraph 2; Article 9 protects the individual against abominable means of police or judicial investigation which deprive the suspect of his intellectual faculties and his consciousness.
Italy has also approved the ICCPR, which contains provisions that are comparable to those of the European Convention, and have the force of law in Italy. It is also worthwhile to recall the European Convention on the Suppression of Terrorism of 27 January 1977.[91]
(2) Developing collaboration between Member States which has been enforced by means of the Convention on Mutual Assistance in Criminal Matters of 20 April 1959 (ratified by Italy with Law No. 215 of 23 February 1961).

90. *The European Court of Human Rights: Italy* (updated as of April 2013), www.echr.coe.int (Accessed June 2015).
91. Ratified by Italy on 28 Feb. 1986 and entered into force on 1 Jun. 1986.

Many issues of mutual assistance in criminal matters are also addressed by EU instruments, such as the European Arrest Warrant adopted with the 13 June 2002 framework decision of the EU Council of Ministers (implemented in Italy by Law No. 69 of 22 April 2005).[92] These warrants are issued by a Member State in order to obtain the arrest and the handover of the arrested person from another Member State.[93]

IV. National Sources

A. *The Constitution*

100. The Constitution sets forth the framework for the penal system, and no law can conflict with the Constitution. The Constitutional Court is charged with insuring that the provisions of Italian criminal law conform to the Constitution.[94]

The Constitution also establishes two fundamental principles: specifically there can be no crime without a law[95] and no penalty without a law.[96] Additional principles founded by the Constitution include: (a) legal responsibility rests solely on the acting individual;[97] (b) rules of penal law are not retroactive;[98] (c) no one can be sentenced without a fair trial (*nulla poena sine judicio*);[99] (d) no one can be considered guilty until a final sentence has been pronounced;[100] (e) penalties cannot consist in treatment contrary to the sense of humanity and must tend to the rehabilitation of the offender;[101] and (f) personal freedom is inviolable, and no one shall be deprived of it except under specific provisions of the law.[102]

B. *Statutes and Legislation*

101. The Italian Constitution provides the principle of legality (*infra*, paragraphs 111–113), and under this provision, criminal offences can only be created and penalties can only be imposed by virtue of a statute, i.e., an Act of Parliament. The primary sources of Italian criminal law are the Constitution and statutes.

In Italy, the primary sources of statutory criminal law are found in the PC, the Italian CCP, and certain special laws (*supra*, paragraphs 37–39).

92. The rules regarding the European Arrest Warrant were modified by Legislative Decree No. 101 of 1 Jul. 2014, adopted to implement EU Directive 13/2012.
93. See ECtHR judgment C-261/09, *Criminal Proceedings against Gaetano Mantello.*
94. Constitution Art. 134.
95. Constitution Art. 25.
96. Constitution Art. 25.
97. Constitution Art. 27.
98. Constitution Art. 25.
99. Constitution Art. 111.
100. Constitution Art. 27.
101. Constitution Art. 27.
102. Constitution Art. 13.

C. Statutory Delegated Legislation

102. Under Article 24 of the Italian Constitution, all criminal laws must be the product of the Italian Legislature (e.g., *Senato* and *Camera*) and have approval of both branches. Regions, provinces and municipalities cannot introduce new criminal laws.

D. Ordinary Laws

103. Italian criminal law is based on the PC, the CCP and the relevant special laws. As mentioned *supra*, paragraph 86, subject to the influence of EU law, the Legislative Power has the monopoly on the production of criminal law (directly or through laws enacted under delegated power) (Constitution Article 117, paragraph 1).

104. Italy also has certain provisions which apply to all laws, civil, criminal and administrative. These laws – *Disposizione sulla Legge in Generale* (Italian General Law Provisions) – are located in the beginning of the Italian Civil Code.

105. In addition to the PC, Italy has a number of special laws, which have always served as an important source of criminalization. The use of special legislation has increased over the years, to the point that for many legal scholars, the Rocco Code is no longer the main source of the Italian criminal justice system, but a secondary and supplementary one.

Among the numerous special criminal laws, it is necessary to mention at least those related to secret associations (Law No. 17 of 25 January 1982); corporate entities (Legislative Decree No. 61 of 11 April 2002); the credit market (Legislative Decree No. 58 of 1998); the banking market (Legislative Decree No. 385 of 24 February 1993); the environment (Legislative Decree No. 152 of 3 April 2006); bankruptcy (Royal Decree No. 267 of 16 March 1942); paedophilia and prostitution (Law No. 75 of 20 February 1958); immigration (Legislative Decree No. 286 of 25 July 1998); drugs (Presidential Decree No. 309 of 9 October 1990); and taxation (Law No. 516 of 7 August 1982).

E. Court Decisions

106. As a civil law country, Italy does not adhere to the common law doctrine that precedents are binding. The only means for defining offences and the related punishment is through statutory law. However, court decisions are nevertheless important in the Italian system – including in the criminal justice system – as lower court judges often refer to prior decisions, in particular decisions of the Court of Cassation, because the judges are aware that if they rule in a contrary manner, there is a substantial likelihood that they will be reversed on appeal.

§5. Classifications and Technique of Criminal Law

107. The Italian PC is separated into two parts: general and specific. The general part consists of provisions that can be applied to all the offences, while the specific part of the Code covers single criminal offences.

The PC is composed of three books. The first book contains the general section. The second and third books are the specific part of the Code and outline the various offences.

108. Under the PC, all offences fall into two broad categories: *delitti*, which are crimes or serious offences and *contravvenzioni*, which are misdemeanours or less serious offences. The distinction between *delitti* and *contravvenzioni* is based on the severity of punishment. The two categories are also used to help to classify special law statutes (drugs, prostitution, weapons, bankruptcy, pollution, hunting, traffic, customs, tax evasion, Military Code in wartime and in peacetime). (See also *infra*, paragraphs 291 et seq.).

The offences are divided into categories and grouped together under headings and sub-headings, e.g., offences against:

(1) the Nation (e.g., espionage, assassination of the president, armed bands, terrorism) (Title I PC);
(2) public authority (for instance, corruption, bribery, embezzlement of public property by an officer) (Title II PC);
(3) judicial authority (e.g., perjury, to suborn a witness) (Title III PC);
(4) religious feelings and against the feelings of pity towards the dead (profanation of a tomb, offences against religion) (Title IV PC);
(5) public order/breach of the peace (for instance, criminal association, particularly of the Mafioso type) (Title V PC);
(6) public safety (poisoning food, water and drugs, arson, provoking a railway, or air disaster) (Title VI PC);
(7) public faithfulness (forgery and counterfeiting) (Title VII PC);
(8) public economy, industry and commerce (commercial fraud) (Title VIII PC);
(9) public morality (rape, indecent exposure); (Title IX PC);
(10) feelings for animals (Title IX*bis* PC);
(11) well-being and soundness of race (Title X PC);
(12) the family (bigamy, incest) (Title XI PC);
(13) the person/violent crimes (murder, assault, non-ransom kidnapping, defamation) (Title XII PC); and
(14) property (theft, money laundering, robbery, extortion, ransom kidnapping). (The PC considers the violent crimes of robbery, extortion, and ransom kidnapping as property crimes because their main intent to gain property.) (Title XIII PC).

Part I. Substantive Criminal Law

Chapter 1. General Principles

§1. The Principle of Legality

I. Limitation on Penalization

109. The principle of legality – also called of strict legality – usually expressed by the Latin maxim *nullum crimen, nulla poena sine lege*, is fundamental for Italian criminal law. This principle was ratified in Article 26 of the Sardinian *Statuto Albertino* of 1848, and is reaffirmed in four texts. Article 1 PC, provides that no penalty can be introduced or imposed other than by force of law. Furthermore, Article 25, com. 2, of the Italian Constitution provides that penalties may be imposed only if they have been provided by statute prior to the commission of the offence. This article also holds the principle of non-retroactivity as the temporal condition of the principle of legality (*supra*, paragraph 101 and *infra*, paragraphs 111–113). Moreover, Article 199 PC, provides that security measures can be imposed only if they are expressly provided by law and in the circumstances provided by the law. Finally, Article 363 CCP provides that the defendant should be acquitted if the fact of which he was declared guilty is not forbidden by force of penal statute.

The essence of the principle of legality is the limitation on penalization by State officials, affected by prescription and application of specific, statutory rules.

The principles have an origin not strictly criminal, in fact it derives from the policy domain and in particular from the period of enlightenment as a reaction against the unlimited power of a judge to supplement or make exceptions to scattered, incomplete and sometimes contradictory penal provisions.

110. The Italian penal law is written according to statutory law, as opposed to customary or case law. This means that the basis of the punishment has to be written with statutory provisions, and that it is forbidden for the judge to apply similar provisions in cases which are not expressly regulated. This is called the *principio di tassatività* ('peremptoriness principle') of criminal law, according to which criminal law is only applicable to facts (or cases) expressly contemplated by law.

II. Legality and Interpretation, and the Prohibition against Using Analogy

111. With regards to the principle of legality, the question of interpretation or construction of penal statutes arises. No doubt, if the language of a statute is plain and its meaning is clear, the judge must give effect to the statute, regardless of what he thinks of its appropriateness: *in claris non fit interpretatio*. However, if the text is ambiguous or unclear on the principle of legality, this then requires the judge to determine the meaning and scope of a penal statute strictly.

112. Interpretation is the mental operation by which one looks for the meaning of the law. Most legal commentators agree that the rules applying to the interpretation of criminal law are the same as applied to other types of statutes, with the only exception that interpretation by analogy is forbidden.

The interpretation can be authentic, when coming from the same authority empowered to issue the law; judicial, when performed by a judge, and doctrinal (also called *opinion doctorum*) when coming from legal scholars.

Interpretation can also be classified as restrictive and extensive when it is not possible to ascribe to the law the meaning which appears prima facie.

Article 12 of the General Provisions of Italian Law provides that in applying the law, one must consider the real meaning of the words with regards to their logic connection and the real intention of the legislator.

When interpreting penal statutes, normal usage of the language shall be taken into consideration, unless the legislator gives a divergent and technical meaning to a word. In order to determine whether a fact is a criminal offence or not, the legislator's goal or intention may be a decisive criterion (i.e., authentic interpretation).

113. The principle of legality and Article 14 of the General Provisions of Italian Law do not allow interpretation by analogy. The Italian penal system does not permit the so-called analogy in *malam partem* as a criterion to ascribe penal provisions to conduct which is not proscribed by them. Doubts can arise in the case of analogy in the defendant's favour. Most legal scholars also accept analogy in the defendant's favour when considering provisions regarding impunity or mitigation of penalties. The prohibition of reasoning by analogy is a direct consequence of the *principio di tassatività* (peremptoriness principle).

Such a prohibition derives not only from Article 25 of the Italian Constitution (principle of legality), but also from Article 14 of the General Provisions of Italian Law, which states that '*criminal statutes and provisions making exceptions to general principles are only applicable to cases and within the time contemplated therein*'.

It is easy to identify the rationale of such prohibition: to prevent judges from creating new rules, applicable to cases not expressly contemplated by law.

§2. The Principle of the Individual Guilty Mind

114. A fundamental rule of substantive Italian criminal law is the principle of individual guilt. Article 42 PC states that no person can be punished for offences committed unless there is conscience and will. This important principle derives from the Classical School of Criminal Law which considers the human being capable of controlling his emotions and selecting those reactions possible under the circumstances.

The central role of this principle is confirmed by Article 27 of the Italian Constitution which underlines the penal principle of *nulla poena sine culpa* (i.e., no punishment without guilt) and rejects the principle of objective responsibility. According to this principle, when evidence shows that the offender was not mentally competent at the time he committed the prohibited act, he cannot be convicted as a criminal – no matter how horrible the offence or how dangerous the offender – because he cannot be held accountable and responsible for his conduct (See *infra,* paragraphs 243 et seq.).

§3. The Principle of Proportionality

115. A third leading principle of Italian criminal law is the principle of proportionality; specifically the punishment must be proportionate to the seriousness of the offence and to the degree of responsibility and culpability of the offender. This principle is based on the concept provided by Article 27 of the Italian Constitution according to which the punishment cannot offend the sense of humanity and must take into consideration the re-education of the condemned. This principle is a guideline of the idea of justice and a parameter of any modern theory on the penalty.

However, there are certain exceptions to the application of this principle: Article 133 PC provides that the judge should consider not only the gravity of the offence, when setting the punishment, but also the defendant's virtual criminal attitude.

Chapter 2. Scope and Application of Criminal Statutes

116. Occasionally, between commission of the offending act and time of trial, the legislature amends the relevant criminal statute. In this event, *quid iuris* (i.e., what is the law) requires the judge choose between the old and the new statute.

§1. Principles concerning the Applicability of Criminal Statutes with Respect to Time

I. Prohibition of Retroactive Criminal Law

117. According to Article 11 of the General Provisions of Italian Law, laws only apply to the future. This means penalties may be imposed only if provided by statute prior to the commission of the offence. Furthermore, Article 2 PC, mentions the principle of *non-retroactivity* i.e., criminal law has no retroactive force and embodies the prohibition against *ex post facto legislation*. This principle is valid both when: (1) a new offence is created by law, and (2) an existing offence is defined in a different way and would result in the case being determined in another manner.

The prohibition against retroactivity expresses the essential temporal condition of the principle of legality: the required criminal law must have existed at the time of the conduct in question. This is also demanded by the Classical School of Criminal Law: a person cannot be judged to be guilty if, at the moment of his act or omission, he could not have known that he had committed an offence. It is unjust to consider something criminal, when it was legal when done, or punish something more severely when a lesser sanction applied at the time of the act.

The prohibition is also set forth in Article 7 of the ECHR:

1. *No one shall be held guilty of any criminal offence on account of any act or omission which did not constitute a criminal offence under national or international law at the time when it was committed. Nor shall a heavier penalty be imposed than the one that was applicable at the time the criminal offence was committed.*
2. *This article shall not prejudice the trial and punishment of any person for any act or omission which, at the time when it was committed, was criminal according to the general principles of law recognized by civilized nations.*

II. Retroactivity of the Favourable Statute

118. Article 2, paragraph 2 PC, sets forth the principle of the retroactivity of the favourable statute. Any modification of substantive criminal law is retroactive if it benefits the defendant. This rule modifies the principle of *tempus commissi delicti*: i.e., the statutes which existed at the time of the commission of the act are applicable to the act. This exception finds its origin in the Classical School of Criminal

Law, which holds that a severe penalty should not be imposed if the criminal law has become less harsh.

It is important to establish what favourable law means for the guilty party. In a judgment, one cannot mix the content of an old rule with the content of a new one. Once the choice is made, the favourable rule should be applied in its entirety (Court of Cassation Decision No. 416 of 17 September 2004).

It is worth noting that only the case at issue is to be evaluated; the judge must consider the various consequences that applying the different rules would have on the specific case.[103]

Additionally, Article 25 of the Italian Constitution provides that '*No one may be punished except on the basis of a law already in force before the offence was committed.*'

The same principle is also affirmed on Article 7 of the ECHR and Article 15 of the ICCPR of 16 December 1966.

Moreover, according to the European Court of Human Rights, not only does ECHR Article 7 guarantee the prohibition against the retroactivity of more stringent criminal laws, but also, and implicitly, the retroactivity of more lenient laws. In other words, when a law is enacted before the final judgment is rendered and the subsequent law is more lenient than the law which was in force at the time of the offence, the court must apply the law which is more favourable to the defendant.[104]

§2. Principles concerning the Applicability of Criminal Statutes with Respect to Space

I. Compulsory Character of Criminal Law

119. The Italian criminal law is compulsory for every person – Italian citizen or foreigner – who is located within the Italian territory, with the exceptions provided for by domestic public and international law (Article 3 CCP).

The rationale of this principle is consistent with the character of criminal law: the law must be applied to everyone, regardless of their citizenship, since the law aims at protecting interests having a particular social value.

120. Specific immunities, however, are granted to certain categories of persons by domestic public and international law (*infra*, paragraphs 134–137).

103. Court of Cassation Decision of 6 Oct. 1979, in *Giust. Pen.*, II (1980), 1; *Ibid.*, 25 Jan. 1978, in *Riv. Pen.* 713 (1978).

104. See *Scoppola v. Italy* (No. 2), ECtHR Grand Chamber judgment of 17 Sep. 2009. In *Scoppola*, the European Court of Human Rights found that in convicting the applicant for murder according to the summary procedure, the Italian courts should have applied the most lenient provision in force during the period between the offence and the final judgment. As the Italian Courts failed to do this, the ECtHR found violations of ECHR Arts 6 (right to fair trial) and 7 (no punishment without law) and awarded the applicant EUR 10,000 in non-monetary damages, EUR 10,000 in costs and expenses, and order the more lenient provision be applied.

II. The Territorial Principle

121. According to Article 6, paragraph 1 PC, when a criminal offence is committed on the Italian territory by either an Italian or a foreigner, it is punishable according to the provisions of Italian law. This rule embodies the territorial principle based on State sovereignty.

However, complications can arise in determining when an offence is considered to be committed on Italian territory. The legislator has chosen the criteria of ubiquity which means that the offence is committed on Italian territory when the act or omission is, completely or partially, committed on this territory or when the consequence of the omission or the act is realized within the territory.

122. The notion of territory is mentioned in Article 6 PC, explained by Article 4 PC, and comprises the territory within the borders and everything belonging to the sovereignty of the State, including Italian ships and aircraft, wherever they are, except in the event they are subject to a foreign territorial law according to international law (Article 4 PC).

The sovereignty of the State extends beyond its land territory and its internal waters to a belt of sea adjacent to its coast, described as the territorial waters. The Italian territorial waters are limited to twelve nautical miles (Article 2 Navigation Code), measured in principle from the low-water line along the coast as marked on large-scale charts officially recognized by the State. Article 4 of the Navigation Code establishes that boats and ships are considered Italian territory. In this case, the Geneva Convention on Territorial Sea and Contiguous Zones (29 April 1958) comes into play (ratified by Italy on 17 December 1964 and entered into force on 16 January 1965). The Convention states that the criminal jurisdiction of the coastal State should not be exercised on board a foreign ship passing through territorial waters to arrest any person or to conduct any investigation in connection with any crime committed on board the ship during its passage, unless the consequences of the crime extend to the coastal State; or if the crime is such that it disturbs the peace of the country of the good order of the territorial sea; or if the assistance of the local authorities has been requested by the captain of the ship or by the consul of the country whose flag the ship flies; or if it is necessary for the suppression of illicit traffic in narcotic drugs.

Article 4 of the Italian Navigation Code extends the sovereignty of the State to the airspace over the territorial waters as well as to the bed of the territorial waters and to the subsoil of the land and the territorial waters.

III. Extraterritorial Criminal Jurisdiction

A. *Principles*

123. Articles 7, 9 and 10 PC constitute an exception to the basic territorial principle and cover certain offences committed outside Italy. Italians and foreigners can be punished for offences occurring outside the territory of Italy only if specifically mentioned by statute. The legislator was guided by the principle of defence and by either the *universality principle* (i.e., for so-called *delicta juris gentium* or offences against the law of nations) or the *opportunity principle.*

The universality principle – i.e., every State has to secure its own legal order as well as that of the other States – embodies the concept of international solidarity in the struggle against criminality. The protection principle, however, extends the application of national criminal law to foreign countries when public or private national interests need protection.

124. The Italian State and Vatican City are independent and have their own laws, and their relations are regulated by the Lateran Pacts[105] and successive treaties. Pursuant to these agreements, under very limited and specific circumstances, Italy's criminal jurisdiction can extend into the Vatican territory.

B. Cases

125. Extraterritorial criminal jurisdiction is primarily covered in Articles 7, 9 and 10 PC.

126. In particular, Article 7 PC regarding 'Offenses Committed Abroad' states that a citizen or foreigner is punished according to Italian law whenever he has committed one of the following offences:

- offences against the Italian State;
- counterfeiting Italian currency;
- offences committed by public officer by abusing of their public position or power;
- all conduct for which international acts establish the applicability of Italian law.

127. Aside from those cases provided by Article 7 PC, a citizen may be punished for offences committed outside the Italian territory if: (1) according to Italian law, the conduct is punishable by life imprisonment or imprisonment of no less than three years; and (2) the Italian citizen if found within the Italian territory (Article 9 PC).

128. Under Article 10 PC, foreigners committing offences outside the Italian territory are subject to punishment in Italy if the crime was committed against an Italian citizen or the Italian State and Italian law provides punishment of life imprisonment or imprisonment of no less than one year, and provided that the offender is present on the Italian territory during the criminal action phase and the Italian Minister of Justice requests prosecution.

105. Constitution Art. 7.

C. Localization

129. It can be challenging to define when an offence is considered to be committed on the Italian territory. The legislator has chosen the *objective doctrine* of *ubiquity*, according to which an offence is considered to have been committed within the Italian territory if: (1) one of the physical acts or omissions constituting an element of the offence was perpetrated there, or (2) the effects of the offence manifested there (Article 6 PC).

D. The Effect of Foreign Adjudication and Execution

130. According to Article 11 PC, if a foreigner or citizen has been sentenced in another country, the Italian courts can adjudicate the defendant again when certain conditions have been met. However, only through a specific proceeding, is it possible to recognize the effects of a foreign adjudication and proceed with extradition (Article 697 CCP).

131. More specifically, the delivery to a foreign country of a person for the execution of a foreign sentence of imprisonment or other measure restricting personal freedom can only take place through extradition. When there is more than one extradition request, the Italian Minister of Justice shall decide the order of precedence, taking into account all the circumstances of the case and in particular the date of receipt of applications, the seriousness and place of commission of the offence, nationality and residence of the person sought, and the possibility of re-extradition from requesting State to another State (Article 697 CCP).

Decisions to extradite must also take into consideration the ECHR (*infra,* paragraphs 552–553) and in particular Article 3 (i.e., the prohibition against torture and inhuman or degrading treatment). In fact, in the 1983 case of *Saadi v. Italy,*[106] the European Court of Human Rights – sitting in Grand Chamber – found Italy in violation of Article 3, when Italy issued an order to deport Nassim Saadi on the basis of Law Decree No. 144 of 27 July 2005[107] (Urgent Measures to Enhance the Prevention of and Fight against International Terrorism). In his application, Saadi asserted that if he were deported, in Tunisia he would be subject to torture or inhuman treatment. The Court agreed with his position finding that Italy had failed to insure that if Saadi were returned to Tunisia, he would be entitled to a new review of the case.

106. *Saadi v. Italy*, ECtHR judgment of 28 Feb. 1983. For other similar cases involving Tunisia, see; *Toumi v. Italy* ECtHR judgment of 5 Apr. 2011; *Abdelhedi v. Italy,* ECtHR judgment of 24 Mar. 2009; *Ben Salah v. Italy*, ECtHR judgment of 24 Mar. 2009; ECtHR *Bouyahia v. Italy*, ECtHR judgment of 24 Mar. 2009; C.B.Z. *v.* Italy, ECtHR judgment of 24 Mar. 2009; *Darraji v. Italy*, ECtHR judgment of 24 Mar. 2009; *Hamraoui v. Italy*, ECtHR judgment of 24 Mar. 2009; *O v. Italy.*, ECtHR judgment of 24 Mar. 2009; and *Soltana v. Italy*, ECtHR judgment of 24 Mar. 2009. See also *Hirisi Jamaa and others v. Italy* ECtHR judgment of 23 Feb. 2012 (Somalian and Eritrean migrants travelling from and sent back to Libya).

107. Converted into Law No. 155 of 31 Jul. 2005.

132. As a Schengen country, Italy is also subject to the provisions of the Convention Implementing the Schengen Agreement Mutual Assistance in Judicial Matters (CISA) as set forth in Chapter 2 of Title III (Police and Security).

133. Of particular interest are the provisions of the CISA regarding the principle of *ne bis in idem* (i.e., a 'not twice for the same' otherwise known as the rule against double jeopardy). According to Article 54 of the CISA:

> A person whose trial has been finally disposed of in one Contracting Party may not be prosecuted in another Contracting Party for the same acts provided that, if a penalty has been imposed, it has been enforced, is actually in the process of being enforced or can no longer be enforced under the laws of the sentencing Contracting Party.

§3. Principles Concerning the Applicability of Criminal Statutes with Respect to Persons

134. Although criminal statutes are generally applicable to all persons (Article 3 PC), according to the above-mentioned principles of the applicability of criminal law with respect to time and space, both national and international public law grant immunities from criminal proceedings to certain persons.

I. Immunities Based on National Public Law

135. Article 90 of the Italian Constitution states that the President of the Republic cannot be prosecuted or punished during the exercise of the public power, except for high treason or attack on the Constitution. Thus, he has the rights of a common citizen for acts committed outside his function.

If the President of the Senate substitutes for the President of the Republic, he has the same immunity during such period.

136. Members of the Parliament (*Camera* and *Senato*) enjoy special immunities as set forth in Article 68 of the Italian Constitution. Specifically, they cannot be persecuted for expressing a vote during the exercise of their function.

Article 68, paragraph 2 (changed by Constitutional Law No. 3 of 29 October 1993), states that no member of either House, throughout the duration of a session, can be arrested for matters which could result in punishment without the authorization of the House of which he is a member, except for flagrant cases.

II. Immunities Based on International Public Law

137. Certain immunities from criminal proceedings derive from International treaties signed or recognized by the Italian Government as stated in Article 10 of the Italian Constitution.

These immunities are:

(1) The Pope is sacred and inviolable (Article 8 of Lateran Treaty).
(2) Freedom from criminal prosecution in Italy is also granted by members of diplomatic missions of foreign States.

The extent of the diplomatic immunity depends upon the status of the member in question and is regulated both by the Vienna Convention on Diplomatic Relations of 18 April 1961 (ratified by Italy on 25 June 1969 and entered into force on 25 July 1969) and by the Vienna Convention on Consular Relations of 24 April 1963 (entered into force in Italy on 25 June 1969). Both Conventions have been ratified by Italy. The immunity of a diplomatic agent from the criminal jurisdiction of the recipient State does not exempt him from the jurisdiction of the sending State, although this State may waive this right. It is interesting to note that Italy has unusually high number of diplomats, as many foreign States have three embassies in Rome: one for Italy, a second for the Holy See (Vatican), and a third for the UN's Agencies in Rome (e.g., WFP, FAO).

By a number of conventions and agreements ratified by Italy, immunity is granted to States and to members of international or supranational organizations, e.g.,:

- General Agreement on Privileges and Immunities of the Council of Europe of 2 September 1949 and accompanying protocols.
- Protocol on the Privileges and Immunities of the European Communities of 8 April 1965.
- European Agreement relating to persons participating in proceeding of the European Commission and Court of Human Rights of 6 May 1969.
- European Convention on State Immunity of 16 May 1972.

Chapter 3. General Principles of Criminal Law

§1. Introduction: The Basic Elements of Criminal Offences

138. An individual is criminally liable if he has carried out an offence which is subject to a criminal sanction.

139. The first step in verifying whether a crime has been committed is to consider the basic elements of the criminal offence. However, this represents one of the major challenges faced by Italian legal scholars, who have approached the analysis in two distinct manners. The theories can be divided into two groups: 'the traditional theory' which requires only two elements, a material and a moral one, for a criminal offence to exist, while according to the second theory, criminal offences require not only the material and moral elements, but also unlawfulness and for some scholars there must also be punishability.[108] The concept of unlawfulness (*antigiuridicità*) concerns the absence of justification for the offence. On the contrary, if a fact can be justified, it can be considered lawful.

According to the first theory, a criminal offence is '*a human fact committed with a culpable mind*' while for the second theory, an offence is represented by '*an unlawful and guilty behaviour*'.

140. It is important to point out that a distinction between the different elements of a certain fact has the character of conventionality; thus, for scientific and educational purposes, it seems more appropriate to look at criminal offences by means of the traditional theory.

§2. The Material or Physical Element (*Actus Reus*)

I. Description

141. According to the traditional theory of criminal offences, the material element is an external human behaviour prohibited by criminal law, which can consist of an act or in an omission.

Without a human behaviour, there is no criminal offence because it is through the behaviour that the breach of criminal law can actually be carried out.

142. In some cases, a conduct is not sufficient to establish the material element because the law may require the behaviour that has an effect or cause an event.

The conduct and the event are different concepts, but they must be linked by a chain of causation, otherwise it would not be possible to consider the event as a consequence of the behaviour. In light of this consideration, when analysing the

108. For more information on the first theory, see F. Antolisei, *Manuale di diritto penale* 211 et seq. (Milano 2006). For further information about the tripartite theory, see Marinucci-Dolcini, *Manuale di diritto penale. Parte generale* 141 et seq. (Milano 2006).

material element, three things must be considered: (a) the conduct, (b) the event, and (c) the chain of causation.

143. As mentioned above, the conduct can consist of an action or an omission. Omission is the opposite of action, but they have a common element in that they are both objectifications of human personality.

The description given by law to a certain material element consists of various specific elements such as those relating to the offender or the victim and those regarding surrounding circumstances such as, for example, time and place or normative elements.

144. It is worth pointing out that a criminal offence is characterized by a modification of the reality, by an external physical act.

Criminal law is not applicable to mere ideas not put into practice and is not concerned with those thoughts and emotions not converted into action. A mere intention which is not converted into action is not relevant for criminal law pursuant to the Latin maxim *cogitationis poenam nemo patitur* (no one can be punished for thinking).

II. Corporate Responsibility

145. Until a few years ago, it was accepted that only an individual could realize the material element of an offence; thus, corporations, enterprises, or legal entities in general could never be held liable for offences, according to the Latin concept *societas delinquere non potest* (i.e., companies cannot commit an offence).

According to contemporary Italian law, entities can be held liable if certain specific offences listed by law are carried out by certain individuals who have specific relationships with the corporation.

146. In accordance with Legislative Decree No. 231 of 8 June 2001 (Decree No. 231/2001), an entity may be held liable for administrative wrongdoings deriving from a crime, when the crime was committed in the interest or to the benefit of the same entity, by:

(1) persons who represent the entity or persons who fill management positions in the entity or in one of its unit, or persons who effectively manage and control the entity (i.e., 'apical persons'); or
(2) persons under the management or supervision of the persons under point (1).[109]

147. The liability of the entity, even if explicitly defined in terms of 'administrative liability' is of a particular nature, with certain characteristics of criminal liability. For example, since the enactment of Decree No. 231/2001, the Italian legislature has expressly provided that an entity can be held *criminally* liable for:

109. Decree No. 231/2001, (5).

(1) offences committed within the sphere of the relations with the public administration[110] (e.g., fraud, bribery and theft of public funds);
(2) forgery of coins, banknotes and duty stamps;[111]
(3) corporate offences, such as misrepresentation of company accounts or statements, forgery of a prospectus or communications of an audit company, obstructing control, fictitious capital formation, fraudulent restitution of contributions;[112]
(4) offences committed for purposes of terrorism or disturbing public order;[113]
(5) offences against personal rights of freedom (*reati contro la personalità individuale*), such as slavery, pornography and exploitation of prostitutes (Article 12 of Legislative Decree No. 286 of 25 July 1988, Article 12 paragraphs 3, 3*bis, 3ter*, and 5);[114]
(6) market abuse offences;[115]
(7) offences against the savings and financial markets;[116]
(8) offences involving female genital mutilation;[117]
(9) offences against a person, such as manslaughter and negligently causing serious injuries resulting from violation of work safety and health requirements;[118]
(10) handling stolen goods, money laundering and use of money, goods or benefits which have illegal origin as per Article 648, 648*bis* and 648*ter* PC;[119]
(11) computer offences[120] (see *infra,* paragraphs 324 et seq.);
(12) offences involving organized crime as per Article 416 and 416*bis* PC, Article 291*quater* of the Consolidation Act which refers to Presidential Decree, No. 43 of 23 January 1973 (Criminal Association aimed at smuggling of foreign processed tobaccos), and Article 74 of the Consolidation Act which refers to Presidential Decree No. 309 of 9 October 1990;[121]

110. Decree No. 231/2001, Arts 24 and 25.
111. Article 6 of Law Decree No. 350 of 25 Sep. 2001, inserting Art. 25*bis* into Decree No. 231/2001.
112. Article 3 of Legislative Decree No. 61 of 11 Apr. 2002, inserting Art. 25*ter* into Decree No. 231/2001.
113. Article 3 of Law Decree No. 7 of 14 Jan. 2003, inserting Art. 25*quater* into Decree No. 231/2001.
114. Law No. 228 of 11 Aug. 2003 inserting Art. 25*quinquies* into Decree No. 231/2001.
115. Law No. 62 of 18 Apr. 2005 inserting Art. 25*sexies* into Decree No. 231/2001.
116. Law No. 262 of 28 Dec. 2005 modifying Art. 25*ter* of Decree No. 231/2001.
117. Law No. 62 of 18 Apr. 2005 inserting Art. 25*quarter*-1 into Decree No. 231/2001.
118. Law No. 123 of 3 Aug. 2007 inserting Art. 25*septies* into Decree No. 231/2001.
119. Legislative Decree No. 231, Art. 63(3) of 21 Nov. 2007 inserting Art. 25*octies* into Decree No. 231/2001.
120. Law No. 48 of 18 Mar. 2008 inserting Art. 24*bis* into Decree No. 231/2001. Recently, Art. 24*bis*, para. 1, of D.Lgs. No. 231/2001, has been amended. In fact, according to Legislative Decree No. 93 of 14 Aug. 2013 privacy violations (i.e., crimes affecting privacy as provided for under sections 167 and subsequent of Legislative Decree No. 196/2003), computer frauds committed by means of identity theft (pursuant to Art. 640*ter*, para. 3 PC), as well as any misuse and forgery of credit cards (pursuant to Art. 55, para. 9, Legislative Decree No. 231 of 21 Nov. 2007), have been included among the crimes covered by Legislative Decree No. 231 of 8 Jun. 2001.
121. Law No. 94 of 15 Jul. 2009 inserting Art. 24*ter* into Decree No. 231/2001.

(13) industrial offences, including unauthorized construction or operation of a nuclear plant and infringement of industrial or intellectual property;[122]
(14) impediment of justice, including inducement not to make statements or to make false statements to the court as per Articles 377*bis* and 378 CCP;[123]
(15) environmental offences.[124]

148. Even if the entity is liable only where a crime is committed by a natural person, the entity's liability is autonomous from the natural person's liability.
The entity is not liable when:

(1) The persons mentioned above acted in their own interest or in the interest of third parties.
(2) The crime was committed by the executives and the entity proves that:
    (a) Its board of directors adopted and effectively implemented – before the crime was committed – organization and management models suitable for preventing offences like the one for which the entity is being sued.
    (b) A body of the entity with autonomous decision-making and control powers was entrusted with the task of supervising the operation and the compliance with the organization and management plans, as well as updating the same plans.
    (c) The persons who committed the crime did it fraudulently and failed to comply with the organization and management plans.
    (d) The supervision of the body with autonomous decision-making and control powers – entrusted with the task of supervising the operation and the compliance with the organization and management plans – was adequate.[125]

149. If the offence was committed by an apical person, the company has the burden of proof. However, if the crime was committed by the people working under the supervision of others (*supra,* paragraph 146, point (2)), the burden shifts to the public prosecutor who must prove that the organization and management plans were not adopted and effectively implemented.[126]

150. Although the Legislative Decree No. 231/2001 gives a central role to the organizational model, it does not provide details on the structure and content of the organizational model. However, Article 6 requires the organizational model to:

---

122. Law No. 99 of 23 Jul. 2009 modifying Art. 25*bis* of and inserting Art. 25*bis*-1 and Art. 25*novies* into Decree No. 231/2001.
123. Law No. 116 of 3 Aug. 2009 modifying Art. 25*decies* of Decree No. 231/2001.
124. Legislative Decree No. 121 of 7 Jul. 2011 inserting Art. 25 *undecies* into Decree No. 231/2001. Recently, Art. 25 *undecies* of Legislative Decree No. 231/2001 has been amended. In fact, according to Law No. 68 of 22 May 2015, environmental pollution (Art. 452*bis* CP), environmental disaster (Art. 452*quater* CP), unintentional crime against the environmental (Art. 452*quinquies*), traffic or desertion of high material radioactivity (Art. 452*sexies* CP) and the offences against specimens of protected wild animal or plant species (Art. 727*bis)* and the damage of archaeological, historical or artistic heritage (Art. 733*bis* CP), have been included among the crimes covered by Law Decree No. 231 of 8 Jun. 2001.
125. Decree No. 231/2001.
126. Decree No. 231/2001, Art. 7.

- Identify the area in which it is most likely that crimes will be committed by managers or employees.
- Lay down special protocols aimed at planning the formation and enforcement of decisions adopted by the corporate body to prevent crimes.
- Identify the safest way to manage financial resources in order to avoid such crimes being committed.
- Make it compulsory for all officers and employees to supply the supervisory body responsible for monitoring the operation of the self-protection model with the necessary information to ensure their compliance with it.
- Introduce disciplinary measures necessary to sanction non-compliance with rules laid down in the model.

III. Acts, Omissions and Causation

151. Criminal offences are defined by law in terms of acts, omissions, or events or consequences caused by acts or omissions.

A. *Action Offences*

152. An action can be defined as a human behaviour intended for a certain purpose. Offences which consist of affirmative acts or conducts, e.g., theft (Article 624 PC) represent the majority of the offences under Italian Law.

The material element of the offence of action exists in doing something which should not have been done, e.g., murder (Article 589 PC). Violation concerns a prohibition and the nature of forbidden acts depends on the offence as defined in the criminal rules. The act or the conduct may consist in verbal acts, as in defamation (Article 595 PC) or in physical movements, as in battery (Article 581 PC).

153. Italian law describes criminal action offences in two ways. In the first manner, the law requires that the action is carried out with certain modalities (constrained form offences); thus, a fact will be relevant only if it has been committed in accordance with the model described by the law. In the second situation, the law sanctions every human behaviour which has caused a certain event, apart from the manner in which it was realized (i.e., 'open form offences').

Basically, the choice of description depends on the importance society gives to the interest protected by the relevant provision of law. Consequently for interests of the utmost importance (e.g., life), the law grants a widespread protection giving relevance to the simple occurrence of an event which damages the protected interest. For example, Article 575 PC punishes the commission of manslaughter, stating that '*one who causes the death of a man is punished*', giving relevance just to the event apart from the way it is actually carried out. Hence death can be the result of an action (shooting) or an omission (letting a man drown).

However, interests considered of less importance (e.g., property) are protected only against certain offensive behaviours described in detail by the law.

B. *Omission Offences*

154. Certain offences are carried out by an omission or negative conduct. The material element of an offence of omission exists in failing to do what should have been done or failing to act in presence of a legal duty to do so (*non facere*). The violation must result from a neglected command as long as it derives from law.

In the PC, there are fewer omission offences than action offences due to the greater potential for the former to interfere with individual freedom.

155. Among the wide range of omission offences, it is possible to draw a distinction between offences of mere omission and commission by omission.

1. Mere Omission

156. An offence of mere omission is the failure to act when the individual had a duty to act, e.g., failure to file a tax return.

2. Commission by Omission (*delicta commissionis per omissionem*)

157. As already seen in relation to the offences of mere omission, an omission to act will suffice as an alternative to an action if there was a legal duty to act. However, in the case of commission by omission, an event must arise from the failure to act, and such event is deemed to be a necessary element of the illicit fact.

It is important to stress that a commission by omission can be carried out only if there is a legal duty to act, to prevent the specific event (e.g., a lifeguard who lets a man drown is guilty of manslaughter). In fact, pursuant to Article 40, paragraph 2 PC '*[n]ot-impeding an event in the presence of a legal duty to do so is equivalent of committing it*'.

With respect to omission, Italian jurisprudence often mentions the necessity of the agent being in a 'position of guarantee'. It has been held that this position not only covers duties and actions specifically designed to prevent the event, but also different and lesser effective duties, such as to solicit a response to the emergency or simply a mere duty to act.[127]

127. In Decision No. 16761 of 3 May 2010 involving multiple manslaughter charges brought against the Mayor and Assessor of Sarno over the deaths of 137 people resulting from the flood of Spring 1998, the Court of Cassation considered the question of whether in order to impute liability, the position of guarantee must be accompanied by impeditive powers that would enable the agent to prevent the occurrence of the event.

In its ruling, the Court excluded such prerequisite, explaining that impeditive powers also include duties different from and less effective than those specifically designed to prevent the event. The Court stated that these powers may also be of the nature of soliciting a response to the emergency or simply a mere duty to act.

Thus, the Court concluded that the legal obligation to prevent an event must be accompanied by the factual existence of powers that allow the agent to put in place, at least in part and in the sense indicated above, appropriate mechanisms to prevent the occurrence of the event.

C. Causation Offences

158. For some offences, the causation of a harmful result is either a constitutive element of the offence or an aggravating circumstance.

In the light of this, Italian law also draws a distinction between: (1) 'offences of mere conduct' or 'formal offences' which do not require the verification of an event (a result); and (2) 'causation offences' or 'material offences' in which the verification of a harmful result is a constitutive element of the offence. In formal offences, the law punishes the commission of an action or an omission (e.g., incest described in Article 564 PC; domestic breaking and entering under Article 614 PC). If an event occurs, it may be considered as an aggravating circumstance of an offence that was already punishable without any harm occurring.

In the second case (i.e., material offences), neither action nor failure to act are punishable as such; the act or omission will only be punishable if it causes a certain harmful result as defined by law.

This distinction can be applied both to action offences and to omission offences and from such dichotomy derives the above-mentioned division in offences of mere omission and commission by omission.

D. The Causal Nexus

159. In order to blame someone for an event, it must be the result of his behaviour. This requirement is set by Italian Law in Article 40 PC which states that '*no one can be punished for a fact that the law considers an offence if the harmful result of the conduct is not a consequence of his action or omission*'.

However, when a criminal provision uses the term 'causation' or a similar expression, problems can arise with respect to determining whether the legal requirement of causation has been met. Specifically, when should a behaviour be considered as the cause of a certain event?

The guidelines for solving the problem of causality are found in the theories of causation, as developed by jurisprudence and doctrine.

160. The main theories about causation are: (1) the theory of equivalence, based on the doctrine of *condition sine qua non*; (2) the theory of adequate causality; (3) the theory of human causality; and (4) the theory of scientific causality.

161. According to the theory of equivalence, a cause lies within a complete set of antecedents which all have to be present in order to produce a certain consequence.

These antecedents can differ greatly, but have one common trait: each element, whatever its quantity (hence the equivalence), is necessary in bringing about the consequence.

Thus, the theory of equivalence holds that every condition necessary to bring a given consequence is to be regarded as a cause. In consideration of the aforesaid, an action is a *condicio sine qua non* (i.e., 'but for') of an event when by eliminating that action, the event would not have occurred (process of mental elimination).

The broad formulation of the concept of causation in the theory of equivalence seems to be excessive for application in law because such theory considers every condition equivalent in determining the event. For example, in a case of homicide, even the murderer's parents would be guilty because the offender's birth could be considered a necessary element of the fact!

162. The theory of adequate causality arose in Germany[128] and states that in order to envisage a *causal nexus*, it is necessary that the actor caused an event with an adequate action. An action is considered adequate when it is appropriate for determining an event in accordance with the experience deriving from similar cases (*id quod plerumque accidit* or what usually occurs). The primary limit of this theory is that it does not consider an action adequate if it is cased by atypical effects of one's conduct, thus widening the area of criminal non-accountability.

163. The theory of human causality arose in Italy and holds that an actor can cause only those results of conduct which he can '*dominate by reason of his cognitive and volitive powers*'.[129] Generally, this theory is criticized on the same grounds of the theory of adequate causality.

164. Nevertheless, since the seventies, the doctrine has started to emphasize the theory of scientific causality which currently is the most supported theory in Italian jurisprudence.[130] In particular, with respect to the *Stava* disaster, the Italian Court of Cassation stated the judge – in order to ascertain what occurred – must refer on one hand to universal and scientific laws and, on the other hand, to statistical rules as long as from these derive a high percentage of risk that an event could occur as a result of the conduct.[131]

IV. Classification of Offences from the Point of View of the Material Element

A. *Momentary and Continuing Offences*

165. Before differentiating between momentary and continuing offences, it is important to note that the distinction only applies to committed offences and not to attempts.

Momentary offences are acts or omissions committed at a given moment (e.g., assault – Article 581 PC). Committing such an offence may take a certain amount of time, but after the act, the offence is completed.

---

128. Von Kries, *Über der Begriff der Wahrscheinlichkeit und Möglichkeit und ihre Bedeutung im Strafrecht*, in *Zeitschrift* (1889).
129. F. Antolisei, *Manuale di diritto penale. Parte generale* 245 (2006).
130. Fiandaca-Musco, *Diritto Penale. Parte generale* 201 (1995); F. Mantovani, *Diritto penale* 139 (Padova 2007).
131. Court of Cassation Decision of 6 Dec. 1990, in *Foro it.*, 1992, II, 36.

Continuing offences, on the contrary, are characterized by the creation and maintenance of a situation forbidden by law due to the persisting of an illicit conduct (e.g., kidnapping – Article 605 PC or criminal conspiracy – Article 416 PC).

166. The distinction between momentary and continuing offences is important for several reasons:

- A continuing offence started under one law and continued under another will be judged according to new legislation if the new penalty is milder; however, if the prior law was milder, the offence will be judged according to both laws, i.e., the new law will apply to the part of the continuing offence that occurred after enactment, while the part of the offence which occurred prior to the enactment will be subject to the older law.
- A continuing offence started abroad and continued in Italy is considered committed in Italy, thus Italian Law applies.
- The period of limitations for a momentary offence starts immediately; while in the case of a continuing offence, the term begins once the offence ceases to be committed.
- Punishable participation in a continuing offence can take place at any given moment, as long as the offence is continuing.
- Self-defence is permissible against continuing offences as long as the illicit conduct lasts.
- From the point of view of criminal procedure, with continuing offences one can be 'caught in the act' as long as the illicit conduct continues.[132]

B. Occasional and Cumulative Offences

167. Unlike other classes of offences, the category of cumulative offences is a creation of doctrine since Italian law provides neither a definition nor a discipline.[133]

An offence is considered cumulative when it requires the repeating of a series of actions or omissions, even if a significant amount of time has passed. Consequently, a single act is not sufficient for criminal liability. For instance, the offence of child abuse (Article 572 PC) requires the commission of a series of acts which must be repeated and cumulative. If the repetition is missing, other offences may be integrated.

168. The qualification of an offence as a cumulative offence is important for the following reasons:

(1) A cumulative offence is a single offence and can be punished only once.

---

132. Fiandaca-Musco, *Manuale di diritto penale. Parte generale* 186 (1995).

133. F. Mantovani, *Diritto penale. Parte generale* 489 (Padova 2007); F. Angelini, *Sull'elemento soggettivo nel reato abituale*, in *Cass. Pen.* 462 (1993); M. Petrone, 'Reato abituale', *N. Dig. It.*, XIV, 941 (1967).

(2) A cumulative offence started under one law and continued under another, will be judged according to the most recent legislation, even in the case the prior law provided milder sanctions.
(3) For the purpose of applying Italian law, a cumulative offence is considered committed in Italy even if only one of the acts of the series required by law has been perpetrated within the Italian territory (Article 6, paragraph 2 PC).
(4) The period of limitation starts to run from the time of the last act of the cumulative offence.[134]
(5) Participation in a cumulative offence only occurs if the participant has contributed to determine the minimum amount of acts of the conduct required to integrate the cumulative offence.[135]

C. *Offences Causing Actual Harm and Endangerment Offences*

169. Italian law distinguishes between 'offences causing actual harm' and 'endangerment' offences depending on whether the interest protected by the criminal provision has been damaged or just threatened. Through endanger offences, the legislator seeks to protect certain interests by punishing behaviours that simply threaten such interests (e.g., threatening the life of a head of State, Article 276 PC).

170. Italian doctrine and jurisprudence also distinguish between 'actual endangerment offences' and 'abstract or presumed endangerment offences' depending on whether the protected interest was seriously threatened, in which case a judge must make a finding accordingly, or the danger is assumed by operation of law (no finding required).[136]

§3. The Moral or Mental Element (*Mens Rea*)

I. Subjective Guilt or Culpability

171. In the Italian system, criminal liability cannot exist simply due to an objective act forbidden by law or the failure to act. There must be a mental element: the subjective guilt or culpability of the offender. The moral element consists of a culpable state of mind which is the result of criminal intent or negligence.

No unlawful behaviour can lead to punishment without a legally blameworthy state of mind in relation to the defendant's unlawful conduct. Thus, the moral element can be considered as a link between the fact and the will of the author.

A verdict of guilt or culpability is a judgment about the legal blameworthiness of one's mental state in relation to his unlawful conduct. It is built on the proposition that the offender can be legally blamed for acting as he did on the condition that he

134. Court of Cassation Decision No. 4636 of 27 Apr. 1995.
135. Fiandaca-Musco, *Manuale di diritto penale. Parte generale* 187 (1995).
136. Fiandaca-Musco, *Manuale di diritto penale. Parte generale* 174 (1995).

can be held responsible for his conduct, and that he acted in the state of mind set forth in the definition of the offence with which he is charged.

The basis of the blame in a finding of guilt is that the offender – who knew or should have known that his conduct was illegal – did not behave himself lawfully, although he was capable of so doing.

172. A 2005 decision by the Italian Supreme Court held that in order to reproach someone, the offender must have had the actual possibility to behave in a lawful manner, but chose to act against the provision of law.[137]

173. The link between criminal liability and culpability is expressly sanctioned in Article 27 of the Italian Constitution which states that '*criminal liability is personal*' and represents a keynote of the Italian criminal system and in Article 42, paragraph 1 PC, which states that '*no one can be punished for an action or omission if he did not carry out it with conscience and willingness*'. The latter expresses the principle of the *suitas* (i.e., free will) according to which an action or omission is considered relevant only if determined or determinable by the author's will.

II. Strict or Objective Liability

174. Strict liability, i.e., guilt without the blameworthy state of mind of the perpetrator, is another form of liability and expressly considered in Article 42, paragraph 3 PC, which states that '*the law determines the cases in which the event is otherwise charged to the agent as a consequence of his action or omission*'. This article concerns the cases of 'objective liability', i.e., based on the casual nexus, independent from intent or negligence. Thus, strict liability still exists in Italian law both in the general provisions of the Code (Article 43, paragraph 3 PC) and in the special provisions covering those crimes which occur when intent is exceeded (Article 584 PC – involuntary manslaughter) and offences aggravated by an event in which the law provides a heavier punishment if an unintended consequence arises from the event (e.g., Article 571 PC – abuse of means of punishment). For example, the director of a school discovers that a student has taken the snack of a classmate, and the director punishes the student in an excessive manner by withholding all food for the day. Being a diabetic, the student then dies from the lack of food. The director would be chargeable under Article 571(2) PC[138] because the consequences of his acts were objectively charged.[139]

175. Unlike other countries' modern PCs which abolished every form of objective liability (Norway, Denmark, Germany, Spain, and Portugal), Italian criminal law still provides for such liability. Although, strict liability should be considered as

137. Court of Cassation (sitting in United Session) Decision No. 9163 of 8 Mar. 2005.
138. Article 571(2) PC: If the fact results in a personal injury, the penalties set forth in Arts 582 and 583 apply, reduced by one-third; if the fact results in death, the imprisonment shall be from three to eight years.
139. See Marinucci-Dolcini, *Manuale di diritto penale. Parte generale* 282–283 (Milano 2006).

conflicting with the principle stated in Article 27 of the Constitution (criminal liability is personal), the Constitutional Court has only had the opportunity to consider the issue on one occasion and its ruling was limited to Article 626, paragraph 1, No. 1 PC concerning theft.

III. Intent

176. Article 42, paragraph 2 PC states that '*no one can be punished for a criminal offence if he has not committed it intentionally, except for unintentional or negligent offences expressly provided by the law*'. Thus, no one can be punished for such offences unless they are expressly provided by the law. Article 43 PC states that a crime is considered intentional when the result of the action or omission is foreseen and wanted by the agent as a result of his conduct.

Intent represents the heaviest degree of culpability and the general standard to attribute a fact to someone.

Equally to every other element of the criminal provision, intent must be specifically proven. It is important to stress that the proof of a moral element is not easy to provide because it requires inferring a mental process from a certain fact.

It would be impossible to refer to fixed standards, as such analysis is quite delicate; thus, the judge must be free to investigate and evaluate every circumstance of the specific case. In order to avoid that the intent becomes impossible to prove (i.e., *probatio diabolic* or 'the devil's proof'), the judge can use general rules of experience but not assumptions (i.e., *dolus in re ipsa*), the latter arising when the intent is assumed by operation of law from the simple commission of a fact.[140]

A. Degrees of Intent

177. An examination of penal law reveals that the legislator does not require the same degree of intent for all intentional offences. The degree of the required intent can be more or less qualified by law. With regards to the legal qualification of intent, the Italian theory of criminal law distinguishes between two degrees: (1) general (*dolo generico*) and (2) wilful or special (*dolo specifico*).

1. General Intent

178. General intent exists when a person consciously, i.e., knowingly and willingly, chooses to do a prohibited act, to omit to comply with a legal command, or to cause a specific forbidden result. The intention must not only encompass the act or omission itself, but also the consequences and the circumstances which make it an offence. Thus, it is only necessary that the agent wants to carry out the fact

140. G. Fiandaca & E. Musco, *Diritto penale parte generale* 367–368 (5th ed., Bologna 2007); F. Mantovani, *Diritto penale* 315 (Padova 2007).

described in the legal provision. For instance, in the case of manslaughter, Article 575 PC does not require any special purpose for causing the death.

2. Special Intent

179. In some cases, acting willingly and knowingly is not sufficient to attract criminal liability: the law requires a special intention, i.e., the offender must have a definite purpose. Such intention is necessitated by virtue of the wording of the provision. For example, Article 624 PC (Theft) requires '*the purpose of the agent to get advantage from the stolen thing*' or Article 642 PC (Fraudulent Damaging of Insured Goods and Fraudulent Mutilation of a Person) requires '*the self-inflicted injury or the destruction of the agent's own property is carried out with the purpose of receiving the proceeds of an insurance policy*'.

B. Types of Intent with Reference to Intensity

180. Intent can be graduated in relation to its intensity, and the judge may evaluate the intensity when deciding the punishment. In fact, Article 133 PC states that when applying a sanction, the judge must consider the severity of the crime, including the level of intent.

To determine the level of intensity, one must consider:

- the intensity of the consciousness of a fact;
- the intensity of the willingness of a fact;
- the length of the evaluation process in deciding whether or not to commit a certain crime.

181. In Italy, with respect to blood crimes, the case law distinguishes three 'levels' of intent, similar to the degrees used for murder in other jurisdictions. The levels are: act of impulse (*dolo d'impeto*); deliberate intent (*dolo di proposito*); and premeditation.

1. Act of Impulse and Deliberate Intent

182. An act of impulse occurs when the criminal decision is taken suddenly, and the action is immediately carried out. For example, a husband murders his wife immediately when he finds her committing adultery.

States of emotion and passion do not have an influence on chargeability. In fact, according to Article 90 PC, they neither exclude nor reduce imputability.

183. Deliberate intent falls between an act of impulse and a premeditated act. The line between deliberate intent and premeditation is minimal, and it is often hard to distinguish between the two. An example of deliberate intent would be when two people begin fighting in a bar, and one of them waits outside to kill the other.

2. Premeditation

184. Premeditation is a particularly severe degree of intent. Premeditation exists when a crime has been committed as a result of a considered decision and when there is a lapse of time between the decision and the action and malice aforethought. Such graduation of intent stands out in the manslaughter and personal injury crimes where it represents an aggravating circumstance (Articles 576, 577 and 585 PC). Some crimes and misdemeanours will be punished more heavily if the offender has acted with premeditation.

The classical theory had identified the core of premeditation in acting *frigido pacatoque animo* (i.e., with a cool and peaceful mind or 'in cold blood'), but it is generally refused because most crimes are committed with a minimum level of emotion, except for those carried out by unethical and immoral psychopathic individuals (i.e., contract assassins).

185. The doctrine identifies the requirements of premeditation as:

(1) a wide lapse of time between the criminal idea and its fulfilment;
(2) the consolidation of the purpose after due consideration;
(3) the persistency of the purpose during the lapse of time *sub* 1.[141]

C. *Types of Intent with Reference to Their Consequences*

186. The subdivision of intent into degrees refers to the more or less qualified intensity of the volitive component of the intent, as already mentioned above.

187. Additionally, the doctrine distinguishes between the two types of intent with reference to the cognitive component, more specifically with regard to direct and indirect intention.

1. Direct Intent (Dolus Directus)

188. Direct intent means that the offender, whatever his motive may be, has the purpose or the aim of accomplishing a certain offence as a consequence of his act or omission.

2. Indirect or Eventual Intent (Dolus Eventualis)

189. Indirect intent involves probable or eventual consequences. It presupposes a will to act or to omit, despite knowledge of the possible, though unwanted and undesired, results of the act or omission. For instance, a person who wants to

141. F. Antolisei, *Manuale di diritto penale. Parte speciale I* 48 (Milano 2006).

frighten people by placing a bomb in a square. His intent is to frighten people; however, he also knows or should know it is probable that people could be injured due to the explosion. If people are injured, even though he hopes they are not, the offender can be punished as if he had committed an intentional crime, since he foresaw or could have foreseen the consequences of his act and he proceeded nevertheless.[142,143]

IV. Negligence

A. Definition

190. Negligence is defined in Article 43 PC as: '*a crime is culpable or against the intention, when the event, although it is foreseen, it is not wanted and happens because of the agent's negligence or recklessness or unskillfulness or because of the non-compliance with laws, regulations, orders or disciplines*'.

Thus, in order to entertain the notion of negligence, three conditions must be fulfilled:

(1) an action or omission is carried out with consciousness and willingness;
(2) the author does not want to realize the fact; and
(3) the fact happens because of negligence, recklessness, or unskillfulness or because of the non-compliance with laws, regulations, orders and disciplines.

The agent carried out the fact punished by the law, but he did not want to do so. If the fact is wanted or even accepted, the moral element is represented by the intent (*dolus*).

1. General Negligence

191. Commonly in Italian doctrine, recklessness and unskillfulness are defined as general negligence. In the cases of general negligence, the precautionary rules have a social root. The rules of negligence are not provided by the law, but by the experience of similar cases.

Negligence occurs when the breached social rule imposes a positive action. Unskillfulness is a form of qualified negligence and refers to activities which require certain technical skills and a specific knowledge (e.g., surgery).

Recklessness is the breach of a duty to avoid a certain conduct or to carry it out with different modalities (e.g., the duty to avoid driving when tired).

---

142. See F. Antolisei, *Manuale di diritto penale, Parte generale* 352 (16th ed., 2003).

143. The definition of eventual intent was clarified by the Court of Cassation, United Sections, in decision No. 38343 of 18 Sep. 2014 (Thyssen case). The Court held that there is dolus eventualis when the agent was aware about the significant possibility to arouse the event and after considering the aim pursued and the eventual consequences, he nevertheless decided to act anyway, even if it meant causing the harmful event.

2. Specific Negligence

192. Negligence arising from the non-compliance with laws, regulations, orders and disciplines is defined as specific negligence. The precautionary rules that must be adopted in this case arise from a juridical root.

The Italian PC mentions laws, as well as regulations, orders, disciplines, and constitutional and administrative rules. Regulations are general rules provided by the Public Authorities in order to discipline certain activities. Orders and disciplines are directed to a specific addressee and can come from both public and private authorities.[144]

B. The Evaluation of Negligence

193. The existence of negligence must be proven. In this connection, it is useful to distinguish between general negligence and specific negligence.

As regards the first one, some legal scholars deem it necessary to resort to the predictability method. Thus, certain behaviour could be considered negligent or imprudent only when it was predictable that the behaviour would result in the illicit event.[145] However, predictability is an insufficient means of evaluation because such fact must actually be avoidable. In fact, if a certain result of a conduct is not actually avoidable by an individual, such event represents a mere fatality. It is important to stress that in evaluating negligence, the judge will have to consider predictability in a relative way. This means that he should consider the particular conditions, states and positions of an individual, because an event can be predictable for one man but not for another.

However, as regards specific negligence, the predictability method is not useful at all. In such cases, criminal liability arises whenever there is a non-compliance with laws, regulations, orders and disciplines. If the agent has actually used every precaution imposed by the rules, he cannot be charged even if the event was predictable.

C. Types of Negligence

194. Conscious or advertent negligence exists when the perpetrator consciously takes an unjustified risk; when he knows that his act or omission may have bad consequences but nevertheless, recklessly or frivolously takes the chance, hoping that the negative result will not follow.

Although this state of mind is near to intention, no intention exists (*culpa dolo proxima*), since the offender would not have acted if he had known the actual consequences. For example, a knife-thrower who trusts in his skills and throws a knife

144. See G. Fiandaca & E. Musco, *Diritto penale parte generale* 490 (3rd ed., Bologna 1995).
145. This method is followed by F. Antolisei, *Manuale di diritto penale. Parte generale* 376 (Milano 2003); F. Mantovani, *Diritto penale* 336 (Padova 2007).

at someone, causing injuries to him. The knife-thrower knows the possible bad consequences of his act, but he is convinced that he can avoid the illicit event and has no desire to hurt anyone.

Unconscious negligence exists when the perpetrator does not predict the risks of his conduct, although he should and would have avoided such risks if he acted reasonably.

The difference between these two kinds of negligence is given by the predictability of the event. In the first case, the perpetrator knows that his behaviour could derive a certain result but he trusts that he can avoid it relying on his skills (e.g., a driver who foresees that he could run over someone crossing the street, but he is sure to avoid him); in the second case, the perpetrator neither foresees the event (e.g., the hunter hiding behind a bush, who shoots a person while firing at a hare).

V. Unintentional Acts

195. Article 43 PC provides a third moral element: *preterintenzione* or unintentional act. This refers to when an act or an omission goes beyond the intention of the perpetrator who wanted to carry out a minor event.

Under the Italian PC, there is only one form of crime involving an unintentional act: involuntary manslaughter (*omicidio preterintenzionale*) (Article 584 PC). The Code states that '*whoever provokes the death of a man through acts aimed at beating him or causing personal injuries to him*' is subject to punishment. Here, the offender's intention is to batter or cause personal injuries, not death. However, the consequence of the conduct is ascribed to the perpetrator even though he did not want to cause the death.

It is important to stress that an unintentional act cannot be considered as a *tertium genus* (i.e., third possibility) intermediate between fault and intention because an event can be wanted or unwanted and it could not be otherwise: *tertium non datur* (i.e., there is no third possibility in the middle).

Some doctrines consider *preterintenzione* as a form of intention mixed with fault because the intention covers the less grave event and the fault covers the heavier event,[146] while the other doctrine considers it as a form of crime aggravated by the event which is charged to the perpetrator even if he did not want the event, introducing in this way a form of strict liability.[147]

VI. The Required Form of Guilt

196. In Italian criminal law, the traditional view is that intent is a requirement of all offences contained in the PC or special legislation unless the law explicitly provides that negligence or excess of intent is sufficient (Article 42, paragraph 2 PC). Crimes (*delitti*) always require intent, except for those cases expressly indicated by

146. See F. Mantovani, *Diritto penale* 348 (Padova 2007).
147. F. Antolisei, *Diritto penale, parte generale* 394 (Milano 2003).

law where negligence is sufficient (the so-called negligent *delitti*) (e.g., culpable homicide).

197. Fault is normally the requirement of *contravvenzioni* or misdemeanours. Article 42, paragraph 4 PC states that '*for misdemeanours (contravvenzioni), negligence is sufficient except as otherwise contemplated by law*'. Such rule is generally construed in the sense that in the Italian criminal system, at least negligence is required to be held liable for committing a misdemeanour; thus, the perpetrator, in order to exclude his liability, must prove that his action was blameless, i.e., neither negligent nor reckless (*azione incolpevole*).

Chapter 4. Justification, Excuse and Chargeability

§1. General Principles

198. Under Italian criminal law, a fact can be considered unlawful (*antigiuridico*) or lawful. A fact is considered unlawful if it is in contrast with the whole legal system, while a fact is lawful even if just one law allows or imposes it.

On the basis of these considerations, Italian criminal law provides for a distinction between justifications and excuses (*cause di giustificazione* or *scriminanti*) which may exempt individuals from criminal responsibility and render not punishable conduct which amounts to an offence under the law. This distinction is of considerable practical importance.

I. Justification: Introduction

199. The rationale of the justifications is the following: there is a law that in order to safeguard a basic right, allows or even imposes the fact be accomplished.

In this case, a conflict of laws could arise between the rule that considers the fact as a crime and the law that imposes the accomplishment of the fact.

In this case, the unity of the legal system requires the conflict be resolved because a conduct cannot be unlawful and at the same time in accordance with law.

The Italian legal system resolves the conflict considering overriding the law that allows or imposes the accomplishment of the fact.

II. Justification: Remarks

200. Justifications concern the material element of the crime and are particular situations in which a fact, normally prohibited, does not amount to a crime.

More precisely, justifications allow facts to be considered lawful although all of the elements of a crime are present. However, a fact generally prohibited is committed to protect an interest having a social value higher or equal to the interest injured.

Consequently, the fact is unlawful in absence of justification. In this case, if should be the other ingredients of the offence (i.e., culpability and punishability) there will be a crime.

On the contrary, the fact is lawful if there is a justification. In this case, the behaviour does not constitute a crime because the other element of the offence – that is the unlawfulness – is lacking.

III. Legal Excuse

201. Unlike justifications, excuses concern the mental element of the crime and regard the culpability. A legal excuse is a particular circumstance that – precluding the formation of a correct nexus between the offender and the prohibited fact – excludes the culpability of the offender.

IV. Difference between Justification and Legal Excuse

202. The difference between justification and excuse is the following: in the former, the fact is considered lawful from the beginning; in the latter, the fact itself could be considered lawful, but the mental element of the crime, necessary for the existence of a criminal violation, is lacking.

§2. JUSTIFICATION

203. The PC provides various justifications. Some are found in the general part of the Code (Articles 50–54 PC), because they can be applied to more or less any type of offence, while other justifications are contained in the specific part of the Code and in special laws, alongside the specific offences to which they can be applied.

204. The justifications contained in the general part of the Code are the following:

(1) consent of the person entitled to the right (Article 50 PC);
(2) exercise of a right (Article 51 PC);
(3) performance of a duty (Article 51 PC);
(4) legitimate use of arms (Article 53 PC);
(5) legitimate defence (Article 52 PC);
(6) necessity (Article 54 PC).

I. Consent

205. The consent of the person entitled to a right is a particular kind of justification. Article 50, paragraph PC states that one who harms or endangers a right, with the consent of the entitled party, shall not be subject to punishment.

The rationale of this justification is that a right cannot be harmed if the subject of the right consents to what would otherwise be a criminal offence.

This justification is particular in that under the Italian system only individual rights, which are protected by law as the exclusive interest of the owner (i.e., the so-called disposable rights) can be waived. Thus, the owner can dispose of such rights giving to a third party the lawful right to harm or endanger them.

On the contrary, public interests, interests of a public body, and so on cannot be waived. Additionally, the right to life cannot be waived.

Property rights and certain individual rights such as honour, moral and private freedom, and so on can be waived.

Physical integrity is freely disposable when the act is useful for safeguarding health, e.g., consent to remove a sick organ. However, the disposal of physical integrity can also be limited if the disposing act would be to the detriment of the health of the consenting person, e.g., donation of organs from one living person to another (Article 5 of Italian Civil Code).[148] Furthermore, an act disposing of one's body is forbidden if it would permanently reduce the physical integrity[149] (quantitative limits) or they are against the public order or morality (qualitative limits).

The limit of the permanent reduction is not considered exceeded when the consent regards the removal of self-reproducing parts of the body (e.g., blood, skin, etc.).

It is considered exceeded and in this case, the consent will be void, when it regards an organ which is not self-reproducing.[150]

206. In order for there to be valid consent, the following conditions must exist:

(1) the person or his legal or voluntary representative must be entitled to give the consent;
(2) the person must be legally competent;
(3) the consent must exist at the moment of the action (thus, it is always a precarious right);
(4) the consent can be tacit or express, and subject to conditions, terms or limitations; and
(5) the consent must be free of faults (mistake, threats of violence, etc.).

II. Exercise of a Right

207. According to Article 51, paragraph 1 PC, there is no crime if the fact took place as a result of the exercise of a right (i.e., excludes the punishment). These rules give the lawful right to commit facts otherwise considered as crime (*penalmente rilevanti* or criminally relevant) and make lawful their accomplishment.

This principle is inspired by the maxim *qui jure suo utitur neminem laedit* (i.e., 'He who uses his own legal right injures no one'). The rationale is that if the law has given a specific right, it recognizes the priority of that right over opposing interests.

However, clearly an action cannot be simultaneously allowed and forbidden by law. Legal logic provides that a conduct is either in conflict with the law or it is not.

148. According to Art. 5 of the Italian Civil Code, the act disposing of one's body is forbidden if it would cause a permanent reduction of the physical integrity, or it would be unlawful against public order and morality.

149. The ban concerning the acts disposing of one's body that cause a permanent reduction of the physical integrity has been infringed by Law No. 458 of 26 Jun. 1967, which considers lawful the donation of a kidney under certain conditions aimed at guaranteeing a spontaneous and not mercenary consent.

150. See Marinucci-Dolcini, *Manuale di diritto penale. Parte generale* 204 et seq. (Milano 2006).

A. *The Concept of Right Ex Article 51 PC*

208. The term 'right' must be examined closely: it includes all subjective rights, as well as those recognized by the Italian legal system, such as constitutional freedom, and those recognized by civil law, and so on.

B. *Sources of the Rights*

209. Rights arise by rule of law and from other sources, such as a judgment, measure of the public prosecutor, administrative act or an agreement.

It is important to stress that in order to avoid punishability, it is not sufficient that the law allows the exercise of a right. The law must allow – at least implicitly – the exercise of the right by a specific action that otherwise would be considered a crime.

Thus, it is necessary to compare rights and make a hierarchy of values. However, in reality, it is not easy to determine when one right prevails over another. For example, the freedom of thought, set forth in Article 21 of the Italian Constitution, finds an explicit limit in offences such as defamation (Article 595 PC).

C. *Actions Aimed at Protecting Property: The Offendicula*

210. Italian law provides certain rights which allow persons to act in order to protect property. A particular mention should be made to the institution known as the *offendicula*.

The *offendicula* is the power of the property owner to put up a boundary, e.g., wall, jutting glass, railings, and so on. The law considers the owner not liable for any harm suffered by a thief when attempting to overcome the obstacle the property owner has established.

However, this does not give the property owner the right to use insidious means such as high-tension cable. Furthermore, where the means adopted create a risk, the owner must provide notice of the danger.[151]

III. Public Duty or Order of the Authorities

211. Article 51, paragraph 1 PC, states that there is no crime if the committed fact took place as a result of the prescription of a statute and on the orders of the authorities.

The rationale of this rule is the same as mentioned for the exercise of a right: a conduct cannot be unlawful and at the same time in accordance with law.

In some cases, there is a conflict of duties. For example, the conflict between the rules to deprive someone of their freedom (e.g., kidnapping Article 605 PC) and the

151. See F. Antolisei, *Manuale di diritto penale* 283 et seq. (Milano 2006).

rule that allows judicial police to detain someone – thus depriving them of their liberty – when they are caught in the act of an intentional crime (Article 380 CCP).

Therefore, in order to avoid a conflict of duties, it is necessary to identify which duty is considered more important, and so that deserves to be protected, in the criminal system.

A. *Fulfilment of a Duty Arising by Law*

212. A duty may arise by law or by other acts having the binding force of a statute, as well as sub legislative sources such as a regulation.

The most important example is the legitimate use of the arms set forth in Article 53, paragraph 1 PC. Under this article, no offence exists when a public official uses arms or other devices in order to fulfil his duty, and such use is necessary to repel a violent act or to overcome resistance to authority.

It is worthwhile to point out that the use of the arms by public officials represents an *extrema ratio* (i.e., last resort); thus, the law requires there be no other appropriate means of defence. Among the available devices, the least dangerous must be used.

The reason for this justification is the necessity of protecting the authority and prestige of public office.

In case of a resistance to authority,[152] the law requires active resistance not merely passive opposition.[153]

B. *Fulfilment of a Duty Arising by an Order of the Authorities*

213. According to Article 50, paragraph 1 PC, the duty may arise also by a lawful order of an authority. The order of the authority has to be lawful both in formal and in substantial terms. The order will be lawful in formal terms if it is:

- given by a public authority competent to give such orders;
- the subordinate had the competence to execute the order; and
- issued according to forms prescribed by the law.[154]

The order will be lawful in substantial terms if all of the conditions provided by law have been met.

The carrying out of an order makes lawful the accomplishment of a fact otherwise considered as a crime.

It is important to underline that if a fact constituting an offence was committed by order of the authorities, the public official who gave the unlawful order is liable.

---

152. For instance, the Italian criminal system allows public officials to use the arms against squatters who do not move out of a flat.
153. *Contra* see Court of Cassation Decision of 7 Jun. 2000, in *Riv. Pen.*, 1140 (2000).
154. For example, see Court of Cassation Decision of 10 Jun. 1982, in *Mass. Pen.*, 882 (1983).

214. Subordinates who carry out an unlawful order can also be responsible for the crime according to Article 51, paragraph 3 PC.

The civil servant is liable because they have a duty to refrain from executing the orders of a superior when the act is forbidden by criminal law.

In fact, civil servants have the right to verify the lawfulness of the order, in formal and substantial terms. Private citizens who receive an unlawful order from the police also have this right.

However, civil servants, soldiers, and so on who carry out an unlawful order – considering it lawful as a mistake of fact – are not criminally liable.

Finally, under Article 51, paragraph 4 PC, one who carries out an unlawful order is not liable when the law does not allow him to verify the legitimacy of the order.

IV. Legitimate Use of Arms

215. With regard to the legitimate use of the arms, please refer *supra*, paragraph 212 and *infra*, paragraph 222.

V. Self-Defence

A. *General Characterization*

216. Self-defence is a justification expressly recognized from time immemorial in most criminal legislations.

217. The principle of self-defence is set forth in Article 52, paragraph 1 PC. According to this article, '*the person who is forced to commit a fact due to the necessity to defend his own rights or those of another against the existing danger of an unfair offence is not subject to punishment, provided the defence is proportionate to the gravity of the offence*'.

Derogating from the principle that the use of force is the exclusive right of public officials, Italian law permits the use of force if necessary to avoid a danger.

This derogation is allowed by the Italian legal system in order to protect the victim, as society places a greater value on the interests of the victim rather than those of the aggressor.

Self-defence involves on one hand an assault and on the other hand a reaction. Both facts are subject to conditions.

B. *Conditions*

1. Conditions Relating to the Attack

218. Legitimate defence is an act against injustice. The assault must be directed against protected goods. In fact, the law provides that the object of the assault has to be a right.

The Italian law extends the right of defence to all rights without distinction. The expression 'rights' covers any individual interest expressly protected by law such as personal rights (e.g., life or physical integrity, personal freedom, etc.), as well as property rights.

219. With regard to the conditions of the assault, the Italian law does not require violence; thus, self-defence is also lawful against a passive attitude.

Furthermore, the right of defence implies that the threat has to be unjust, i.e., in contrast with the rules provided by legal system.

Thus, one can defend oneself against offences of subjects that enjoy immunity from prosecution (e.g., a diplomatic representative) and subjects that are *non compos mentis* (e.g., not of sound mind). The legitimate defence is allowed against the illicit fact.

The law provides that the risk of an unjust offence is present, forthcoming and imminent.

Consequently, a justified defence is excluded if the attack was only hypothetical or if the attack has already taken place.

2. Conditions Relating to the Reaction

220. Defence has to be necessary, i.e., the only way to avoid the adversary's threatened harm.[155]

It is important to point out that necessity is not considered in the abstract, but in actual fact, weighing the conditions of the party assaulted, the means he had, the time, the place, and the way of the attack.

Defence is allowed when there are no possible means of escaping without danger or obtaining effective help immediately.

Therefore, flight or other alternatives should be preferred above acts of defence, and consequently, one who can safely retreat has no right to use force.

221. Defence must also be proportionate to the attack. Thus, the amount of the force the defender may use must be proportional to the threatened harm which he seeks to avoid.

The proportionality between attack and defence has to be determined *ex ante*, referring to the moment of the action and considering all the circumstances of the actual case.

From the text of Article 52 PC, it follows that Italian criminal law does not distinguish self-defence and the defence of another. The conditions of legitimate defence are the same. Thus, reaction is allowed in order to protect a personal right or the rights of another. The actual circumstances of each case must be examined to determine whether the limits of necessity were crossed.

For example, a person subject to rape can defend his or her sexual freedom even by killing the aggressor. On the contrary, there is no justification for protecting one's

155. See Court of Cassation Decision of 27 Feb. 1993, in *Riv. Pen.* 52 (1994).

property rights by killing or wounding an aggressor climbing a tree; in this case there is no proportionality. Thus, if the landowner has no devices other than a gun, a justified action would be to shoot in the air, rather than at the aggressor.

C. Self-defence at Home and in the Workplace

222. In 2006, the Italian Parliament passed legislation allowing people to shoot robbers in self-defence. Law No. 59 of 13 February 2006 regarding self-defence issues introduced two new paragraphs (2 and 3) to Article 52 PC.

The law, extending the limit provided for self-defence, permits the use of guns and knives by people in homes or workplaces to protect lives or belongings. The amended law allows people to use legally registered weapons to protect themselves or others, and their property and the property of others, from harm. It applies if there is a danger of aggression and the attacker does not desist.

223. At present, the Italian law on self-defence is similar to that of Britain. A killing is not considered an offence if the killer has been 'obliged by necessity' to end the life of another person. However, the use of force must be proportionate to the threat. The victim may only do what is indispensable for his or her protection.

VI. Necessity

A. Generally

224. Article 54 PC provides that a person is not subject to punishment if he is forced by necessity to save himself or another from an imminent danger of serious harm, and such harm has not been voluntarily caused by him or is not otherwise avoidable. Necessity legitimizes conduct that is technically illegal, but is justifiable on the basis of common sense, principles of justice and/or utilitarian concerns.

Like self-defence, the necessity must relate to an imminent risk of an unfair offence. Consequently, a justified defence is excluded if the attack was only hypothetical or if the attack had already taken place.

Necessity is only limited to protect life, physical integrity, or sexual or personal freedom. Thus, property rights and public rights are excluded.

225. Moreover, it must be stressed that although necessity shows affinity with self-defence, the two are very different. In fact, with regards to self-defence, the action harms the aggressor; while necessity involves the harm of a third party, namely one who did not cause the dangerous situation.

B. Conditions

226. In order for necessity to apply as a justification, two conditions must be met. First, Italian law provides that the fact, considered as an offence, is necessary to avoid a significant risk of harm and there was no adequate lawful alternative for escaping the harm.

This point is important in order to understand the difference between self-defence and necessity. In the case of self-defence, as mentioned above, the reaction is allowed when it is impossible to escape without danger or to obtain effective help immediately (the so-called *commudus discessus*). However, with necessity if there are lawful alternatives, even dangerous, for escaping the harm, there is no justification.

227. Second, the person who acts must be forced by necessity to break a law in order to save himself or another from an imminent danger of serious injury. Thus, another important element is need: there must be a need for the law to be broken. The meaning of the term 'need' is a decisive factor in determining whether the necessity is a justification or an excuse.

In fact, this is a crucial and controversial issue because determining whether the basis of the necessity lies in justification or in excuse is not a simple task.

Two interpretations are possible. According to the first one, the need represents only the objective impossibility of saving a good from an imminent danger of serious damage without sacrificing the good of an innocent third party. The second interpretation identifies the need with a restriction of the freedom of action and supposes the acting subject had an awareness of the risk and a psychological perturbation.

Following the former interpretation, necessity is considered a justification, while the latter interpretation classifies justification as an excuse. In this case, the rationale, affecting the mental element of the crime, is that as result of the extreme pressure of the circumstances, all perception of freedom of choice or of freedom to act, has been lost; thus, there is no voluntary act, culpability or guilt.

The latter seems to be the predominant opinion, and it is confirmed also to the literal meaning of the law.

228. Finally, as with self-defence, in the case of necessity as justification, the fact – considered as a crime – must be proportionate to the danger escaped. Therefore, it is possible to sacrifice a good greater than the one at risk, provided that the gap between the two is not excessive.

§3. Legal Excuse

I. Introduction

229. As explained above, in order to consider an actor guilty, it is not sufficient that he or she committed an unlawful act with intent or negligence.

The law also requires the act is not committed in presence of legal excuse.

230. Legal excuses are particular circumstances that influence the will or the psychophysical capacity of the actor.

The Italian criminal system identifies these cases with the concept of *insegibilità* i.e., it is not possible to expect a different behaviour from one who acted under the pressure of abnormal circumstances.

Legal excuses are only those strictly provided for by law. They preclude the formation of a correct psychic nexus, namely the conditions required by Article 42, paragraph 1 PC which states, '*no one can be punished for an action or omission foreseen by the law as a crime if he or she did not commit it with awareness and will*'.

II. Type of Legal Excuses

231. The legal excuses provided by law are the following:

(1) fortuitous event (Article 45 PC);
(2) force majeure (Article 45 PC);
(3) duress (Article 46 PC);
(4) mistake (Articles 5 and 47 PC).

A. *Fortuitous Event*

232. The placing of the fortuitous event (*caso fortuito*) among legal excuses is a controversial issue.

Italian legal scholars have approached the analysis in two different ways. The objective theory places the fortuitous event in the field of the causation. According to this theory, if there is a fortuitous event, there is no chain of causation between the behaviour and the event.

On the contrary, the subjective theory places the fortuitous event in the field of culpability. The fortuitous event is considered to be an unforeseeable and unavoidable fact that the offender could not impede. As a consequence, the criminal liability of actor must be excluded. Courts and legal scholars predominantly prefer this theory.

B. *Force Majeure*

233. There is no easy way to make a distinction between fortuitous events and force majeure as both concepts are similar.

Generally, a fortuitous event is marked by unforeseeability and can be negative or positive, while force majeure is marked by the unavoidability.[156] Force majeure (act of God) is an unforeseeable force against which the offender could not resist or had no control (Article 45 PC). Force majeure is often referred by the Latin

156. See R. Garofoli, *Manuale di diritto penale, Parte generale* 595 (3rd ed., Milan 2006).

expression action *cui resisti non potest* (i.e., 'superior force against which it is useless to struggle').

In this perspective, for instance, there is no criminal liability if a worker kills a passer-by due to a seismic tremor that throws him off a scaffolding, i.e., there is force majeure.

C. Duress

234. According to Article 46 PC, duress (*costringimento fisico*) is a physical coercion to which a subject could not resist. The coerced subject actually has carried out the offence; however, the act was performed in order to avoid some threatened or actual harm. The coerced subject is only outwardly the author of the fact; in reality, he is the tool of someone else. The basis of the excuse is the lack of guilt due to the lack of freedom of choice on the part of the person reacting, and criminal liability arises for the author of the violence, not the one who acts.

For example, criminal liability of a sentry does not arise in the event he fails to give the alarm because seditionists have tied him to a tree.

It is important to stress that duress should not be confused with the psychological coercion (i.e., undue influence) set forth in Article 54, paragraph 3 PC.

Thus, with physical coercion, the behaviour is of the subject who uses another to carry out the offence. Accordingly, the behaviour is based on a human factor and consequently the will is lacking.

On the contrary, with psychological coercion, the coerced subject acts with will but under a psychological perturbation (the so-called *vis compulsiva*).[157] In this case, there is the will, but it is vitiated, making it obligatory to verify the existence of the state of necessity.

D. Ignorance of the Criminal Law

235. In the Italian criminal system, a mistake (i.e., an incorrect representation of the reality) can be 'of fact' or 'of law'.

In order to address mistake, it is necessary to make a brief reference to the general rule set forth in Article 5 PC. According to this article, *ignorantia legis neminem excusat* or '*ignorance of the law excuses no one*'.

Consequently, in the Italian criminal system, the mistake of law or the erroneous interpretation of the law does not exclude the criminal liability of the actor.

Typically, there is no *mens rea* capable of being negated by an actor's ignorance or mistake of law. Thus, no one can justify his conduct on the grounds that he was not aware of the law.

157. See R. Garofoli, *supra*, 597 (3rd ed., Milan 2006).

However, this rule has been mitigated[158] by a judgment of the Italian Constitutional Court. In fact, the Constitutional Court ruled that the ignorance of criminal law excludes the crime when the ignorance is inevitable.[159]

E. Mistake of Fact

236. Mistake of fact is regulated by Articles 47 and 48 PC.

According to Article 47, paragraph 1 PC, the error of fact excludes the criminal liability of the offender.

To start, mistake of fact must be defined: it is an error regarding the essential elements of the prohibited fact. For instance, there is a mistake of fact when an individual takes something incorrectly believing that it is his own.

Moreover, it is important to point out that a mistake of fact excludes the mental element (intent) of the crime. However, it is also worth noting that there will be a criminal violation if the material mistake was due to the negligence of the offender and the offence is a negligence crime. In this case, there is no fault liability.

§4. CHARGEABILITY

I. Introduction

237. Article 85 PC states that no one can be punished for a fact provided by law as crime, if at the moment of its commission, he or she was not capable of understanding and intent[160] (chargeable – *compos mentis*).

In order for a person to be charged with a crime, he must be mentally competent at the time of its commission. The Italian PC uses the expression *capacità di intendere e di volere*, namely capable of understanding and intent. The expression *capacità di intendere* (capable of understanding) covers not only the capacity to know what is occurring, but also the capacity to understand the social value of the act that has been carried out.

It is worth noting that it is not necessary that the actor is able to understand his conduct is unlawful, but it sufficient that he generically understands that his conduct is in contradiction with 'life's exigencies'.

However, the expression *capacità di volere* (capable of intent) means the capability of a person to control his own impulses and to act in accordance with reason. It is important to point out that there are persons who are able to distinguish good

---

158. On this question see F. Antolisei, *Manuale di diritto penale* 412 (Milan 2006); G. Fiandaca. *Principio di colpevolezza e ignoranza scusabile della legge penale: 'prima lettura' della sentenza n. 364/88*, in *Foro it.*, I, 1385 (1988).

159. Constitutional Court Decision No. 364 of 24 Mar. 1988 in *Giur. It.*, 1988, I, 1, 1076.

160. On this matter, see G. Baftttaglini – Grifo, *Imputabilità*, in *Novissimo Digesto* Ital., VIII, 451 (1962); A. Crespi, *Imputabilità (diritto penale)*, in *Enciclopedia del diritto*, XX, 763 et seq. (Milano 1970).

from evil but are unable to act in accordance with their own opinion and knowledge. In these cases, the *capacità di volere* is lacking.

Thus, the law provides that to be charged with a crime, there must be understanding and intent (*intendere and volere*). If only one of these is lacking, a person is not chargeable.

It is important to underline that one cannot be charged if he lacks mental health or maturity.

II. Exclusions

238. According to Articles 86–88 PC, there are certain cases in which chargeability is excluded or reduced. In particular, there is an exclusion or reduction of chargeability for:

(1) minority;
(2) insanity;
(3) deaf-mutism;
(4) intoxication;
(5) drug abuse.

A. Minority

239. The Italian legal system sets the age of majority at 18 years in most cases. In line with this, the Italian PC generally sets the age of the criminal responsibility at 18; however, there are certain factors that must be considered with regards to minority.

In fact, it is important to distinguish the case in which the perpetrator of the crime is under the age of 14 from the situation in which the perpetrator is between 14 and 18 years.

240. According to Article 97 PC, if the offender is under the age of 14 at the moment of the offence, he cannot be charged with a crime. Thus, the minimum age of criminal responsibility is set at 14 years. Children under the age of 14 are in principle presumed to lack a sufficient level of maturity to be held responsible and are presumed to be incapable of criminal responsibility. Therefore, there is an absolute legal presumption that the minor is incapable of understanding and intent, and the minor can never be punished and indicted for any type of illegal activity.

241. Pursuant to Article 98 PC, if the offender is between the ages of 14 and 18 at the time of the offence, he can be charged with a crime, if mentally competent. In this case, the punishment is reduced and a more lenient criminal sanction is imposed.

242. It is important to point out that in this case, i.e., the person is between the ages of 14 and 18, there is no legal presumption that the offender is incapable or capable of understanding and intent, but the matter falls within the discretion of the judge. The latter has to be ascertained on a case-by-case basis; if the offender was chargeable, he can be held responsible. In particular, the judge must make a psychological survey in order to verify the level of maturity and the moral and psychological development of the perpetrator of the crime.

It must also be noted that if the minor is under 14 at the time of the crime, but is not capable of understanding and intent, and cannot be punished and indicted, there still can be consequences to the offender. When there is a *delitto* (crime) and the minor is considered to pose a danger to society, he can be subjected to security measures such as probation (*libertà vigilata*) or reformatory school.

Instead, when the offender is between 14 and 18 years, he is considered liable and is punished but, as said, a more lenient criminal sanction is imposed. If the judge considers the offender a danger to society, the judge can order that after the execution of the penalty, if the risk persists, the offender is sent to a reformatory school or put on probation.

B. Insanity

243. Insanity is covered by Articles 88–89 PC. It is a pathological state: a mental disorder that causes a lack of the normal capacity of understanding and intent. As a consequence, one acts without the mental and physical health sufficient to be capable of understanding the unlawfulness of certain behaviour and to act in accordance with such understanding. A diagnosis of insanity alone may be a basis for certain types of detention.[161]

The mental disorder may cause both the lack of the capacity of understanding and intent. There is a lack of the capacity of understanding in cases of dementia, idiocy and derangement, while there is a lack of the capacity of intent in cases of kleptomania or pyromania, in which the actor is capable of understanding the unlawfulness of the behaviour but is unable to act according to his understanding because of a mental disability which prevents him from commanding and controlling his conduct.

---

161. Under Art. 5(1)(c) of the ECHR, persons of unsound mind, alcoholics, drug addicts and vagrants may be detained; however, in order for the detention to be allowed under the Convention, the Contracting State must prove the persons' condition. In this regard, in *Luberti v. Italy,* the European Court of Human Rights stated:

> *the mental disorder must be of a kind or degree warranting compulsory confinement: and the validity of continued confinement depends on the persistence* of such a disorder. Moreover, *in deciding whether an individual should be detained as a person of unsound mind the national authorities are to be recognized as having a certain margin of appreciation since it is in the first place for the national authorities to evaluate the evidence adduced before them in a particular case.*

Luberti v. Italy, ECtHR judgment of 23 Feb. 1984.

1. Insanity at the Moment of the Act

244. In order to obtain a reduction or an exclusion of the chargeability, the Italian PC requires that the offender was insane at the time he committed the prohibited act.

245. It is possible to distinguish the different degrees of mental insanity. The PC provides for: (a) total mental insanity (Article 88 PC) and, the (b) partial mental insanity (Article 89 PC). In the former, the capacity of understanding and intent is lacking; while in the latter, it is only reduced (i.e., diminished capacity).

If the offender is considered not guilty by reason of insanity (i.e., total mental insanity), he must be acquitted. However, often in this situation the offender is recognized to be socially dangerous and must undergo compulsory hospitalization in a special mental institution for offenders.

In the case of partial insanity, there is a reduction of the punishment and in addition to the penal sanction, compulsory hospitalization in a clinic or in a *casa di custodia* or secured mental health facility is provided as security measure.

It must be stressed that the offender must first serve the sentence and in addition, compulsory hospitalization in a clinic or in a *casa di custodia* or secured mental health facility is provided.

2. Insanity at the Moment of Trial

246. When the insanity manifests itself after the commission of the act, if the offender shows his insanity before an irrevocable judgment of conviction, and if he must not be acquitted for another reason, he is subject to compulsory hospitalization in a special mental institution for offenders and the proceeding is suspended.

The proceeding will restart when, after a psychiatric examination, the offender is found to be mentally competent, i.e., he has a sufficient degree of mental and physical health to be capable of trial.

Instead, if the insanity appears after the irrevocable judgment of conviction, the offender must undergo compulsory hospitalization in a special mental institution for offenders and there is no suspension of the sentence.[162]

3. Mental Incompetence Caused by Another

247. According to Article 86 PC, when someone causes the mental incompetence of another in order to make the second person commit a crime, the person causing the incapacity is responsible for the act.

The mentally incompetent subject will be held responsible if he gives his consent to the inducement, and he shares the unlawful purpose or when in his behaviour, there are the essential elements of negligence and thus the fact is punishable as such.

---

162. In the past, the judge had the power to suspend the sentence. Subsequently, the Constitutional Court stated that this rule was unlawful (Constitutional Court Decision No. 146 of 19 Jun. 1975).

C. Alcoholic Intoxication, Drug Abuse and Deaf-Mutism

248. The Italian criminal system also regulates those cases in which the offence was committed by a subject after drinking or consuming drugs. In fact, a person can be considered criminally liable, even if he is found partly mentally incompetent because of intoxication deriving from alcohol or drug abuse, although in this case more precise information is needed.

1. Alcoholic Intoxication

249. With regard to the alcoholic intoxication, it is important to distinguish real drunkenness from the chronic intoxication.

a. Real Drunkenness

249.1. Real drunkenness may be:

(1) involuntary;
(2) voluntary;
(3) preordained;
(4) habitual.

250. Involuntary drunkenness (Article 91 PC) is due to a fortuitous event and force majeure, as in the case in which the offender was made drunk against his will (e.g., victim of a joke).

In this case, if the intoxication causes a lack of the capacity of understanding and intent, the offender, who unintentionally committed an offence, is not chargeable with a crime and shall be acquitted.

Otherwise, the offender shall be punished, but there will be a reduction of punishment.

251. Voluntary drunkenness (Article 92, paragraph 1 PC) is where one uses liquor of his own free will and thus could foresee that he could be careless due to the alcohol. In this case, the offender shall be punished.

In particular, according to the dominant jurisprudence,[163] if the perpetrator of the crime foresaw and wanted the action or omission as a result of his conduct, there is intent.

If the action is the result of his carelessness, the offender shall be punished as being negligent, because he knew that his act or omission may have negative consequences, but trusted that the damaging result would not follow.

163. See Court of Cassation Decision of 30 Apr. 1990, in *Riv. Pen.*, 162 (1991); Court of Cassation Decision of 29 Apr. 1977, in *Mass. Dec. Pen.*, No. 135.724 and 135.725 1977; See F. Antolisei, *Manuale di diritto penale* 638 et seq. (Milan 2006).

252. Preordained drunkenness (Article 92, paragraph 2 PC) is when the offender drank in order to commit the criminal offence and to find an excuse. In this case, he shall be punished, and there will be an increase in punishment.

It must be stressed that, in order to justify punishment, in pursuance of the principle of the *actio libera in causa* (lacking the will to act) (Article 87 PC), the law considers that the guilt precede intoxication. Thus, the offender can be punished since as the action originated when he was sober, namely he was rational and responsible when he formed his intent.

253. Habitual drunkenness (Article 94 PC) presupposes that the subject has the habit of using liquor and consequently is often in a drunken state. In this case, after the execution of the penalty, if the offender is recognized to be socially dangerous, compulsory hospitalization is provided.

b. Chronic Intoxication

254. Chronic intoxication (Article 95 PC) deriving from alcohol represents the last phase of alcoholism. In this case, there are deep psychological disturbances,[164] and the subject is considered to be mentally ill; thus, the rules relating to insanity apply (Articles 88 and 89 PC) (*supra*, paragraphs 243–246).

2. Drug Abuse

255. The same rules establishing for the intoxication deriving from alcohol are provided (Articles 93 and 95; Article 94, paragraph 3 PC) for drug consumption.

3. Deaf-Mutism

256. According to Article 96 PC, a deaf-mute cannot be held responsible if, at the moment of the commission of the act, he lacked the capacity of understanding and intent due to his illness.

If the deaf-mute is recognized as being capable of understanding and intent, he is treated as a normal person and guilt is determined in the normal way.[165]

If it is ascertained that at the moment of the commission of the fact, he was incapable of understanding and intent, the rules of total mental insanity apply, the offender must be acquitted, and he must undergo compulsory hospitalization in a special mental institution for offenders. If it is proven that the capacity of understanding and intent was diminished, the offender shall be punished, but there will be a reduction of punishment and usually in addition to the penal sanction, compulsory hospitalization in a clinic or *casa di custodia* or secure mental health facility is provided as a security measure.

---

164. The most serious conditions are *delirium tremens*, the alcoholic psychosis of Korsakoff, and alcoholic paranoia.
165. See Court of Cassation Decision of 30 Jul. 1996, in *Giur. It.* II, 584 (1997).

Chapter 5. Incomplete or Partly Perpetrated Criminal Offences

§1. Criminal Attempt

I. Introduction

257. As mentioned previously, criminal liability may arise when a criminal offence has been carried out.

258. On occasion, a criminal offence falls short of completion and the offender make a substantial, but unsuccessful effort to commit a crime, e.g., the perpetrator shoots with a defective gun. The Italian criminal system addresses this situation in Article 56 PC, which extends liability to attempts.

This provision complements the rules concerning specific offences and creates other forms of offences by combining two rules: the rule regarding the specific crime and Article 56 PC. This combination gives rise to a new form of the offence (e.g., attempted murder, robbery, etc.).

The essence of attempt is to deter and reform the person attempting a crime or who has unsuccessfully attempted a crime.

II. Italian Attempt Statutes

259. Article 56, paragraph 1 PC provides that if the offender carries out suitable acts unequivocally directed at committing a crime, but the conduct has not been completed or the event has not occurred, an autonomous crime called 'attempt' occurs.

It is important to point out that the crime of attempt is contemplated with respect to crimes (*delitti*) but not with respect to misdemeanours (*contravvenzioni*).

Furthermore, according to Article 42, paragraph 2 PC – which states that '*no one can be punished for a criminal offence if he has not committed it intentionally*' – criminal liability may arise only when the offender has committed the criminal attempt with intent.

From a subjective point of view, the criminal attempt is complete, but from an objective point of view, only part of the required conduct has been carried out. As a result, the typical offence is incomplete.

Consequently, it is possible to distinguish the two forms of attempt: the so-called unfinished attempt and the completed attempt.

In the former, the action has not been entirely completed, as happens when the person attempts to steal, but is discovered and escapes. It is worth noting that this form of attempt cannot be represented by an omission, since an omission cannot be divided into a series of acts.

With completed attempt, the action has been entirely finished, but the event has not occurred, e.g., a person shoots in order to kill someone, but fails.

III. Conditions

260. There are three elements that characterize criminal attempt:

(1) The action has not been entirely completed or the event has not occurred.
(2) The acts carried out by the offender are unequivocally directed to commit the crime.
(3) The acts carried out by the offender are able to endanger a right protected by a rule.

261. Under Italian criminal law, the acts carried out by the offender must be suitable to create the probability that a crime will be committed. Specifically, the law requires a conduct that enables harm or endangers a right protected by a rule.

262. It is important to point out that not all preparation for an offence is a punishable attempt. In fact, the law establishes which conducts may be significant in order to have an attempt. The criminal course (*iter criminis*) must begin in order to have attempt.

The doctrine and the jurisprudence agree that the acts '*unequivocally directed to commit the crime*' are only acts of execution[166] equivalent to at least a part of the required conduct.

Consequently, preliminary acts are irrelevant (e.g., the agreement or the instigation of a crime that is not subsequently committed) (Article 115 PC).

These acts have only an instrumental role and could be significant only if they represent a separate type of crime (e.g., watermark making (Article 461 PC) or incitement to bribe (Article 322 PC).

IV. The Judgment of Suitability (*il giudizio di idoneità*)

263. As explained *supra*, paragraphs 260 et seq., in order to have an attempted crime, the acts of the offender must be unequivocally directed to commit the crime and not simply preliminary acts of the scheduled offence.

Therefore, it is important to verify if the acts carried out by the offender were sufficient to complete the crime. Namely, were the acts sufficient to create a probability that the crime would be completed, and if so, did they endanger a right protected by a rule?

264. It is the task of the judge to evaluate the facts. The judge must consider the completed crime and compare it to criminal attempt. Namely, he must make a

166. Constitutional Court No. 177/1980, GC 1980, I, 1548. See also G. Petrocelli, *Il delitto tentato* 75, 138 (Padova: Studi 1966); Marinucci – Dolcini, *Diritto penale, Parte Generale* 292 et seq. (2002); O. Vannini, *Il problema giuridico del tentativo* 24 (1950). *Contra*, I. Caraccioli, *Il tentativo nei delitti omissivi* 246 (Milano, 1975); F. Mantovani, *Diritto Penale, Parte Generale* 451 (4th ed., 2001).

judgment of the suitability (*il giudizio di idoneità*) to determine if the acts were sufficient.

265. On this subject, it is important to distinguish 'conduct offences' from 'event offences'.

In offences consisting of one or more actions (in which the committing of the offence takes place when the conduct is performed), the judgment of suitability has to be related to the actions required by law in order to complete the offence. For example, in the offence of escape from incarceration, if the subject is discovered while he is scaling the boundary wall with a rope, the judge must evaluate if the acts carried out could lead to the accomplishment of the action and thus the commission of the offence.

On the contrary, in 'event offence' (in which the committing of the offence takes place when the event occurs), the court must carry out the judgment of suitability by considering the event or the events. For example, with regard to intentional homicide by firearm, the trier of fact evaluates the probability that the act of aiming a gun could lead to the completion of the action and to death.

266. This judgment has to be formulated *ex ante*, on the basis of a posthumous prognosis. Thus, the judge must consider the moment when the action began, using the maximum knowledge available, at the moment the ascertainment is carried out, including eventually the knowledge of the offender.

Moreover, the judge has to take into consideration the actual circumstances in which the means used by the offender were utilized. It is sufficient for it to say that a punch usually does not lead to death, but if it is thrown by a boxer, his fist could become a lethal weapon.

As mentioned above, with regards to attempt, the rule set forth in Article 42, paragraph 2 PC is relevant. Consequently, '*no one can be punished for a fact provided as attempt if he has not committed it intentionally*'. Therefore, criminal liability may arise only if the offender has intentionally committed the criminal attempt.

V. Object of Intent

267. In the Italian criminal system, attempt is not an independent offence, but rather a punishable mode of a specific offence.

Consequently, the mental state required for criminal attempt is the intent to commit a certain criminal offence. In fact, the required mental state is not the intent to engage generally in criminality, but the intention to commit a specific offence.

Thus, the intent is the same for the completed crime and the attempted crime; the object is the accomplishment of the relative complete crime.

On the contrary, some doubts arise with regard to the kinds of intent. In particular, whether or not the kinds of intent significant to the completed crime are relevant with regard to criminal attempt. For example, the compatibility of the eventual intent (*dolo eventuale*) with attempt is a debated question. Some people rule out this hypothesis,[167] on the contrary, others[168] consider the eventual intent compatible with the attempt.

VI. Incompletion of the Offence and Perpetrator's Will

A. *Intentional/Voluntary Withdrawal*

268. According to Article 56, paragraph 3 PC, if a person voluntarily withdraws from the action, there is no punishable attempt if the portion of action performed does not amount, by itself, to a different kind of crime.

In this case, the law assumes that there has already been an unlawful act punishable as attempt that, because of the voluntary withdrawal, becomes unpunishable.

For example, a person enters a house in order to steal valuables locked in a safe, opens it and takes the items. In this case, there is already an attempt to steal. If the perpetrator voluntarily decides to abstain from completing the action, leaves the stolen goods and exits, there will be not an attempt to steal, but the acts performed will amount to trespass and damage (Article 635 PC).

In action offences (*reati commissivi*), there is a withdrawal when the action is not completed, as in the example mentioned above.

With omission offences (*reati ommissivi*), there is a withdrawal when the action initially omitted is performed (e.g., failure to assist – Article 593 PC).

The law requires a voluntary withdrawal. This happens when the perpetrator, of his own free will, abstains from further activities or prevents the harmful results of the act before completing the offence. In this case, the perpetrator must be convinced that he can complete the action, but he does not want to do so.

However, it is also worth noting that there is also voluntary withdrawal if the perpetrator acts out of self-interest (e.g., he enters a house in order to steal something but decides to abstain because he is planning to go back when the stolen goods are more considerable).

B. *Active Withdrawal*

269. With regard to the event offences (*reati di evento*), when the action is entirely completed, but the perpetrator willingly impedes the completion of the event, according to Article 56, paragraph 4 PC, there is 'active withdrawal'. Namely there is an attempt, but not an event and generally the law provides a reduction of the punishment established for the criminal attempt (e.g., a person is thrown into the water by the agent, but then the agent enters the water and saves the victim).

The law requires that the perpetrator's action is able to impede the event, so if he tries to impede it, but fails, there will be a completed crime.

---

167. Caputo – Captano, *Delitto tentato e dolo eventuale*, RP 1073 (1974); *Cass. Pen.*, 8 Nov. 1995, PCCPolo; 17 Mar. 1995, Papagni; 28 Feb. 1992, Scialpi.

168. E. Morselli, *Il tentativo*, *Giust. Pen.*, II, 40 (1988); G. Petrocelli, *Il delitto tentato*, *supra*, 36; *Cass. Pen.*, 22 Oct. 1993, Galatolo; 23 Mar. 1990, Lavia; 27 Apr. 1989, CalvaNo.

VII. Attempt and Legally Impossible Offences

270. With regard to attempt, it is worthwhile mentioning Article 49 PC, paragraph 2, regarding legally impossible offences. According to this article, there is no punishment when the harmful and dangerous event is impossible because of the unsuitability of the action or the inexistence of its object.

Determining whether there is an attempt or a legally impossible crime is crucial. In order to make a distinction, the legislator requires that the inexistence of the object has to be absolute, e.g., attempt to kill an already deceased man. Thus, there is not a legally impossible crime, but an attempt to steal when the pocket of the victim is empty.

An event can also be impossible because of the unsuitability of the action (e.g., an attempt to shoot someone who is clearly behind a bullet-proof shield).

In these cases, according to the principle of offensivity, there is no punishment, and it is a task of the judge to understand if the perpetrator is socially dangerous. If the prognosis of the judge is affirmative, the judge could order that he is subjected to security measures as probation (*libertà vigilata*).

VIII. The Penalty for Attempt

271. The distinction between an attempt and the completed offence has significance with respect to the level or severity of penalty imposed.

In fact, in line with the principle of offensivity, as there is a less serious offence, the law provides a reduced penalty (*pena diminuita*) with respect to that provided for the completed crime.

In particular, the punishment for attempt could be imprisonment for no less than twelve years, if the penalty provided for the accomplished crime is life imprisonment; or, in the other cases, the penalty provided for the accomplished crime can be reduced by one-third to two-thirds (Article 56, paragraph 2 PC).

§2. Participation in, or Parties to Criminal Offences

I. General Remarks

272. Generally, when establishing offences, the Italian legislator considers and describes the conduct of one perpetrator.

However, on occasion, two or more persons are involved in the commission of the offence. Thus, there is one offence and a plurality of offenders. In this case, the law provides a specific legal institute called 'participation in the crime'.

The rules concerning punishable participation serve the purpose of making atypical behaviours relevant and extending liability to all the participants of the criminal offence.

It is also worth noting that offences involving multiple participants frequently entail particular danger.

II. Italian Participation Law

273. The general principles concerning punishable participation are set forth in Articles 110–118 PC.

274. Italian criminal law makes a distinction between three categories of parties to the criminal offences, establishing different forms of liability.

In particular, the categories are determined by the degree of participation and cooperation, providing, as a consequence, differences in the penalties.

This means participation requires the existence of a principal offence in which an actor participates and to which his liability is related. The character of liability for participation has important consequences for the level of sentence. The three categories are:

(1) *Principal*: The qualified person who commits the qualified crime. More specifically, the principal carries out the action that, by itself, qualifies as a crime. The principal directly engages in the criminal act or omission as described by the law.
(2) *Co-author/Joint author*: When the execution of the qualified fact is carried out by means of more than one person on the basis of an agreement between them and each of them performs a part of the fact, the participants are called joint authors (*coautore*). This form of participation is similar to that of a principal. The co-authors, in fact, are principal actors, who directly engage in the criminal act or omission.
(3) *Accessory*: One who carries out an action that, in itself, does not constitute the fact provided by law as a crime (e.g., the accessory who buys a gun for an assassin).

275. Before describing the features of participation, it is important to distinguish between the offences that may be performed by one or more persons, from those offences which require two or more agents.

In the former, the so-called mono-subject offences (*reati monosoggettivi*), such as theft and intentional homicide, in order to have participation, it is necessary that another person cooperate in the commission of the crime (i.e., necessary participation). This person is the so-called accomplice to distinguish him from the principals, namely the perpetrator of the crime as stated by the law.

In the latter, so-called multi-subject offences (*reati plurisoggettivi*), there must be at least two people participating (eventual participation) (e.g., bigamy requires the participation of the perpetrating husband and the second spouse).

III. Conditions of Participation

276. According to Articles 110–118 PC, for participation to be punishable, the following requirements must be met:

(1) plurality of persons;
(2) realization of a principal offence;
(3) a chain of causation between the activity of the accessory and the realization of the event prohibited by the law; and
(4) awareness and will to play a part in carrying out the fact.

A. *Plurality of Persons*

277. The law requires a plurality of offenders cooperating (as principal, co-author, accessory) in the commission of the offence.

B. *The Requirement of a Principal Offence (Performed or Attempted)*

278. According to Article 115 PC, participation requires the existence of a principal criminal offence, i.e., a crime covered by law.

Consequently, in order to have participation in a crime, the law requires a principal offence be carried out by the principal, namely the author in a strict sense. Because a crime can occur both when there is a complete crime and an attempted crime, participation is possible both in offences and attempts.

C. *Chain of Causation*

279. The law requires also that the conduct of the accessory contributes in carrying out the fact. In addition, there is debate over the type of conduct which is necessary for there to be participation.

In fact, many legal scholars[169] assert that the accessory's action must be *condicio sine qua non* (e.g., an essential part) of the offence, or, more simply stated, the crime would not have occurred but for the action of the accessory.

Other scholars,[170] on the contrary, consider significant all the actions carried out by the accessory, sufficient to have an influence on the accomplishment of the crime. Thus, on the basis of this theory, also one who stands guard for another, participates and contributes to the crime, because, without his contribution, there would be a different distribution of the tasks between the parties. Consequently, also simple advice or dissuasion is enough if they bolster the intent to commit a crime. However, there will not be participation, if the one who has received the advice, had already resolved to commit the crime. Participation is possible also in omission offences, e.g., the caretaker of a villa who makes an agreement with the thieves to leave a door open intentionally in order to facilitate the theft.

---

169. E. Maezger, *Diritto Penale (Strafrecht), Italian translation by Att. Mandatari* 430 (Padova 1935).
170. M. Gallo, Lineamenti di una teoria sul concorso di persone nel reato 57 et seq. (Milano 1957); A. Magliaro, Principi di diritto penale. Parte generale 561 (Milano 1998); G. Grasso, in Romano e Grasso, Commentario, v. II, 150 et seq.; See F. Antolisei, supra, 563 et seq. (Milano 2006).

280. Commission by omission finds a juridical basis in the principle set forth in Article 40, paragraph 2 PC, according which the '*not-impeding an event in the presence of a legal duty to prevent it is equivalent to committing it*'.

The law has two requisites: (1) the violation of a legal duty to act, and (2) the omission is a condition necessary to the commission of the crime.

It must be noted that participation by omission must be distinguished from connivance. A conniver is one present during the commission of a crime, who does not object. As the Italian criminal system does not provide for a general duty of individuals to impede offences, criminal responsibility does not arise for the connivers.

D. Awareness and Will to Participate

1. The Required Intent

281. Criminal responsibility for participation does not arise if the principals and the accomplices do not intentionally, i.e., knowingly and willingly, cooperate in order to achieve a common criminal result.

Thus, the party has to be not only conscious to participate, but also has to be the will to contribute to the commission of the crime.

However, there is a debate over what constitutes consciousness: according to some legal scholars,[171] there must be consciousness of the participation of another. Other scholars[172] contend reciprocal consciousness is not necessary, the consciousness of at least one of the parties is sufficient.

2. Special Cases

282. On occasion, the crime committed is different from the agreed crime. According to Article 116 PC, in this case each participant is responsible for the crime actually committed if a chain of causation exists between his conduct and the prohibited event. Thus, the event is considered as wanted, even if the intent of the parties is lacking.

This rule represents a case of strict liability and raises a question of constitutional legitimacy with respect to the proportionality principle (regarding the relationship between the degree of liability and the penalty). In fact, in this case, the law could punish a negligence offence with a penalty provided for an intentional offence (*a titolo di colpa*).

---

171. Court of Cassation Decision of 9 Feb. 1987, Graziani, CED 175260, FI 1987, II, 409; F. Antolisei, *supra*, 568 (Milano 2006); A.R. Latagliata, *I principi del concorso di persone nel reato*, Napoli, 1964.

172. Court of Cassation Decision of 5 Dec. 2003, M., CED 228424; Court of Cassation Decision of 27 Feb. 1995, Gherrino, CP 1997, 56; Court of Cassation Decision of 20 Dec. 1989, Pistoia, CED 184044, RP 1991, 197; Court of Cassation Decision of 1 Jun. 1989, Caveduri, CED 183083, GP 1991, II, 214.

The rigidity of this rule is mitigated by the exception set forth in the second paragraph of the Article 116 PC. In fact, under this article, if the crime committed is different and more serious than the crime agreed, the applicable punishment can be reduced.

IV. Forms of Participation Provided for by Law: Material and Moral

283. The doctrine provides two kinds of participation: material and moral.

The participation is material when it takes place during the execution phase. In this case, the subject cooperates in the commission of the offence, but does not carry out a qualified conduct, e.g., he furnishes the gun used for the commission of the crime. In this case, it is necessary to ascertain if the actions had an influence on the commission of the crime.

Moral participation, however does not involve a physical action, but an intellectual one (e.g., incitement). In this case, the law requires there be a *causal nexus* between the non-qualified conduct and the principal offence. Thus, the instigation has to inspire the criminal intention or to strengthen it, and the crime has to be committed. In fact, according to Article 115 PC, criminal liability may only arise when the instigation is accepted and the crime is committed; otherwise, there is no punishment.

Italian legal doctrine sometimes distinguishes between the *determinatore*, i.e., the party who provokes the original intent and the *instigatore*, i.e., a person who reinforces a pre-existing intent. In each case, the causal influence has to be ascertained in actual terms. Issues commonly arise regarding the nature of the accessory's conduct.

V. Punishment for Participation

284. As said above, the Italian Criminal Law bases liability for participation on the degree of participation and cooperation, providing, as a consequence, different penalties.

Article 110 PC introduces a general rule regarding participation: when a plurality of persons takes part in the same crime, each one is considered an offender and is subject to the penalty established for the respective offence.

However, this does not mean that all participants receive the same penalty, because the punishment must be based on each individual's own contribution to the crime.

285. Furthermore, aggravating and mitigating circumstances (Articles 112 and 114 PC) have an effect on the criminal liability. In particular, it is interesting to note that the rules which establish that the aggravating circumstances apply even if some of the participation in the crime is not chargeable and punishable. However, Article 119, paragraph 1 PC, provides that the subjective circumstances, which exclude the punishment for those who concurred in the crime, have an effect only with regard the subject to which they refer.

VI. Withdrawal from Participation and Proactive Withdrawal

A. *Withdrawal from Participation*

286. At times, one or more of the parties may withdraw from the participation. In case of voluntary withdrawal of the principal, there is no punishment if he has not performed the action provided by law as a crime.

The position of the accessory is different. On this point, some hold that, in order to have a voluntary withdrawal of the accessory, it is necessary that he hinder the execution of the intended offence, stopping the activity of all other parties. However, this opinion is considered to be far too rigid.

Others contend that the accessory only needs to hinder the effects of his action, e.g., he takes back the gun he gave to the principal. Thus, the subsequent conduct of the principal will be completely autonomous, and there will be no chain of causation between the accessory's conduct and the conduct of the principal.

B. *Proactive Withdrawal*

287. On the contrary, in order to proactively withdraw, the accessory must hinder the execution of the intended offence. Thus, if the principal is going to shoot someone using a gun furnished by the accessory, there will be a proactive withdrawal if the accessory hinders the death of the wounded by transporting him to hospital.

VII. Agent Provocateur

288. Occasionally, a law enforcement agent or citizen participates in a criminal enterprise and instigates a crime solely in order to entrap the other parties. By instigating the crime, the person is acting as an agent provocateur as opposed to a simple undercover agent. In the case of an agent provocateur, the question arises whether or not the person is guilty as a principal or as an accomplice, and whether he is responsible for a completed crime or an attempt.

This issue has been historically controversial. And in fact, according to the European Court of Human Rights, the use of agents provocateurs equals entrapment and is not allowed as it infringes on the defendant's right to a fair trial.[173]

289. Under the more rigid view of the issue, the purpose of the agent provocateur – that is to deliver the guilty to justice – does not excuse the conduct and its contribution to the crime committed. However, the prevailing view under Italian law, excludes the liability of the agent provocateur.

173. See *Teixeira De Castro v. Portugal,* ECtHR judgment of 9 Jun. 1998 paras 31–39. A defendant's right to a fair trial is violated if the undercover agent acts in a way so as to encourage and instigate the commission of a crime thus causing the defendant to have a criminal intent that would otherwise have been absent.

Some scholars,[174] and certain jurisprudence, exclude liability based on the existence of a justification of legal duty.

The prevailing doctrine considers the agent provocateur not punishable because there is a lack of intent. In fact, the agent does not want to contribute to the commission of the crime, but rather he wants the commission of the crime to be hindered, i.e., intervention by the police.[175,176,177]

VIII. Negligent Participation

290. Up to this point, the topic of participation has been analysed considering only intentional offences. The Italian PC also provides for participation in negligent crimes. In fact, Article 113, paragraph 1 PC, establishes '*when a negligent crime has been caused by the cooperation of several persons, each of them is subject to the penalties provided for that crime*'.

Moreover, paragraph 2 specifies '*the penalty is increased for the leader of the crime, when the conditions established by Article 111 PC (inducement of a non-chargeable offence) and the aggravating conditions set forth in Article 112, paragraphs 3 and 4 PC occur*'.

174. F. Antolisei, *supra,* 569; Califano, *L'agente provocatore* 73 (1956); Court of Cassation Decision of 27 Sep. 1989.
175. T. Delogu, *La responsabilità penale dell'agente provocatore*, STSA 19, 34 (1938); Fiandaca – Musco, 468; Marinucci – Dolcini, *Manuale di diritto penale, Parte generale* 276 (2004).
176. See also Delogu, *supra*, 34; Mantovani, *Diritto penale. Parte generale* 518 (5th ed., 2007).
177. See also Grasso, in CommSist II, Arts 110, 172; Mantovani, *supra*, 554.

Chapter 6. Classification and Survey of Criminal Offences

§1. General Classification of Criminal Offences

291. As explained, under Italian law, criminal offences can be classified in a variety of ways, for example qualified and non-qualified offences, or offences of action and offences of omission.

292. However, generally criminal offences are divided into two main categories: crimes (*delitti*) and misdemeanours (*contravvenzioni*).

This criterion is used by the PC and within the framework of the complementary laws.

I. Legal Classification

293. The distinction provided by the Italian PC between crimes and misdemeanours has fundamental importance. Usually, crimes are considered more serious offences and misdemeanours less severe. This distinction is based on the gravity of the crime and, in particular, on the severity of the punishment and the different types of penalties envisaged, as underlined by Article 39 PC.

In particular, crimes may be punished by life imprisonment, imprisonment and *multa* (i.e., fine) (*infra*, paragraphs 339–343). Misdemeanours may be punished by imprisonment and *ammenda* (i.e., fine) (*infra*, paragraphs 344–346).

These categories of crimes are described into the second and third books of the Italian PC.

II. Italian Penal Code Framework

294. The Italian PC is divided into a general part, which contains provision applying to all the offences, and a special part, which provides for single criminal offences.

The general part is contained in the first book, entitled *Offences in General*, while the specific part is contained in the second and third books entitled *Types of Crimes* and *Types of Misdemeanours* respectively.

§2. Survey of Criminal Offences

295. As it is impossible to provide an exhaustive survey of all offences under Italian criminal law, the following survey is limited to a brief representation of the structure and the content of the second book of the Italian PC.

It is also worth noting that in addition to the criminal offences of the PC, there are a multitude of criminal offences provided for by special statutes. For reasons of brevity, only the most important of these offences are covered.

I. Offences of the Penal Code

296. The second book of the Italian PC contains the various different crimes. It generally classifies each crime under a specific heading, showing a catalogue of definitions of the various criminal offences as well as the punishment provided for each of them. It is subdivided into thirteen Titles.

A. Title I: Crimes against the Nation

297. Crimes against the Nation (*delitti contro la personalità dello Stato*) are found in Articles 241–313 PC and are offences detrimental to the State political affairs. They concern both the relation between the State and other nations, e.g., revealing a State secret (Article 261 PC), espionage (Articles 257–258 PC), and domestic affairs, e.g., attempt on president's life (Article 276 PC), armed gangs (Article 309 PC), terrorism (Articles 280–280*bis* PC).

B. Title II: Crimes against the Public Authority

298. Title II contains Crimes against Public Authority (*delitti contro la pubblica amministrazione*) (Articles 314–360 PC).

This title includes all the offences that obstruct the due course of the executive, legislative, and judicial activity of the State, as well as the public bodies. The code distinguishes offences committed by civil servants in the exercise of their function from offences committed by private citizens.

The first part deals with embezzlement of public property by an officer (Article 314 PC), corruption, malfeasance (Article 317 PC[178]), bribery (Articles 318–321 PC), and abuse of authority (Article 323 PC).

299. As regards bribery, recently there have been a number of modifications to the law. In fact, Italy has ratified several anti-corruption conventions, among which the most important is the Organisation for Economic Co-operation and Development (OECD) Anti-Bribery Convention of December 1997. As a consequence of Italy implementing the OECD Anti-Bribery Convention, new articles were introduced into the PC.

In particular, Article 3 of Italian Law No. 300 of 29 September 2000 introduced Article 322*bis* PC. This article extends the domestic bribery offences in the PC to foreign public officials (including the EU and others, i.e., members of the Commission of the European Community (EC), the European Parliament, the European Court of Justice, and the Court of Auditors of the European Communities; officials and contracted agents within the meaning of staff regulations of officials of the EC

178. This Article was amended by the last anti-corruption law, Law No. 69 of 27 May 2015 which introduced also the position of the public service officer.

or the conditions of employment of agents of the EC; any person seconded to the EC by the Member States or by any private or public body which carries out functions equivalent to those performed by EC officials or other agents; members and employees of bodies created on the basis of Treaties establishing the EC Community; those who, within other Member States of the EU carry out functions or activities equivalent to those performed by public officials or persons in charge of a public service).

300. In late 2012, Italy passed a long-debated law on Anti-Corruption.[179] Law No. 190 of 6 November 2012 introduced two new offences: inducement to give or promise undue advantages (Article 319*quarter* PC) (induced bribery)[180] and illicit trafficking of influence (Article 346*bis* PC).[181] This law also amended Italian Civil Code Article 2635,[182] making private corruption an offence. Furthermore, the Law specifically identifies those areas and activities which are considered to be

179. Law No. 190 of 6 Nov. 2012, entered into force on 28 Nov. 2012, published in the Official Gazette No. 265 of 13 Nov. 2012 *Disposizioni per la Prevenzione e la Repressione della Corruzione e dell'Illegalità nella Pubblica Amministrazione* (Dispositions for the Prevention and Repression of Corruption and Illegality in the Public Administration). In Italian: http://www.publinforma.com/pdf/Legge%20anticorruzione%20n.%20190-2012.pdf (Accessed in June 2015).

180. Law No. 190/2012, Art. 1, para. 75(i) – Inducement to give or promise undue advantages (ICC Art. 319*quarter*) This provision was subsequently amended by Art. 1, para. 1 (h) of Law No. 69 of 27 May 2015 which increased the penalties.:

> It is an offence for one to leverage on their existing relationships with a public official or an employee of a public service, by unduly giving or promising, money or another economic advantage, in exchange for the public official to perform an act contrary to his official duties or with the delay or omission of an act of his office. The penalty is imprisonment from three to eight years, and also applies to anyone who unduly gives or promises money or other pecuniary advantage.

181. Law No. 190/2012, Art. 1, para. 75(r) – Illicit trafficking of influence (Criminal Code Art. 346*bis*):

> Unless the act constitutes a more serious offence, the public official or public service, abusing his position or his powers, induces another person to unduly give or promise to him or a third party, money or other benefits shall be punished with imprisonment from three to eight years. In the cases covered by the first paragraph, who gives or promises money or other benefits shall be punished with imprisonment up to three years.

182. Law No. 190/2012, Art. 1, para. 76 – Private Corruption (Italian Civil Code Art. 2635):

> [T]he directors, general managers, managers responsible for preparing corporate accounting documents, auditors and liquidators, who, following the giving or the promise of money or other benefit, for himself or for others, perform or omit acts in violation of the obligations inherent in their office or duties of loyalty, causing harm to the company, shall be punished with imprisonment from one to three years. If the offence is committed by a subordinate, the penalty of imprisonment of up to one year and six months. The person giving or promising the money or other benefits are also subject to the same penalties. If the company is listed, the penalties are doubled.

particularly at risk for corruption. In addition, the law[183] increased the penalties for certain corruption-related offences, created protection for whistle-blowers,[184] and changed the denomination of the Independent Commission for Evaluation, Transparency and Integrity (*Commissione Nazionale per la Valutazione, la Trasparenza e l'Integrità delle Amministrazioni Pubbliche* or 'CiVIT')[185,186] in Italian Anti-Corruption Authority (thereby fulfilling Article 6 of the ONU Convention and Articles 20 and 21 of the Strasbourg Convention regarding anti-corruption).

Moreover, in order to reduce the risk of corruption in public administration, according to Article 67 of the Law No. 190/2012 was introduced the Decree No. 235 of 6 November 2012, which contains '*Provisions on the ineligibility and ban on holding elective and government position which result from final convictions for intentional crimes*'.[187]

Recently, Law No. 69 of 27 May 2015 introduced '*Provisions relating to crimes against the public administration, of mafia type organizations and false accounting*'. Aforementioned law, whose aim is to strengthen the penalties for crimes of corruption, malfeasance and embezzlement, further increased the penalties for certain corruption – related offences (Articles 317, 318, 319 and 319 *quarter* PC) and also amended Articles 2621 and 2622 of Civil Code (dealing with false corporate reporting in case of listed and unlisted companies).

301. With regard to offences by private citizens, these include, among other things, violence and threats against a civil servant (Article 336 PC), insulting a public prosecutor (Article 343 PC), and unlawful practice of a profession (Article 348 PC).

C. Title III: Crimes against Judicial Authority

302. Crimes against Judicial Authority (*delitti contro l'amministrazione della giustizia*) are contained in Articles 361–401 PC.

This title includes all the offences that disturb and obstruct the due course of the judicial activity. It also assures that the judicial activity is carried out by the body

183. Law No. 190/2012, Art. 1, para. 75 (d, f, g, h) – Malfeasance (Criminal Code Art. 317) – Corruption for the exercise of the function (Criminal Code Art. 318) – Corruption for an act contrary to official duties (Criminal Code Art. 319) – Inducement to give or promise undue advantages (Criminal Code Art. 319*quarter).*
184. Law No. 190/2012, Art. 1, para. 51 inserting Art. 5*bis* - *Tutela del dipendente pubblico che segnala illeciti* ('Rules for Public Employees who Report Illicit Acts', i.e., whistle-blowers) into Legislative Decree No. 165 of 30 Mar. 2001.
185. Law No. 190/2012, Art. 1.
186. CiVIT was set up originally by Law No. 15/2009 and further regulated by Legislative Decree No. 150/2009. The Anti-corruption Law assigns new functions to CiVIT concerning Anti-corruption, complementary to those previously assigned by Legislative Decree No. 150/2009, thus enlarging CiVIT functions and powers. http://www.civit.it/ (Accessed June 2015).
187. The TAR (i.e., the Regional Administrative Court) of Campania raised an issue of the constitutional legitimacy of the Decree No. 235/2012, because the decree allows the suspension from office for the municipal, provincial, district and regional administrators who have committed crimes before the entry into force of the law. The matter is still pending before the Constitutional Court.

appointed. Under the heading of crimes against judicial authority, the Italian legislator criminalizes, among other things, the crime of perjury (Article 372 PC) and the subornation of witnesses (Article 377 PC).

D. *Title IV: Crimes against Sentiments regarding Religion and against the Dead*

303. Crimes against religious sentiments and against the feelings of pity towards the dead (*delitti contro il sentimento religioso e contro la pietà dei defunti*) are covered in Title IV (Articles 402–413 PC).

This title deals with the crimes that are detrimental to religion and the sentiment for the dead, e.g., offences against religion, profanation of tomb.

Due to the abrogation of the principle that Catholicism was the established religion, now the protection provided by law is extended to all the religions and cults recognized by the Italian State.

E. *Title V: Crimes against Public Order*

304. Title V (Articles 414–421 PC) addresses crimes against the public order (*delitti contro l'ordine pubblico*).

This title includes all the offences that could endanger, disturb and breach the peace, e.g., solicitation (Article 414 PC), criminal association (Article 416 PC), Mafia-style criminal organization (Article 416*bis* PC).

F. *Title VI: Crimes against Public Safety*

305. Crimes against public safety (*delitti contro l'incolumità pubblica*) are set forth in Title VI (Articles 422–452 PC).

This title includes all the offences that might harm or endanger life and physical well-being of an unspecified number of people. These offences include, among other things, massacre (Article 422 PC), arson (Article 423 PC), provoking a railway disaster (Article 430 PC), intentional removal, and omission of measures against accidents at work (Article 437 PC), and poisoning food or water (Article 439 PC).

Recently, this title has been amended by Law No. 68/2015, which introduced an unintentional crime against the environment (Article 452*quinquies*) and the crimes of environmental pollution (Article 452*bis* CP), crime of environmental disaster (Article 452*quater* CP) and crime of traffic and desertion of highly radioactive material (Article 452*sexies* CP).

G. *Title VII: Crimes against Public Faithfulness*

306. Those crimes against public faithfulness (*delitti contro la fede pubblica*) are found in Title VII (Articles 453–498 PC).

Under this title are included the counterfeiting of coins (Article 453 PC), negotiable instruments, and instruments such as credit cards (Article 458 PC) and bank notes (Article 460 PC), and the counterfeiting of stamps, seals and marks (Article 459 PC).

In order to punish these offences, the law requires the false currency or instrument to be sufficient to deceive the majority of people, and it is sufficient to break, endanger and harm the interest protected by law. Moreover, the law requires a specific intent, namely consciousness and will to counterfeit and to harm someone else.

H. *Title VIII: Crimes against Public Economy, Industry and Commerce*

307. Title VIII addresses crimes against public economy, industry and commerce (*delitti contro la l'economia pubblica, l'industria e il commercio*) (Articles 499–518 PC).

This title protects the due course of the economy, punishing all the facts that bar freedom of production and exchange of goods, such as agiotage (Article 501 PC) and commercial fraud (Article 515 PC).

I. *Title IX: Crimes against Public Morality*

308. In Title IX (Articles 519–544 PC), crimes against public morality (*delitti contro la moralità pubblica ed il buon costume*) are addressed.

309. Originally, this title covered offences against sexual freedom and those involving the aiding, abetting or fostering of prostitution, or the debauchery of minors.

However, in 1996 this title was completely modified. Law No. 66 of 15 February 1996 moved offences against sexual freedom to among those crimes against individual freedom (see Articles 609*bis* et seq.). Title IX punished offences regarding indecent exposure (Article 527 PC), now the Legislative Decree No. 8 of 15 January 2016, change this crime in administrative offences

310. Prostitution is still regulated by Law No. 75 of 20 February 1958 and punishes those who lead another to prostitution or abet or foster prostitution.

It is important to note that the mere act of prostitution is not punishable under Italian law.

J. *Title IXbis: Crimes against Feelings for Animals*

311. Title IX*bis* covers crimes against feelings for animals (*delitti contro il sentimento per gli animali*) (Articles 544*bis*–544*sexies* PC).

This title was added by Article 1 of Law No. 189 of 20 July 2004 and was subsequently amended by Article 3, paragraph 1 of Law No. 201 of 4 November 2010 which increased the penalties for the offences referred to in Articles 544*bis* and 544*ter* PC. These articles punish all offences against animals carried out for cruelty and without need. This title includes offences involving, among others: killing or mistreating animals, organizing, encouraging and directing fighting between animals such as dogfights or cockfights.

Moreover, Decree No. 121 of 2011 introduced in the Criminal Code two new offences to protect plants and animals. Article 727*bis* penalizes the capture or killing of animals and plants belonging to protected species. Furthermore, Article 733*bis* punishes the deterioration of a habitat within a protected site.

K. Title X: Crimes against Well-being and Soundness of the Race

312. Crimes against well-being and soundness of the race (*reati contro l'integrità e la sanità della stirpe*) were addressed in Title X (Articles 545–555 PC). Abortion is covered in this section. However, this title has been abrogated by Article 22 of Law No. 194 of 22 May 1978.

Abortion is no longer punishable if the conditions provided by law are fulfilled. Normally, the abortion must be performed within the first ninety days of pregnancy, and the pregnant woman must be in an emergency situation with respect to her physical conditions, as well as the economic, social and family conditions. The consent of the pregnant woman is required. Only in special case of necessity and emergency may an abortion be justified if performed after the term mentioned.

L. Title XI: Crimes against the Family

313. Title XI sets forth those crimes against the family (*reati contro la famiglia*) (Articles 556–574*bis*[188] PC).

This title includes all offences that could harm or endanger the institution of the family. Among the criminal offences against the family covered in this title are bigamy (Article 556 PC), incest (Article 564 PC), crimes directed to concealing the civil status of a child (Article 568 PC) and the mistreatment of children (Article 572 PC).

M. Title XII: Crimes against the Person

314. Crimes against the person (*delitti contro la persona*) are found in Title XII (Articles 575–623*bis* PC).

This title concerns all offences that harm or endanger the citizens' basic goods, such as life, integrity, honour and freedom. Among these crimes, the most important offence is the homicide (Article 575 PC).

315. Italian criminal law distinguishes between intentional, negligent and so-called preterintentional homicide.

188. Introduced by Art. 3, para. 29, let. B) of the Law 15 Jul. 2009, No. 94.

The Italian PC considers the homicide intentional (Article 575 PC) when the offender kills with the purpose of ending the victim's life.

Negligent homicide (or manslaughter) (Article 589 PC) occurs when the killing was committed as a result of carelessness, negligence and unskillfulness.

The homicide *ex* Article 584 occurs when death is beyond the intention of the agent: the author, in fact, wants a crime less serious than the one that occurs. In that case, it is possible to speak of a 'preterintentional' homicide, which is characterized by a mixed *mens rea*, partly intentional and partly unintentional. Cases of intentional homicide (or voluntary homicide) include infanticide (i.e., killing of an infant) (Article 578 PC) and the homicide with consent (Article 579 PC), (i.e., killing with the consent of the victim).

316. Under the general heading 'crimes against the person' are also included offences concerning bodily harm, such as personal injury. Article 582 PC establishes that '*anyone who causes bodily harm to another person resulting in that person's mental or bodily injury is punishable with a term of imprisonment ranging from three months to three years*'.

This title also included offences such as insult (Article 594 PC) which it was repealed by Article 1 of Legislative Decree No. 7 of 15 January 2016, defamation (Article 595 PC), offences against individual freedom such as the prostitution of minors (Article 600*bis* PC), pornography of minors (Article 600*ter* PC), kidnapping (Article 605 PC) and sexual assault (Article 609*bis* PC). Moreover, this section also covers offences against the sanctity of the domicile (Articles 614 et seq. PC).

317. Also included in Title XII are certain computer crimes, which were introduced into the PC by Law No. 547 of 23 December 1993, Law No. 273 of 12 December 2002; No. 48 of 18 March 2008; and Law No. 1 of 24 January 2012; law No. 93 of 14 August 2013. The PC divides cybercrimes into two general categories: (1) those which considered crimes against the person (i.e., acts against the will of the victim's legitimate right to protect their systems and communications; and (2) those crimes, such as computer fraud (Article 640*ter* PC) which are considered property crimes. For more on this topic, see *infra*, paragraphs 324–327 on cybercrime.

N. Title XIII: Crimes against Property

318. Crimes against property (*delitti contro il patrimonio*) are found in Title 13 (Articles 624–649 PC).

The Italian PC contains a great variety of offences against property. First of all, it distinguishes crimes against property committed by means of violence from those committed by means of fraud. With regard to the first categories, the most serious and important crimes are theft (Article 624 PC) and robbery (Article 628 PC).

1. Offences against Property Committed by Means of Violence: Theft and Robbery

319. The Italian PC makes a distinction between theft and robbery. In the case of theft, Article 624, paragraph 1 PC establishes:

> *anyone who takes possession of the movable object of another person with the aim of gaining profit from it for himself or for others, is subject to punishment of a term of imprisonment of six month to three years and with a fine of between one hundred and fifty (154.00) to five hundred and sixteen (516.00) Euro.*

Moreover, Article 624*bis* PC addresses those thefts committed by means of breaking into a house or similar.

320. Article 628 PC describes robbery as:

> *anyone who, with the aim of gaining an unlawful profit for himself or for others, and with the threat of violence, takes possession of a movable object of another person by subtracting it from that person, is subject to punishment of a term of three to ten years of imprisonment and with a fine of between five hundred and sixteen (516.00) Euro to two thousand and sixty-five (2,065.00) Euro.*

321. In cases of robbery and theft, the Italian PC provides for a very wide range of aggravating circumstances.

These aggravating circumstances result in an increase in the term of imprisonment envisaged for theft. The aggravating circumstances regarding theft include, acts of violence on things, the use of fraud, the use of arms or drugs, the commission of the offence with skill, the commission of an offence in groups of three or more persons, stealing travellers' baggage, goods which are in public premises or three or more heads of cattle.

Robbery is aggravated when arms are used, when it is committed by a group of people, or if the violence makes some one incapable of understanding or intent.

322. Finally, other kinds of offences against property committed by means of violence are extortion (Article 629 PC), kidnapping for ransom (Article 630 PC), damaging in general (Article 635 PC), damaging of a data processing system (Article 635*bis* PC), damaging of information, data and programmes used by a government or other public bodies or anyway data of public interest (Article 635*ter* PC), damaging of information technology or telecommunications (Article 635*quater* PC), and damaging of information technology or telecommunications systems of public utility (Article 635*quinquies* PC). These offences will be discussed in more detail in the next sub-sections).[189]

189. These items were included in the Criminal Code by Art. 5, para. 2 of the Law No. of 18 Mar. 1948 on the Ratification and implementation of the Convention of the Council of Europe on crime 'computer', made in Budapest 23 Nov. 2001.

2. Offences against Property Committed by Means of Fraud

323. The Italian PC describes fraud as the act of misleading someone, with devices and trick, gaining profit from it for himself or for others (Article 640 PC).

The Code contains a great variety of offences against property committed by means of fraud, such as computer fraud (Article 640*ter* PC), fraudulent insolvency (Article 641 PC), embezzlement (Article 646 PC), receiving of stolen goods (Article 648 PC), recycling (Article 648*bis* PC), and so on.

Article 3, paragraph 3 of Law No. 186 of 15 December 2014 introduced in the Criminal Code the crime of self-laundering. The new Article 648*ter*1 PC punishes the conduct of anyone who, having committed or participated in committing an intentional crime, employs, replaces, moved, in economic activities, financial, entrepreneurial or speculative, money, goods or other benefits from the commission of this crime, so as to hinder concretely the identification of their criminal origin.

II. Cybercrimes

324. As mentioned in paragraph 317 *supra*, the Italian PC generally classifies computer offences into two parts: those considered crimes against the person and those categorized as property crimes.

The majority of the crimes listed under general heading of crimes against persons were introduced into the PC by Law No. 547 of 23 December 1993, as amended.[190] The crimes in this section include: unauthorized access to a computer or telematic system (Article 615*ter* PC); unlawful withholding or disseminating *of* access codes to a computer or telematic system (Article 615*quarter* PC); dissemination of equipment, devices or computer programmes intended to damage or disrupt a computer or telematic system (Article 615*quinquies* PC); illegal interception, impediment or disruption of computer or telematic communications (Article 617*quarter* PC); installation of equipment designed to intercept, impede or disrupt computer or telematic communications (Article 617*quinquies* PC); and forgery, alteration or deletion of the content of computer or telematic communications (Article 617*sexies* PC).

325. Italy has taken further steps by signing, ratifying and adopting the provisions of the Convention on Cybercrime of 23 November 2001[191,192] (Cybercrime Convention), which aims to harmonize the domestic substantive and procedure laws regarding cybercrime.

326. Many of the new laws added by adopting the Cybercrime Convention involve crimes against property and thus are found in Title XIII. The new laws as

190. Law No. 48 of 18 Mar. 2008.
191. Law No. 48 of 18 Mar. 2008.
192. As the Convention has now been adopted in whole or in part by a number of States outside of the European Union (e.g., USA, Japan and Canada), at present the Convention is also sometimes referred to as an International Convention, rather than EU.

per Law No. 48 of 18 March 2008 include: damaging of information, data, and programmes used by governments or other public body or anyway data of public interest (Article 635*ter* PC); damaging of computer or telecommunication systems Article (635*quater* PC); and damaging of public computer or telecommunications utilities (Article 635*quinquies* PC). Under Article 7 of Law No. 48 of 18 March 2008,[193] criminal liability has been extended to entities under Legislative Decree No. 231 of 8 June 2001. See *supra,* paragraphs 145 et seq.

327. Moreover, the adopting of the Cybercrime Convention has impacted a number of provisions of the Italian CCP, in particular those regarding inspection (Article 244 CCP), searches (Articles 247 and 352 CCP), and sequestration (Articles 254 and 254*bis* CCP). See *infra,* paragraphs 598 and 602.

III. Misdemeanours

328. As known, criminal offences are divided generally into two main categories: *crimes and misdemeanours*, the last are less serious offences than the first one and are forbidden for public order reasons.

The criteria to make a distinction between crimes and misdemeanour, adopted by the Italian PC (Article 39 PC), are the severity of the punishment and the different types of penalties envisaged.

In particular, there will be a crime when the law inflicts life imprisonment, imprisonment or a heavy fine/penalty (*multa*), while there will be a misdemeanour when the law inflicts arrest or a fine (*ammenda*).

329. The third book of the PC concerns misdemeanours and is subdivided into two titles (Articles 650 et seq. PC). Title I (Articles 650–730 PC) deals with the misdemeanours involving the police, while Title II (Articles 731 et seq. PC) addresses misdemeanours regarding the social activity of public authority.

IV. Criminal Offences in the Special Laws

330. The PC is the main source of the Italian criminal justice system, but not the only one.

In fact, Italy has many special laws that represent another source of criminalization. A large part of the incriminating provisions are contained in the so-called *complementary legislation*, the use of which has increased over the years.

Among the numerous special criminal laws, it is useful to mention at least those related to secret associations (Law No. 17 of 25 January 1982), corporate offences (Legislative Decree No. 61 of 11 April 2002, Legislative Decree No. 231 of 8 June 2001 and Legislative Decree No. 190 of 6 November 2012), financial brokerage/ credit market (Legislative Decree No. 58 of 24 February 1998, Legislative Decree

193. Article 7 of Law No. 48 of 18 Mar. 2008, introducing Art. 24*bis* to Legislative Decree 231 of 8 Jun. 2001.

No. 37 of 6 February 2004), banking market (Legislative Decree No. 385 of 1 September 1993, Legislative Decree No. 37 of 6 February 2004), environment (Legislative Decree No. 152 of 3 April 2006), bankruptcy (Legislative Decree No. 5 of 9 January 2006), prostitution (Law No. 75 of 20 February 1958), prostitution regarding a minor (Law No. 269 of 3 August 1998 and Law No. 46 of 11 March 2002), and drugs (Presidential Decree No. 309 of 9 October 1990).

This list, even if only indicative, makes it clear that there is frequent recourse to the complementary legislation.

Nevertheless, it is also necessary to point out that at times complementary legislation poses considerable problems because certain subject matters are already regulated in depth by the law, thus creating divergence or overlap between the sources.

Chapter 7. The Sanctioning System

§1. The General Sanctioning System

331. In the Italian criminal system, the punishment is the sanction or penalty that criminal law provides for a particular crime. More exactly, the punishment represents the direct consequence of the crime.

If, on the one hand, the punishment has the function of punishing the offender, on the other hand, it also has a rehabilitative function.

In fact, Article 27, paragraph 3, of the Italian Constitution, which establishes the rehabilitative function of a penalty, states, '*penalties cannot consist in treatment contrary to the sense of humanity and must tend to the rehabilitation of the offender*'. For instance, as discussed in paragraph 372 *infra*, one of the ways in which Italy is approaching restorative justice is through the use of juvenile criminal mediation, in particular victim-offender mediation (VOM).

332. The Italian criminal law distinguishes the following categories of punishment:

(1) principal penalties;
(2) accessory penalties;
(3) substitute sanctions.

333. Principal penalties are imposed by the judge with the conviction on the basis and within the limits the law provides for that specific crime. They are a direct consequence of the crime.

Principal penalties are the following:

(1) life imprisonment (*ergastolo*);
(2) imprisonment (*reclusione*);
(3) fines (*multa and ammenda*);
(4) misdemeanour imprisonment (*arresto*) (Article 17 CCP).

Life imprisonment and imprisonment are considered custodial penalties, while fines such as *multa* and *ammenda* are considered pecuniary penalties (Article 18 CCP).

334. Accessory penalties are inflicted in certain cases, and generally in connection with principal penalties. Accessory penalties – as set forth in the CCP and special laws – are generally connected to specific crimes (see *infra,* paragraph 347).

335. Substitute sanctions are used as an alternative to short-term imprisonment and are inflicted in the presence of particular circumstances. In fact, in pronouncing a sentence for minor offences, the judge may replace imprisonment with substitute sanctions such as semi-liberty or monitored release.

§2. The Death Penalty

336. Historically, Italy has adopted an abolitionist policy with respect to the death penalty, and in fact, Italy is now at the forefront of an effort to ban capital punishment worldwide.

Despite this, prior to abrogation, the death penalty was among the principal penalties as set forth in Article 21 CCP, '*[d]eath is to be carried out inside a penitentiary or in any other place suggested by the Ministry of Justice. The execution is not public unless the Ministry of Justice determines otherwise*'.

In 1944, the death penalty was generally abolished by Law Decree No. 224 of 1944; however, it was retained under certain circumstances pursuant to Law Decree No. 159 of 27 July 1944 (for serious crimes related to fascism) and Law Decree No. 234 of 10 May 1945 (for exceptional cases of serious criminal offences such as extortion and armed robbery).

Italy's definitive choice to renounce the death penalty was confirmed in 1947 in the original version of the Constitution (in the final paragraph of Article 27) which states: '*the death penalty is not admitted, except for the cases provided for by the military laws in times of war*'.

The abolitionist policy achieved its definitive goal in 1994, with Law No. 589 of 13 October 1994, which completely abolished the death penalty by removing even the exceptions envisaged in case of war and substituting the penalty with life imprisonment.

In 2007, Article 27 of the Constitution was amended to reflect the excluding of all capital punishment. In addition, on 3 March 2009, Italy ratified the thirteenth Protocol of the ECHR, concerning the abolition of the death penalty in all circumstances.

§3. Punishment Features

337. With respect to punishment, the Italian sanctioning system provides certain features:

(1) Punishment is strictly personal (Article 27, paragraph 1 of the Constitution).
(2) A penalty is inflicted only in the cases established by law according to the basic principles 'no penalty without a law' (*nulla poena sine lege*).
(3) The penalty is always inflicted to the perpetrator as consequence of a commission of a crime.
(4) The punishment is proportionate to the crime.

Moreover, the Italian sanctioning system complies with other basic constitutional principles that follow as well:

(1) Rules of penal law are not retroactive.
(2) No one can be sentenced without a fair trial (*nulla poena sine judicio*).
(3) No one can be considered guilty until a final sentence has been pronounced.

(4) Penalties cannot consist in treatment contrary to the sense of humanity and must tend to the rehabilitation of the offender.
(5) Personal freedom is inviolable and no one shall be deprived of it except under specific provisions of the law (Article 27 of the Constitution).

§4. PUNISHMENTS

I. The Principal Penalties

338. The Italian law provides different principal penalties for crimes and misdemeanours. And although some of these penalties are similar, in Italian legal parlance, different words are used depending on whether a crime or misdemeanour is involved. For example, imprisonment is referred to as *la reclusione* for a crime and *l'arresto* for a misdemeanour.

A. *Crimes*

339. As regards crimes, the principal penalties are the following:

1. Life Imprisonment (*ergastolo*)

340. Life imprisonment is a custodial sentence of an indefinite period and represents the most severe penalty foreseen by the Italian criminal law system. This penalty replaced capital punishment when the death penalty was eliminated from the PC. In fact, life imprisonment is generally envisaged in those cases for which the death penalty was originally applied (Article 22 PC). However, although the penalty is considered 'permanent', under the 1986 penitentiary reform, after serving ten years (eight in cases of good behaviour) in prison the offender may be entitled to special leave (*permessi premio*). After twenty years of prison, the defendant also may be considered for semi-liberty – allowing the defendant to spend up to forty-five days at home annually (*infra*, paragraphs 365–366). And, after twenty-six years (twenty-one for good behaviour), the defendant may be eligible for parole if approved by the Surveillance Court. Offenders sentenced for mafia-related activities or terrorism are not eligible for parole, unless they cooperate with the authorities.

In addition, the Italian Constitutional Court has held it is unlawful to give a life sentence to a minor under the age of 16 as it constitutes a form of 'cruel and unusual punishment' and is in conflict with the rehabilitative function required under the Italian Constitution.[194] Life imprisonment is provided for in cases of crimes against the Nation, against public safety and against life. When an offender has received more than one life sentence, they are required to spend a period of six months to three years in solitary confinement.

194. Constitutional Court Decision No. 168 of 27 Apr. 1994.

2. Imprisonment (*reclusione*)

341. In cases involving crimes, the custodial sentences which can be imposed by a judge range from fifteen days to twenty-four years, and up to thirty years when several aggravating circumstances are present (Articles 23 and 66 PC).

3. Fine (*multa*)

342. The pecuniary penalties provided for crimes which can be imposed by the judge range from EUR 50 to EUR 50,000 (Article 24 PC as amended by Law No. 94 of 15 July 2009), and up to EUR 10,329 when several aggravating circumstances are present. If there are aggravating circumstances and the court decides to exercise its power under Article 133*bis* PC, in determining the amount of the fine, the judge may also consider the economic conditions of the offender and may triple the fine (up to EUR 30,987) or reduce it to one-third. (Article 66 PC).

343. In order to prevent non-payment of the penalty by the offender, the Italian criminal system introduced the principle of the conversion of the pecuniary penalty. Thus, if the offender is not able to pay the amount established, it is possible to convert it into a custodial penalty. The rate of conversion is EUR 250 – or the applicable fraction of EUR 250 – of pecuniary fine for each day of detention (Article 135 CCP, as amended by Article 32(62) of Law No. 94 of 15 July 2009). If a pecuniary sanction is not paid or not paid in full, the judge will re-convert the penalty remaining to an equal period of imprisonment or arrest.

B. Misdemeanours

344. With regard to misdemeanours, the principal penalties are imprisonment and fine.

1. Misdemeanour Imprisonment (*arresto*)

345. Misdemeanour imprisonment is a custodial penalty imposed by the judge in a range between five days to three years, and up to five years when several aggravating circumstances are present (Articles 25 and 66 PC).

2. Misdemeanour Fine (*ammenda*)

346. For misdemeanours, the pecuniary penalties which may be imposed by a judge range from EUR 20 to EUR 10,000 (Article 26 PC), and up to EUR 2,065 when several aggravating circumstances are present (Articles 25 and 66 PC). If the court decides to exercise its power under Article 133*bis* PC, the judge may also consider the economic conditions of the offender and may triple the fine (up to EUR 6,197) or reduce it to one-third. (see *infra*, paragraph 382). It should be noted that the conversion mentioned *supra*, paragraph 343 is also available for *ammenda*.

II. Accessory Penalties

347. Usually, accessory penalties are automatically inflicted with principal penalties as a consequence of the commission of specific crimes. However, in certain situations, the application of accessory penalties is within the discretion of the judge. For example, in cases of life imprisonment, the defendant typically loses certain legal rights, but under Article 32(3), the judge has discretionary power over the application of the accessory penalty.

These penalties are basically forms of legal interdiction or disqualification.

348. The Italian PC provides for the following accessory penalties:

(1) disqualification from holding public office;
(2) disqualification from practising an art or profession;
(3) legal disability;
(4) temporary disqualification from managing corporations and enterprises;
(5) disqualification from entering into contracts with the public administration;
(6) removal and suspension of parental authority;
(7) suspension from practising an art or profession;
(8) publication of the conviction.

It should be noted that other special accessory punishments are provided for by specific criminal provisions, contained in the complementary legislation.

A. *Disqualification from Holding Public Office*

349. A disqualification from holding public office (Articles 28 and 29 PC) can be definitive or temporary. The first one deprives the offender of the following rights: to vote, to be eligible for any other political right; to exercise of public functions, offices and employment; to have the status of public officer/civil servant; to have honorary titles and public pays, pensions and benefit, and so on.

Temporary disqualification ranges from less than one year to a maximum of five years. During the period of disqualification, the offender may be deprived of the above-mentioned rights.

B. *Disqualification from Practising an Art or Profession*

350. The disqualification from practising an art or profession (Article 30 PC) deprives the offender of the ability to exercise a profession, an art or an employment for which is necessary a specific qualification, license or authorization.

The ban ranges from a minimum of one month to a maximum of five years.

C. Legal Disqualification

351. This kind of penalty deprives the offender of the legal capacity regarding property rights (Article 32 PC). It may arise from a life imprisonment sentence or from a prison sentence of five years. This kind of penalty also causes the loss of the parental authority.

D. Temporary Disqualification from Managing Corporations or Enterprises

352. The temporary disqualification from managing corporations or enterprises arises from a prison sentence of no less than six months inflicted for crimes committed by means of abuse of powers or violation of public duties (Article 32*bis* PC).

E. Disqualification from Entering into Contracts with the Public Administration

353. Under this section, the offender may be temporarily disqualified from entering into contracts with the public administration or authority (Article 32*ter* and 32*quater* PC). The penalty is a direct consequence of the conviction for the crimes indicated in the Article 32*quater*, such as criminal association, mafia-style criminal organization, crimes against public authority,[195] economy and property. The disqualification ranges from a minimum of one year to a maximum of five[196] years.

F. Removal and Suspension of Parental Authority

354. The Italian PC distinguishes the removal of parental authority from its suspension. The former causes the definitive loss for the parents of all powers over their children and their property. It arises from a life imprisonment sentence and from the convictions for crimes such as, among others, incest, sexual offences regarding parents, and so on.

The suspension instead causes the temporary deprivation of the rights abovementioned (Article 34 PC).

G. Suspension from Practising an Art or Profession

355. This penalty prevents the practice of an art, trade, industry or profession, which requires the obtaining of a qualification or license to practice. The penalty ranges from a minimum of fifteen days to a maximum of two years. Moreover, this penalty is applied for any misdemeanour committed by abuse of profession, art,

---

195. Article 32*quater* as amended by Law No. 190 of 6 Nov. 2012, inserting inducement to give or promise undue advantages among the crimes covered by this article.
196. Article 3*ter* PC, as amended by Law No. 69 of 27 May 2015.

industry or trade, or by misconduct, when the penalty is not less than one year of arrest (Article 35 PC).

H. *Publication of the Conviction*

356. This accessory penalty determines the publication, at the offender's expenses, of the estreat of the conviction in one or more journals in the jurisdiction where the sentence was issued, where the offence was committed or the offender's last place of residence. The sentence is also published on the website of the Ministry of Justice. The duration of the publication on the website is established by the court in an amount not exceeding thirty days. Failing this, the duration is fifteen days.

This penalty is a direct consequence of life sentence, of crimes against public safety committed with fraud, or crimes regarding trademarks and service marks (Article 36 PC).[197]

III. Substitute Sanctions

357. When the criminal judge pronounces a short sentence for a minor crime, he may replace imprisonment with a substitute sanction (*sanzioni sostitutive*) as a means for preventing the defendant from going to prison.

358. Substitute sanctions include the following:

(1) Semi-detention (*semidetenzione*)[198] – Semi-detention entails a period of at least ten hours a day in a penal institution, along with a number of prohibitions, duties and disqualifications, such as suspension of driving license, prohibition to possess firearms, and so on. Semi-detention may substitute a custodial penalty of up to one year.
(2) Monitored liberty (*libertà controllata*)[199] – Monitored liberty involves the prohibition against leaving the municipality or residence without a specific authorization, and the duty to appear before the police, checking in on established days at the local police station. It also implies a number of further prohibitions, duties and disqualifications. Monitored liberty may substitute a custodial penalty of up to six months.
(3) Pecuniary sanctions (*pena pecuniaria*) – Under Law No. 689 of 1981, pecuniary sanctions may be used to substitute a custodial sentence of up to three months.[200] The monetary penalty as an alternative sanction is subject to certain restrictions and subjective (relapse, etc.) and objective (which would militate against crime) conditions.

197. Article 36 PC, as amended by Law No. 69 of 18 Jun. 2009.
198. Law No. 689 of 24 Nov. 1981, Art. 55.
199. *Ibid.*, Art. 56.
200. *Ibid.*, Art. 53.

When there is an inability to pay the fine, it can be converted into a period of monitored liberty for a maximum period of one year for a crime and six months for a misdemeanour.

(4) Substitute service (*lavoro sostitutivo*) – When the pecuniary penalties do not exceed one thousand Euro, the offender may request substitute service, instead of monitored liberty. The surveillance judge then determines the work to be carried out, and, when necessary, the social services to be involved.[201] The substitute service consists of unpaid activities carried out to the benefit of State or local institutions, organizations, such as educational, conservation, civil protection, and so on. The work is coordinated by the Ministry of Justice, which can also delegate the work to the surveillance judge. The substitute service is to be carried out within the province of residence of the offender and generally involves one day of work a week, unless the offender requests additional days. The work is subject to certain subjective (relapse etc.) and objective (prevention of crime) conditions.[202] If the conditions are violated, the surveillance judge forwards the file to the Surveillance Court, which converts the service back into a fine or period of imprisonment, depending on the original penalty (i.e., fine for a crime or misdemeanour).

IV. Alternative Measures to Imprisonment

359. Alternative measures to imprisonment (*misure alternative alla detenzione)* were introduced by Law No. 354 of 26 July 1975[203] within the framework of an international effort to create alternative sanctions to detention, in order to ensure the rehabilitation role of penalties as envisaged by the Italian Constitution. Subsequently, Law No. 663 of 10 October 1986 and Law No. 165 of 27 May 1998 implementing this subject, extended and modified the requirements for the application of these measures.

Alternative measures are requested by the offender and granted by the Surveillance Court during the execution phase of the penalty, as compared to substitute sanctions, which are given by the judge when the sentence is issued.

360. The most significant alternatives measures to imprisonment are:

(1) assignment of the offender to the Probation Service;
(2) house arrest;
(3) semi-liberty;
(4) assignment of special categories of offenders to the Probation Service;
(5) community service;
(6) juvenile criminal mediation.

201. *Ibid.*, Art. 107.
202. *Ibid.*, Arts 59 and 60.
203. Law No. 354 of 26 Jul. 1975, *Norme sull'ordinamento penitenziario e sull'esecuzione delle misure privative e limitative della libertà.* (Rules on the Prison System and the Execution of Measures Depriving or Limiting Liberty).

A. Assignment of the Offender to the Probation Service

361. As explained in paragraph 64 *supra*, the Directorate General for the Execution of Sentences in the Community (*la Direzione Generale dell'Esecuzione Penale Esterna*) is the primary provider of Italy's probation services.

362. Assignment of the offenders to the Probation Service (*affidamento in prova al servizio sociale*) – Article 47 of Italian Law No. 354 of 26 July 1975 provides that an offender may be placed under the supervision of the Probation Service if his prison sentence is less than three years or there are only three years remaining on the sentence. The period of the probation must correspond to the sentence to be served, or remaining to be served.[204] The assignment to probation service is allowed also for convicts who must atone a penalty, even residual, not exceeding four years, if their attitude demonstrated that they are unlikely to commit other crimes.

363. As mentioned, it is a task of the Surveillance Court (*Tribunale di Sorveglianza*) to apply this alternative measure.

The Surveillance Court may assign community service on the basis of the personality tests and when there is reason to believe that the measure will contribute towards rehabilitating the offender. It must also be noted that the so-called Simeone Law (Law No. 165 of 27 May 1998) established that it is no longer a prerequisite for testing that the offender has served at least part of the prison sentence.

Once assigned, the offender has to carry out activities under the control of the social services. The latter control the behaviour of the person and assist in his or her reintegration into society. If the assignment proves to be constructive, the remainder of the penalty is reduced. If it fails, the measure is revoked, and the offender must serve the rest of his or her sentence in prison.

B. House Arrest

364. Pursuant to Article 47*ter* of Italian Law No. 354 of 26 July 1975, house arrest (*detenzione domiciliare*) is a measure by which a person is confined by the authorities to his or her residence or a private residence or clinic. Apart from a few exceptions, the offender is not allowed to leave. This measure can be applied to persons aged over 70 (60 in case of health problems) and to some categories of persons who have to serve a prison sentence not exceeding four years (e.g., pregnant women, minors under the age of 20), even if it constitutes the remainder of a longer sentence.

204. The application of alternative measures to imprisonment has been widely used in the Italian system. Recent years have seen an increase of this kind of measure (in 2003, has been granted 17,500 community service sentences with an increase of 408% more than 1991).

C. Semi-liberty

365. According to Article 14 of Law No. 663 of 10 October 1986,[205] semi-liberty (*semilibertà*) allows the offender to spend a part of the day outside prison in order to participate in educational, work or other activities that are useful for his or her social rehabilitation. The law provides that in order to request and be granted semi-liberty, the offender must have already served at least a certain percentage of the sentence (twenty years in the case of a life sentence). The applicable percentage is based on the crime involved. If the sentence is less than six months and the offender has not been assigned to the probation services, the offender may be granted semi-liberty from the beginning.

366. Semi-liberty may be revoked when the offender loses his job, the Surveillance Court deems the offender is not suitable for treatment or has violated the requirements of the release. The measure may also be revoked if the offender does not return to the prison facility at the designated time without a justified reason (if the absence is less than twelve hours, revocation is optional).

367. The State must use diligence in granting semi-liberty and monitoring the offender. If the State fails to do so and the offender commits another offence, it may be held liable for damages.[206]

D. Assignment of Special Categories of Offenders to the Probation Service

368. Certain categories of offenders, such as alcoholics and drug addicts may be assigned to the Probation Service *(Affidamento in prova in casi particolari*). Addicts may request to be assigned if their sentence or remaining sentence is six years or less. The request is made in order for the offender to begin or continue treatment. The Italian Health System (ASLA) must pay for the treatment, which must be carried out at an authorized private or public treatment programme. This type of assignment can only be granted twice.

369. Offenders diagnosed as having AIDS or other serious illnesses or immune deficiencies who are currently or about to take part in medical programme at an

205. Article 14 of Law No. 663 of 10 Oct. 1986 replaced Art. 48 of Law No. 354 of 1975.

206. See *Maiorano and Others v. Italy*, ECtHR Decision of 15 Dec. 2009. In this case, the European Court of Human Rights has found that the State was responsible in relation to a double murder committed by Angelo Izzo, a dangerous offender who had been granted semi-liberty. The Court awarded damages to the relatives of two women who had been brutally murdered by Izzo during his release. In particular, the ECtHR unanimously found that the State had violated applicants' rights under ECHR Art. 2 (right to life) for failing to conduct a satisfactory investigation into individual negligence within the judicial system. The Court took the view that the granting by the Palermo sentence execution court of day release to Angelo Izzo, despite his criminal record and behaviour in prison, together with the failure by the public prosecutor's office of Campobasso to forward information on his criminal activities to the sentence execution judge, had constituted a breach of the duty of care required by Art. 2 of the Convention. Accordingly, the Court held unanimously that there had been a violation of Art. 2 under its substantive head.

infectious disease hospital, university hospital, or other sanitary unit, may request either to be assigned to the Probation Services[207] or given house arrest[208] even when the penalties exceed the limits. The Surveillance Court may not grant the request, if within the last year the offender has been granted an alternative measure, which has subsequently been revoked.

370. If the offender is not detained, the request is made to the public prosecutor, who has thirty days to respond, as provided by Article 656 CPP as amended by Law No. 165 of 27 May 1998 and by Decree No. 241 of 24 November 2000 (Article 10). The public prosecutor then transmits the request to the competent Surveillance Court, which fixes a hearing on the matter. If the offender is in protective custody, the competent surveillance judge may suspend execution, order the offender to be released, and then transmit the documents to the competent Surveillance Court.

If during the measure, another custodial sentence is issued, the director of criminal enforcement informs the surveillance judge of the extension of the provisional measure. The judge then forwards the file to the Surveillance Court which must decide within twenty days to continue or end the measure.

The surveillance judge may suspend the assignment and send the documents to the Surveillance Court when offender commits another offence after the granting of the measure or when the offender acts improperly.

In case of revocation of the measure pursuant to Article 168*bis* PC, the prosecutor, as he determines the penalty to be enforced, deducts a period equivalent to the one the tested person performed. For deduction three days test match one day in jail.[209]

E. Community Service

371. Originally introduced by Article 54 of Legislative Decree No. 274 of 28 August 2000 (i.e., the jurisdiction of the Justice of the Peace courts), community service involves the unpaid performance of work for the community to be implemented by the State, regions, provinces, municipalities or agencies, and organizations focusing on social work or volunteering. The work – in the sense of Ministerial Decree No. 151 of 26 March 2001 – is to be for the benefit of those with HIV, the handicapped, sick, elderly, children, prisoners, foreigners, or in the field of civil protection, the protection of public property, environmental or other activities relevant to the specific skills of the offender. In 2005, in the context of preparing for the Winter Olympic Games in Turin, the drug-related laws were amended to include community service as an alternative measure.[210]

---

207. Law No. 354/1975, Art. 57.
208. Law No. 354/1975, Art. 47*ter*.
209. Article added by Law No. 67 of 28 Apr. 2014, named 'Powers to the Government regarding custodial sentences but not in jail and reform of the system of sanctions. Provisions on the suspension of the proceedings with probation and against untraceable'. This measure constitutes a delegation of the Parliament to the government in order to reform the no prison penalty system.
210. See Art. 73 (para. 5*bis*) of Presidential Decree No. 309 of 9 Oct. 1990, subsequently modified by Law No. 49 of 21 Feb. 2006. The Constitutional Court declared the unconstitutionality of Art. 4*bis*

F. Juvenile Criminal Mediation

372. As a means of implementing restorative justice, Italy has begun using mediation in juvenile crime matters. The juvenile mediation movement started in Torino in the mid-1990s, and began being supported in 2002 by the Juvenile Justice Department of the Italian Ministry of Justice.

A juvenile criminal matter may be mediated at any stage of the proceeding; however, only the public prosecutor can request it during the pre-trial investigative stage, while both the prosecutor and judge can suggest mediation during the trial phase. Only the judge has the power to suspend the case and refer it to mediation. Most often mediation is initiated based on the assessment of the charged offender's personality as per section 9 of Presidential Decree No. 448 of 1998.

The main problem preventing the further development of the mediation system in Italy is the limited legislation on the topic; thus, there are no uniform practices or quality standards. Despite this issue, at the time of the publishing, there are nineteen juvenile criminal mediation centres in Italy.[211]

§5. General Rules Concerning Sentencing

I. The General Principles

373. Sentencing in the sense of judicial choice and the meting out of punishment is regulated by the principle of legality. As seen above (*supra*, paragraphs 111–113), this principle means that penalties may be imposed only if they have been provided for by statute prior to the commission of the offences.

II. Length of the Sentence

374. The Italian PC provides certain minimum and maximum time limits for sentences. It is a task of the judge to determinate the effective extension of a prison sentence or the effective extent of a fine.

375. The Code grants the judge discretional power to determine the sentence, within the limits provided for by law. This means that, although the judge has discretional power, it is not absolute. Thus, the criminal judge is not free to decide on the length of the sentence, but he is bound by the law (Article 132 PC).

In order to guide the judicial discretion of the judge, Article 133 PC establishes parameters that the judge has to take into account when determining a sentence.

---

of Decree No. 27 of 30 Sep. 2005, which amended Art. 73. This article has been replaced by Art. 1, para. 24*ter*, l. b) of Decree No. 36 of 20 Mar. 2014 and amended by Law No. 79 of 16 May 2014.

211. Centres are located in Ancona, Bari, Boe, Brescia, Cagliari, Caltanissetta, Catanzaro, Florence, Foggia Genoa, Latina, Milan, Naples, Palermo, Salerno, Sassari, Turin, Trento and Reggio Calabria.

In particular, the law establishes that he has to take into account the following:

– the seriousness of the offence (taking into consideration the type of offence committed, the seriousness of the damage caused or of the threat posed, and the level of guilt); and
– the capacity of the offender to commit an offence (including the offender's reasons for committing the offence, his or her precedents and life conditions, and his or her behaviour before committing the offence).

Moreover, the judge has the duty to state the reasons for the decision. The grounds for a decision have to be analytical and specific.[212]

376. With regard to fines, in addition to the criteria above-mentioned, the judge must also take into consideration the economic conditions of the offender. The law provides that the judge may increase the maximum limit provided for *multa* and *ammenda* up to three times or decrease it by up to one-third when, considering the economic conditions of the offender, he thinks the fines are inefficacious or too high respectively (Article 133*bis* PC). If the offender is unable to pay the fine, the judge may even decide to convert the fine into a custodial penalty (*supra*, paragraph 343).

III. Grounds for Increasing or Mitigating Punishment

A. *General Principles*

377. For each criminal offence, the Italian legislator has provided the applicable penalty or penalties, either by fixed amount or by indicating the maximum and minimum penalties which may be imposed for a given offence.

378. Furthermore, there are rules which allow the judge, under certain circumstances, to raise the statutorily provided maximum (i.e., aggravating circumstances) or to impose a penalty lower than the minimum provided for the offence (i.e., mitigating circumstances).

The aggravating and mitigating circumstances are incidental elements (*circumstantial*) of the crime, added to legally provided conditions for basic offences.

B. *Classification of Circumstances*

379. In the Italian criminal system, it is possible to distinguish between the various kinds of circumstances:

(1) aggravating and mitigating;

---

212. On the judicial discretion of the judge, see Court of Cassation (Section II) Decision No. 7362 of 2 Feb. 1978, 10 Jun. 1978, *Cassazione penale massimario annotato*, 1140; Court of Cassation Decision of 19 Nov. 1982, *Kitzeler*, CED 157312.

(2) common and special;
(3) circumstances with a common efficaciousness (*efficacia comune*) and special efficaciousness (*efficacia speciale*);
(4) objective and subjective circumstances;
(5) definitive and discretional circumstances.

The most important is the distinction between aggravating and mitigating circumstances.

1. Aggravating and Mitigating Circumstances

380. Aggravating circumstances cause an increase of the punishment provided for a criminal offence, while mitigating (or extenuating) circumstances cause a reduction of the punishment provided for a criminal offence.

The increase or the decrease of the punishment can be quantitative or qualitative. In the former, they affect the *quantum* or amount of the penalty, i.e., the basic punishment is increased up to one-third; in the latter, they affect the kind of penalty. For example, with intentional homicide (Article 575 PC), aggravating circumstances (Articles 576 and 577 PC) cause a conversion from imprisonment (*reclusione*) to life imprisonment and under Article 280 PC (attacks upon another's life or physical integrity and kidnapping for the purpose of terrorism or for subverting the democratic order), aggravating circumstances are deemed to be present if the attempt to the safety of any person causes a serious injury or the death of the person, or if the action is directed against persons who perform legal, penitentiary, or public safety functions, while they are performing their duties.

Moreover, circumstances may be distinguished as being common or special.

2. Common and Specific Circumstances

381. Common circumstances are provided for an unspecified number of people and may be added to all the criminal offences.

Specific circumstances, on the contrary, are provided for certain offences. For example, Article 605 PC addresses the offence of kidnapping. If the offence is committed by a public official as the result of an abuse of power, it is considered as a (specific) aggravating circumstance under Article 61(9) PC.

3. Circumstances *Efficacia Comune* and *Efficacia Speciale*

382. Circumstances *efficacia comune* cause an increase or a decrease up to one-third of the punishment provided for by law for the basic criminal offence.

Circumstances *efficacia speciale* are those that may impose a punishment different than the one provided for by law; or may cause the punishment to be determined independently to the punishment provided; or may cause an increase or decrease of the base penalty by more than one-third.

For example, under Article 437 PC, if one fails to place, removes or damages facilities, equipment and signals designed to prevent disasters or accidents at work, the punishment provided is imprisonment from six months to five years. However, if the fact results in a disaster or accident, the punishment is imprisonment from three to ten years.

4. Objective and Subjective Circumstances

383. According to Article 70, paragraph 1(1) PC, objective circumstances relate to the object, the place, the time and all of the modality of the action, the seriousness of the damage and to the danger, conditions, and personal qualities of the offender.

Subjective circumstances, instead, concern the intensity of intent or negligence, the conditions or personal qualities of the offender, and the relationship between the offender and the victim.

5. Definitive and Discretional Circumstances

384. Definitive circumstances are provided for by law in detail. On the contrary, discretional circumstances are those selected by the criminal judge using his discretionary power.

C. Sentencing and Circumstances

385. The legislative framework of the sentencing process must be considered alongside the particular circumstances of the fact that, as said, may increase or reduce the punishment.

With regard to the rule concerning the evaluation of circumstances – set forth by Article 59 PC – it must be noted that this rule has been modified by Law No. 19 of 7 February 1990.

In particular, Article 59, paragraph 3 PC establishes that the court is to consider irrelevant any aggravating and mitigating circumstances that the offender mistakenly believed were present.

The mitigating circumstances are considered in favour of the offender, even if unknown by him or believed by mistake not to exist.

The aggravating circumstances are charged to the offender objectively.

D. Concurrence of Circumstances

386. It must also be noted that when there is only one aggravating or mitigating circumstance, there will be a two-phase judgment. During the first phase, the judge has to identify and quantify, according to the principles laid down in Article 133 PC, the penalty provided for the basic crime; in the second phase, he has to consider the circumstances and increase or decrease the penalty.

Moreover, if there is a concurrence of more than one circumstance, all aggravating or all mitigating, the judge has to determine the increase or the reduction with regard to just one circumstance, then on the penalty resulting from the first increase or reduction, he has to determine the further increases or reductions (*homogeneous concurrence*, Article 63, paragraph 2 PC).

However, in case of *heterogeneous concurrence* – namely if there is a concurrence of aggravating and mitigating circumstances – the judge has to balance the concurrent circumstances. If the judge considers that the mitigating circumstances prevail, he applies only the relative reduction of penalty; if he considers prevalent the aggravating circumstances, he applies only the increase in penalty. If the judge considers equivalent the aggravating and mitigating circumstances, he will apply the penalty that he should have inflicted if no circumstances were present (Article 69, paragraph 4 PC).

E. Recidivism

387. Recidivism can be generally described as the situation when someone commits an offence after having been convicted previously of another.

In the Italian criminal system, recidivism (Article 99 PC) represents an aggravating circumstance (Article 70, paragraphs 1 and 2 PC) and may cause an increase of the punishment, if some conditions are fulfilled.

In order to have recidivism, two conditions are required: the commission of an offence, and a previous conviction, with a final judgment, for an intentional crime.

Recidivism may always be taken into consideration in deciding the appropriate level of punishment. In addition, recidivism causes an increase of the punishment and may have other effects, such as the impossibility of receiving a plea bargain,[213] house arrest,[214] amnesty, pardon, conditional release,[215] and so on.

388. There are three forms of recidivism:

(1) simple;
(2) aggravated;
(3) repeat.

1. Simple Recidivism

389. Simple recidivism occurs when the offender, who has been previously convicted for a crime which does not involve negligence (*delitto non colposo*), commits a new offence within five years after that conviction.

213. Article 444 CCP.
214. Articles 47*ter*, 50*bis*, and 58*quater* of Law No. 354 of 26 Jul. 1975 and Art. 94 of Presidential Decree No. 309 of 9 Oct. 1990.
215. Article 30 of Law No. 354 of 26 Jul. 1975.

2. Aggravated Recidivism

390. Aggravated recidivism occurs if the new offence not involving negligence:

(1) is equal to the previous one;
(2) is committed during the five years following the previous conviction; or
(3) is committed during or after the execution of the punishment or during the time when he is released from the punishment.

3. Repeat Recidivism

391. Repeated recidivism occurs when the new offence is committed by an offender who was already a recidivist.

§6. Security Measures

392. In addition to penalties, the Italian PC contains security measures. Security measures do not have the repressive function of penalties. In particular, security measures are different from penalties because of:

– the function;
– the subjects; and
– the length.

First, these are educational and protective measures that may be taken, in place of or in addition to the penalty, against offenders considered socially dangerous. Second, their aim is either to protect society against dangerous offenders or to reform offenders, or both to protect society and to reform offenders.

These measures are imposed on those perpetrators of a crime or quasi-crime that are considered socially dangerous because there is a significant risk that the defendant will probably commit other offences in the future (Article 203, paragraph 1 PC).

As said above, according to the Italian PC, a person is socially dangerous if he or she has committed a crime and there is a strong likelihood that he or she will commit another crime in the future, considering the characteristics of the offence and the offender.

Security measures are also imposed on individuals who are not criminally liable, or if liable, are subject to lesser penalties because they were found totally or partially mentally incompetent at the time of the crime (in case of mental disease, chronic intoxication deriving from alcohol, drug abuse, etc.).

393. The length of the measure imposed is usually indefinite: in fact, only the minimum length is set. If, at the end of the fixed period, the surveillance judge believes that the person is still socially dangerous, he can decide to impose another minimum period. At the end of this second period, the behaviour of the offender is examined again, and so on. When the judge believes the person is no longer socially dangerous, he withdraws the measures (Article 207 PC).

The judge has discretionary power when deciding on the type of security measure to be applied. Nevertheless, some measures are specifically envisaged for certain types of perpetrators of crimes. Thus, mentally disabled offenders are sent to a judicial psychiatric hospital, while minors are sent to reformatories.

Security measures are separated into two types: personal and property.

I. Personal Measures

394. Personal measures are divided further into two forms: custodial and non-custodial.

A. *Custodial Security Measures*

395. Custodial security measures are the following:

- assignment of offender to prisons, prison farms or work houses;
- recovery of offender in health and custodial houses;
- recovery of offender in judicial psychiatric hospitals; and
- assignment of offender to reform houses.

B. *Non-custodial Security Measures*

396. Non-custodial security measures are the following:

- assignment to the Probation Service;
- prohibition from residing in one or more towns;
- prohibition to frequent public houses or places in which alcohol is served; and
- expulsion of foreigners from the country.

II. Property Measures

397. There are two forms of property or patrimonial measures: bail and confiscation (Article 236 PC). While technically, the two are classified as safety or protective measures, they are still subject to the general regime on penalties.

Bail involves the offender's depositing of a sum of money as a guarantee of good behaviour during the term of a non-custodial measure (Article 237 PC). If the offender does not commit another crime requiring arrest during this term, the security is returned. If bail is not posted, the court may order release under surveillance (Article 238 PC).

The court may also order seizure of the offender's property. If the offender is convicted, the court may order confiscation of any objects used in the commission of the crime, as well as any profits or products resulting from the offence (Article 240 PC). Moreover, for certain offences (e.g., usury,[216] mafia-related offences,[217] terrorism[218] corporate crimes[219]), seizure and confiscation is possible not only for goods and profits related to the crime, but also other goods of the equivalent value. This provision aims to prevent that the use of economic goods of criminal origin may allow the offender to benefit from the advantages arising from the illicit activity. In this way the offender is deprived from any economic benefit arising from the crime.

§7. Concurrence of Offences

398. When someone commits more than one offence, there is a concurrence of offences.

The Italian criminal system provides for three forms of concurrences of offences:

(1) real concurrence (*concorso materiale*);
(2) formal concurrence (*concorso formale*);
(3) apparent concurrence (*concorso apparente*).

I. Real Concurrence

399. Real concurrence (*concorso materiale*) arises when the offender commits, with more than one punishable act or omission, more than one offence (e.g., the offender kills someone, hides the dead body, after stealing, etc.).

In order to determine the sentencing of a real concurrence of offences, the Italian law applies the principle of consecutive sentences (*cumulo delle pene*). Thus, all of the penalties which are provided for each offence must be imposed cumulatively. In the case of concurrence of offences punishable with the same kind of penalties, the judge will make a sum of the penalties provided for each offence. In the case of concurrence of offences punishable by different kinds of penalties, the judge will apply all the penalties without distinction.

However, Italian law establishes that the maximum value of the total punishment cannot exceed five times the most serious penalty.

II. Formal Concurrence

400. Formal concurrence (*concorso formale*) deals with the situation where the offender commits several offences by one act or omission. It may happen that by one act or omission, the offender violates more than one criminal law (*concorso eterogeneo*) (e.g., the same shot kills a person and wounds another). It also often happens that by one act or omission, the offender violates the same criminal law

216. Article 644 PC.
217. Article 416*bis* PC.
218. Article 270*bis* PC.
219. Article 2641 of the Italian Civil Code.

several times (e.g., someone with one expression insults more than one person) (*concorso omogeneo*).

In this case, the sanctions are less strict than the previous provided for *concorso materiale*. In fact, in order to determine the sentencing of a real concurrence of offences, the penalties provided for the most serious offence are increased up to triple.

III. Apparent Concurrence

401. An apparent concurrence (*concorso apparente*) of offences occurs when it appears that there were multiple offences, but substantially only one rule was violated (e.g., robbery includes the crimes of theft and criminal violence).

§8. Continued Offences

402. If the offender violates more than once the same or a different statute with one or more acts or omissions, interrelated by the same criminal intention, there will be a continued offence (Article 81, paragraph 2 PC).

The elements of these forms of concurrence of offences are:

(1) the plurality of acts or omissions;
(2) more than one violation of the same or different statutes;
(3) the same criminal intention.

Thus, if the offender steals a car in order to commit an armed robbery, he will be responsible for continued robbery rather than for robbery and illegal possession of firearms.

In this case, the judge applies the penalty provided for the most serious crime, increased up to triple.

Chapter 8. The Causes for Extinguishing the Crime and/or the Penalty

§1. Introduction

403. Both the crime and the penalty can be extinguished. If the crime is extinguished, it is no longer possible to effect a penalty with regards to such offence.

If, however, the penalty is extinguished, the cause of the extinguishment presupposes the conviction and impedes infliction of the penalty.

§2. The Causes for Extinguishment

404. The extinguishing causes of offences and/or penalties are set forth in Articles 150 et seq. PC. In particular, there are the following causes:

(1) death of the offender;
(2) amnesty;
(3) pardon;
(4) *grazia* (presidential pardon);
(5) statute of limitations;
(6) payment of a fine;
(7) judicial pardon;
(8) suspension of the conditions of the penalty;
(9) no mention of the conviction in the criminal history registry;
(10) conditional liberty;
(11) application of the penalty upon request;
(12) withdraw of the *querela* (i.e., victim's complaint);
(13) rehabilitation.

I. Death of the Offender

405. Death of the offender can extinguish the crime (Article 150 PC) or the penalty (Article 171 PC), depending on whether the death occurs before or after the conviction. In any event, the civil liabilities of the deceased relating to the crime still remain charged to his estate and heirs.

II. Amnesty

406. Amnesty (Article 151 PC) is an act of general clemency in which the State renounces its right to put into effect its punitive powers. Amnesty, if granted before a final conviction, is referred to as *propria* and has a completely abolishing effect, while if granted subsequently, it is referred to as *impropria* and stops the execution of the conviction also with regard to the accessory penalties, but not to the other penal effects, such as the usability of the conviction for future declarations of recidivism, habitual offender and professional criminal (e.g., contract killer).

III. Pardon

407. Pardon (Article 174 PC) is also an act of general clemency, which does not operate on either the crime or the accessory penalties – unless the decree of clemency provides otherwise – but only on the principle penalty.

IV. Grazia (Presidential Pardon)

408. Grazia (literally 'grace') is a presidential pardon (Article 174 PC) and a particular act of clemency which can be granted only by the head of State, who may intervene on a final conviction. *Grazia* only operates on the principle penalty.

V. Statute of Limitations

409. The statute of limitations can bar either the prosecution of the crime (Article 157 PC) or the execution of the penalty (Articles 172–173 PC). This occurs when, for a certain period of time, the State has not exercised its punitive power. Crimes punishable by life imprisonment do not have a statute of limitations.

410. The statute of limitations on an offence runs when there is no prosecutorial or judicial intervention. However, the accused can always renounce the limitations by making an express declaration. In addition, in calculating the term, it is not possible to consider the time passed during a manifestly unfounded appeal[220] to the Court of Cassation.

Nevertheless, in every case, the term cannot be less than six years if a felony is involved and four years if the crime is a misdemeanour (Article 157 PC).

411. To determine the statute of limitations, one must consider the penalty established by law for the offence carried out or attempted, without considering reductions for attenuating circumstances or increases for aggravating circumstances. However, when the law establishes a penalty different from the ordinary and there are special effects, then the maximum increase of the penalty provided for aggravating circumstances is to be considered. The judgment of equivalence or prevalence between the aggravated and the attenuating (or mitigating) circumstances as covered in Article 69 PC (*supra*, paragraph 379) have no influence on the calculation of the statute of limitations.

When the law establishes joint or alternative prison sentences and pecuniary penalties, to determine the statute of limitations, only the prison term is regarded. When

220. As established by the Court of Cassation with the Decision No. 15599 of 19 Nov. 2014.

the law establishes a penalty other than incarceration and pecuniary penalties, a term of three years applies.

The terms indicated above are doubled for cases of negligent disaster (Article 449 PC), multiple manslaughter, or manslaughter in connection with violation of highway ordinances or in connection with violations of the regulations related to safety at work (Article 589 PC, paragraphs 2 and 3 PC) as well as certain offences related to organized crime and terrorism (Article 270 PC).[221]

In the case of criminal attempt, the term of limitations runs from the cessation of the activity.

For permanent crimes, the statute of limitations starts running from the cessation of the permanence. The statute of limitations remains suspended in cases of authorization to proceed, questions deferred to another proceeding, request for postponement by the accused, and in every other case provided by law (Article 159 PC). When the cause of the suspension of the case ends, the clock starts running again.

412. The statute of limitations is interrupted in the presence of a specific activity by the prosecutor (e.g., convictions which are not definitive (see Article 160 PC). To verify the interruption, it is not necessary for the prosecutor to provide notification of the specific activity,[222] deposit of an act (e.g., motion or criminal complaint) is sufficient.[223] The interrupted limitations recommence from the day on which the interruption is verified. If there are more interruptive acts, the statute of limitations runs from the last of these (Article 160 PC).

The original period of the statute of limitations indicated above cannot be extended more than one-fourth. However, a longer extension is provided for offences related to organized crime and terrorism, as well as for cases of recidivism; repeat or habitual offenders, and professional criminals (e.g., hired killers) (Article 161 PC).

413. The limitations of the penalty presuppose that there has been a final conviction not yet extinguished. The penalty of (felony) prison detention extinguishes with lapse of a time equal to twice the penalty inflicted and, in any event, not less than ten years and not greater than thirty years while felony fines (*multa*) are extinguished after ten years. (Article 172). The misdemeanour penalties of arrest and fine (*ammenda*) lapse after five years (Articles 172 and 173 PC).

VI. Payment of a Fine (Oblation)

414. Oblation is the extinguishment of single misdemeanours and consists of the payment of a sum of money before the debate in court or the criminal conviction.

221. The Constitutional Court has recently intervened in the matter by a judgment of 28 May 2014, No. 143, and declared Art. 157, para. 6 unconstitutional in so far as it provides that the terms of the preceding paragraphs of that article are doubled for the crime of negligent arson.
222. Court of Cassation Decision of 14 Jan. 1998.
223. Court of Cassation Decision of 8 May 1996.

For those misdemeanours punishable only by fine, the interested party has the right to pay a fine which consists of the payment of a sum of money equal to one-third of the statutory penalty. For misdemeanours punishable alternatively by fine or arrest (Article 162*bis* PC), the judge is given discretionary power.

However, the payment of a fine is not allowed if there remain damaging or dangerous consequences of the crime avoidable on the part of the offender and otherwise in cases of repetition, recidivism, habitualness and professional crime. The fine corresponds to one-half of the maximum of the provided *ammenda* (i.e., fine).

VII. Judicial Pardon

415. Judicial pardon can be granted not more than one time to those who at the time of the commission of the crime were under the age of 18 and have no prior criminal convictions (Article 169 PC).

VIII. Suspension of the Conditions of the Penalty

416. Conditional suspension of the penalty (Articles 163–168 PC) may be granted by the judge when the penalty inflicted – including both detention and pecuniary fines, taking into account in the latter, the criteria set forth in Article 135 PC – does not exceed two years of incarceration (i.e., *arresto* for misdemeanours and *reclusion* for crimes). Different limits are provided for those under the age of 18, between the ages of 18 and 21, or over the age of 70. The suspension includes both the principle sanctions and the accessory sanctions on the condition that within a certain period of time (five years for crimes and two years for misdemeanours), the offender does not commit another crime. If the offender commits another crime, the judge may order him to serve the old and the new sentences. If there are no additional offences at the end of the term provided, the conviction is extinct, and there is no execution of the penalty. According to Article 166 PC, the conditional suspension may also be extended in the event that the punishment imposed is not a prison sentence.

IX. No Mention of the Conviction in the Criminal History Certificate

417. If requested by the private party, the judge may decide there be no mention of the conviction in the criminal history certificate, if it is a first conviction and the penalty inflicted is not more than two years of imprisonment, or EUR 516 if pecuniary (Article 175 PC).[224] The judge may also grant the request if the imposed sentence is a combination of imprisonment of less than two years and a fine – which when converted to imprisonment (see *supra* paragraph 343) creates a total detention of thirty months.

224. Constitutional Court Decision No. 304 of 17 Mar. 1988.

If the offender commits a subsequent offence, the order is revoked and the original conviction is listed on the criminal history certificate.

X. Conditional Liberty

418. Conditional liberty (Articles 176 and 177 PC) represents a reward granted to the convicted, who maintained good behaviour during the time already served. If at the end of the period corresponding to the time remaining on the penalty, there are no motives for revoking the conditional liberty, the residual penalty is extinguished and the measures of personal security are revoked.

XI. Plea Bargain

419. The application of the penalty upon request (i.e., plea bargain) determines the extinguishment of the crime, with respect to every penal effect, if in the term of five years when the offence is a felony, or two years when the crime is a misdemeanour, the accused does not commit a crime or a misdemeanour of the same type (Article 445 PC).

XII. Withdrawal of the *Querela*

420. The withdrawal of the *querela* (Articles 152–156 PC and Article 340 CCP) occurs in those cases of crimes involving a *querela* by the offended person (except certain cases of irrevocability), and extinguishes the crime if the *querela* is expressly or tactically withdrawn. The intervention must be made before final conviction.

XIII. Rehabilitation

421. Rehabilitation (Article 178 PC) extinguishes neither the crime nor the principle penalty, but the accessory sanctions and the other penal effects of the conviction. The convicted who is granted rehabilitation must prove effective and constant good behaviour in the five years (or ten years in the case of aggravated recidivism or repeated crime) since the principle penalty was executed or extinguished.

Part II. Criminal Procedure

Chapter 1. Principles, Institutions, Stages

§1. The Judicial Organization

422. In the furtherance of the overview of the criminal justice system in the General Introduction (*supra*, paragraphs 18–35), the following provides a more detailed explanation of the composition and the competences of the trial jurisdictions.

I. Trial Jurisdictions

423. The Italian criminal law system is divided into various judicial bodies, as explained (*supra*, paragraphs 28–29).

The criminal jurisdiction is entirely exercised by ordinary judges, regardless of the kind of the crime, with the exception of military crimes (Article 1 CCP).

424. On the basis of the reform introduced by Legislative Decree No. 51 of 19 February 1998, and by Law No. 479 of 16 December 1999, the judicial bodies are:

(1) Justices of the Peace (*Giudice di Pace*).
(2) Tribunals (*Tribunale Ordinario*).
(3) Courts responsible for the Enforcement of Sentences (*Tribunale di Sorveglianza*).
(4) Juvenile Courts (*Tribunale per i Minorenni*).
(5) Courts of Assizes (*Corte di Assise*).
(6) Courts of Appeal (*Corte di Appello*).
(7) Courts of Appeal of Assizes (*Corte d'Assise d'Appello*).
(8) The Court of Cassation (*Corte di Cassazione*) – the highest Court of Appeal.
(9) Judges for the Preliminary Investigations (the so-called *GIP*) and for the Preliminary Hearing (the so-called *GUP*).

A. The First-Instance Level: The Justice of the Peace, Tribunal and Court of Assizes

425. At the first-instance level, the trial jurisdiction is made up of the Justice of the Peace, the Tribunal and the Court of Assizes.

426. The Justice of Peace is a sole judge with jurisdiction on minor offences (*supra*, paragraph 30).

427. The Court of Assizes has jurisdiction to try crimes carrying a maximum penalty of twenty-four years in prison or life imprisonment, and other serious offences. The prosecution is conducted by the public prosecutor at the Court of Assizes (*Pubblico Ministero presso la Corte d'Assise*) (Article 51 CCP). In the Court of Assizes and Court of Appeal of Assizes (*Corte d'Assise* and *Corte d'Assise d'Appello*), the judicial panel consists of two stipendiary and six popular or lay judges (*giudici popolari*). There is no jury (*supra*, paragraph 29).

428. The Tribunal (*Tribunale*) has jurisdiction over all other offences. Depending on the gravity and on the characteristics of the criminal offence, the Tribunal can try a matter as a solo judge or in a collective composition made up of three judges. The prosecution is conducted by the public prosecutor at the Tribunal (*Pubblico Ministero presso il Tribunale*). The prosecution for organized crime (i.e., *Mafia*), ransom kidnapping, drug trafficking, and related offences is conducted by the Antimafia Public Prosecutor (*Procuratore Distrettuale Antimafia*) and the twenty deputy prosecutors working under him (Article 51 CCP).

429. A special judicial body is represented by the Juvenile Court, which is a special court and has jurisdiction on offences committed by minors between 14 and 18 years old (*supra*, paragraph 25).

B. The Second-Instance Level: The Court of Appeal and the Court of Appeal of Assizes

430. Appeals against Tribunal and Justice of Peace decisions are decided by the Court of Appeal (*Corte d'Appello*). Appeals against Court of Assizes' decisions are decided by the Court of Appeal of Assizes (*Corte d'Assise d'Appello*). In the appeal stage, prosecution is conducted by the public prosecutor at the Court of Appeal (*Procuratore Generale presso la Corte di Appello*) (Articles 51, 593, and 605 CCP), (*supra*, paragraph 31).

C. The Court of Cassation

431. The Court of Cassation (*Corte di Cassazione*), which is the third instance, decides appeals concerning questions of formal legitimacy. The prosecution is conducted by the Prosecutor General at the Court of Cassation (*Procuratore Generale presso la Corte di Cassazione*) (Article 606 CCP), (*supra*, paragraph 33).

It is possible to appeal to the Court of Cassation against unappealable sentences as well as against the decisions rendered by the Appeals Court. The Court of Cassation is the highest court of the Judiciary and decides on specific cases provided for by Article 606 CCP, which are the following:

(1) *ultra vires* of the judge;
(2) non-compliance or wrong application of the criminal law or other regulations that must be taken into account in order to apply the criminal law;
(3) non-compliance with the trial regulations regarding nullity, forfeiture, unusableness and inadmissibility;
(4) when a decisive proof was not gathered and the party made a specific request;
(5) when reasoning is missing, contradictory or manifestly illogical, and such defects result from the appealed decision or from the acts of the trial.

At the end of the hearing, the Court of Cassation can decide whether to confirm or annul the decision that was brought before it. In specific cases, the Court of Cassation can annul the decision without remanding it to the lower courts when it believes that the return is superfluous or when it can inflict directly the punishment or take the necessary actions (Article 620 CCP).

II. The Investigative Powers

432. The investigating power is divided between the public prosecutor and the judicial police, who are active in the preliminary investigations phase and can be described as the public prosecutor's executive. Thus, the public prosecutor conducts the pre-trial investigation either directly or indirectly by employing the judicial police.

An investigation takes place to establish when there is enough circumstantial criminal evidence to prompt a criminal action. Depending on the type of crime, the investigation must be completed within a legally fixed period of time. (Articles 326 and 358 CCP) (see *infra*, paragraphs 441 et seq.).

433. It is worthwhile to point out that the accused has the right to defence (Constitution Article 24, comma 2 and 111) which consists in the right to have adequate time and facilities to prepare his defence. The right to defence also includes the right to legal counsel.

In fact, the accused has the right to defence at any stage of the proceeding, and this right may not be waived.

In particular, the CCP provides that the defence counsel must be present during the questioning carried out by the judicial police and have the right to be present in other specific cases (i.e., local inspections, seizure, etc.) (Articles 360, 364, paragraph 1 and 365 CCP).

A. The Public Prosecutor

434. As mentioned *supra*, paragraphs 44–47, the public prosecutor is responsible for the prosecution and for directing the investigation and collecting of evidence.

The public prosecutor in the Italian criminal system has a monopoly in prompting the criminal action and once a criminal proceeding has started, the public prosecutor becomes part of the process on behalf of the State, which he represents. The other party is the accused person.

The prosecutor's activity is bound by the principle of mandatory prosecution, according to which the public prosecutor is always obliged to prosecute any crime. Such principle, as known, does not operate in common law jurisdictions and some civil law jurisdictions, where prosecutorial discretion is applied.

The compulsoriness of penal action is sanctioned by the Constitution (Article 112). According to this provision, the public prosecutor, when becoming acquainted with the commission of a crime (*notitia criminis*), is legally bound to start the investigation and, if there is enough circumstantial evidence, to take penal action against the alleged culprit of that particular crime.

In conclusion, the prosecutor is therefore without discretionary power to withhold prosecution. Prosecution is not simply a right, but a duty of the public prosecutor (Articles 358 and 405 CCP).

435. Nevertheless, since, on the one hand, the public prosecutor has the theoretical duty to always prosecute any crime, and since, on the other hand, the number of offences to prosecute is higher than the actual possibilities for the public prosecution, it can be stated that, de facto, the prosecutor has some leeway in choosing the proceedings to prosecute first (see *supra*, paragraph 45).

However, certain offences can only be prosecuted under specific conditions; penal action cannot be taken unless a specific requirement is met. Offences prosecutable by initiative (i.e., submission of a *querela* or complaint) of the offended person (*reati perseguibili a querela dell'offeso*) can range from forcible rape to minor personal injury and can be prosecuted only if the offended person requests the public prosecutor to proceed against someone for the alleged commission of a crime. Excluding rape and similar sex offences, this request can be withdrawn, and this essentially eliminates the crime (Articles 120, 152 PC; Article 340 CCP).

436. For offences allegedly committed by members of the two Houses of Parliament (*Camera dei Deputati* and *Senato della Repubblica*), a special authorization of the Parliament is required in order to both, carry out certain types of investigation procedures (search and seizure, wire tapping) and to arrest or otherwise limit MPs' personal freedom.

437. It should be noted that the public prosecutor, throughout his investigation acts, must seek not only evidence against the defendant, but even elements in the accused's favour because he must pursue a just result. With regard to this, the Italian Constitutional Court has pointed out that the public prosecutor is a public body having a duty of accuracy and indifference to the result, i.e., the public prosecutor does not have to pursue the defendant's conviction, but he must act in order to get a just sentence, even if the defendant deserves to be acquitted. In fact, acting on behalf of the State, the public prosecutor does not represent a particular interest but simply acts in order to guarantee the abidance of the law.[225]

B. The Judicial Police

438. The judicial police have a repressive function, instead of the pre-emptive one typical of the State police. In fact, the first one intervenes when the second one could not avoid the commission of a crime.

Article 55 CCP indicates the functions of the judicial police. It states that:

> *the judicial police must receive, even on their own initiative, information about offences, impede the worsening of their consequences, look for their authors, ensure the collection of evidences and everything that could be useful in order to guarantee the application of the criminal law.*

It is easy to infer that the judicial police operates on receipt of the *notitia criminis*, aside from any order eventually issued by the public prosecutor.

Hence, it is possible to assume that in Italy the principle of 'atypicalness of the judicial police's investigating acts' applies.[226] In fact, once a *notitia crimis* is received and until the public prosecutor fails to issue guidelines about an investigation, the judicial police are obliged to continue executing investigative acts on their own initiative, in order to collect every necessary proof.

The Italian Court of Cassation has pointed out that the only limit is the prohibition to carry out acts eventually conflicting with the guidelines given by the public prosecutor.[227]

439. With regard to the duty of the judicial police to impede the worsening of the consequences of offences, it is worthwhile to point out that such rule does not give the police the power of seizure other than in those cases specifically provided by the CCP. In fact, Article 321, paragraph 3*bis* CCP states that the preventive seizure can be carried out by the judicial police only in emergency cases, and in any case it must be validated by the judge.[228]

Once the public prosecutor issues investigating guidelines, the police still maintain certain autonomy. In fact, on the one hand the police are obliged to carry out every order issued by the public prosecutor; on the other hand, it can also lead in executing every activity necessary in order to verify whether a crime has been committed, provided that they inform promptly the public prosecutor (Article 348, paragraph 2 CCP).

225. Constitutional Court Decisions No. 190 of 1970, 88 of 1991, 111 of 1993, and 241 of 1994.
226. Court of Cassation, Second Section, Decisions No. 2655 of 8 Apr. 1997 and No. 2655; Court of Cassation Decision of 1 Apr. 1998.
227. Court of Cassation, First Section Decision of 4 May 1994.
228. Court of Cassation, United Sections, Decision of 18 Jun. 1991.

§2. The Stages of the Penal Process

440. The criminal procedure commences when an offence is reported, and is completed when a decision by a court is given. It is divided into two phases. These are the investigative phase or preliminary investigation (*indagini preliminari*), which precedes the trial and in which the public prosecutor has an important role, and the Court hearing or trial during which the contending parties present the evidence to the Court.

In the Italian criminal system, it is important to distinguish between the investigation and the trial, according to the technical terminology adopted by the Italian CCP, which establish that the preliminary investigations are not part of the trial but part of the criminal proceeding. The preliminary hearing, on the contrary, is considered part of the trial because it is conducted before a judge after the exercise of the criminal action by the public prosecutor. Thus, the 'borderline' between the criminal investigation and the trial is the point in time when the public prosecutor makes a request for trial to the judge (*richiesta di rinvio a giudizio*).

I. Preliminary Investigation

A. The Notitia Criminis

441. Preliminary investigations start when the public prosecutor is informed with a *notitia criminis*, i.e., when he or she receives sufficiently detailed and specific information about the commission of a criminal offence.

Such information, which is not evidence of a crime, can be specific (*notizia specifica*), containing the indications about the person who committed the fact, or generic (*notizia generica*), when the author of the crime is unknown.

It is a prerequisite of the process, but it cannot be considered a part of it because under Italian law, the criminal proceeding starts with the commission of the first investigating act carried out by the police or by the public prosecutor. This is the reason why, unlike all other judicial deeds which must be written in Italian to be effective in any Italian trial, the *notitia criminis* produces the aforesaid effects even if it is drawn up in a language other than Italian.

The public prosecutor and the judicial police receive information about the commission of a crime, but they are not merely the passive recipients of information from third parties. According to the Italian Court of Cassation, in order for a *notitia criminis* to be admissible at trial, it must be contained in a document which has an identifiable author. Thus, information coming from a confidential or anonymous source cannot be considered as a *notitia criminis* unless verified to determine if the notice is grounded.[229] However, anonymous reports or tips can give rise to criminal proceedings de facto by providing the public prosecutor or the judicial police with the possibility to act on the information received and thus create a valid *notitia criminis*.

229. Court of Cassation Decision of 8 Mar. 1995.

In addition, public prosecutors and judicial police can also discover cases themselves in accordance with Article 330 CCP. And, the judicial police have a duty to report to the public prosecutor all offences of which they are aware, regardless whether the knowledge arises as a result of their office or otherwise (Article 361 CCP).

Finally, it is possible to distinguish between two different types of *notitia criminis* depending on whether they are provided by the CCP (*notizia nominata*) or other means (*notizia innominata*).

1. *Notitia Criminis* under the CCP

442. The CCP expressly provides for two kinds of *notitia criminis*:

(1) The complaint (*denuncia*) is a declaration made by any person, except doctors (see below sub letter (b)), through which a public prosecutor or the judicial police is informed about the commission of a crime. (See Article 361 PC; Articles 331 and 333 CCP). The *denuncia* is a duty criminally sanctioned for a public officer or a person in charge of a public service, while private persons are generally free to decide whether to denounce a crime or not, except for some cases explicitly provided by law in which they are obliged to denounce (i.e., crimes against the State punishable by life imprisonment). In these obligatory cases, if the private citizen does not report the crime, he or she may be subject to a penalty of up to one-year imprisonment or a fine of EUR 103–EUR 1,032 (Article 364 PC).

(2) The medical report (*referto*) is a declaration through which, a healthcare professional refers to the public prosecutor or the judicial police information regarding the commission of a crime that the professional knows due to his activity. The *referto* is a criminally sanctioned duty (with a fine of up to EUR 516), except when the report would lead the patient to a criminal charge. The reasoning is that the law does not want to discourage those individuals needing care to contact a doctor, notwithstanding the commission of a crime. In these cases, the doctor has the option of reporting to the public prosecutor or to the police (Article 334 CCP and Article 365 PC).

2. Other Forms of *Notitia Criminis* (*Notizia innominata*)

443. A *notitia criminis innominata* (i.e., 'anonymous') can be made in a variety of ways, such as a defendant caught in the act, confidential information provided by a secret informer to the police or the public prosecutor, or a self-incriminating declaration given by a witness during examination. (See also *supra* paragraph 430).

B. The Preliminary Investigation Phase

1. Generally

444. Once the prosecutor is informed about the commission of an offence, the preliminary investigation phase commences. During this pre-trial phase, the public prosecutor has a dominant position in carrying out the investigation.

It is important to point out that a specific time limit is fixed for the investigation phase since, on the one hand, the public prosecutor cannot delay *sine die* the exercise of the criminal action, and, on the other hand, the law cannot provide an indefinite length for an investigation.[230]

445. The time limit for the investigation does not start on the day the offence is reported, however, but on the day when the offender is identified and listed on the criminal registry, in other words, from the moment in which a given person is investigated for a certain offence (Article 405, paragraph 3 CCP). The time limit set to investigate a specific person is six months, but in the case of more serious offences, the limit is one year (Article 407, paragraph 2, letter (a) CCP). On request of the public prosecutor, the time limit can be extended by six months one or more times, up to a maximum length of eighteen months and, in the case of more serious offences, up to two years. The public prosecutor must ask the judge for the preliminary investigations (GIP) for the extension before the expiry date, and he must indicate the reasons for that extension. In particular, the first extension must be justified by a 'just cause' (*giusta causa*) while for the subsequent requests, the investigation must be particularly complex, or there must be an objective impossibility to conclude the investigation within the extended time limit (Article 406, paragraphs 1, 2, and 2*bis* CCP). When the extension is denied by the judge, he or she grants a ten-day period to the public prosecutor within which the prosecutor must close the investigation, either dismissing the charge or exercising the criminal action (Article 406, paragraph 7 CCP).

When the author is unknown (*notitia criminis generica*), the public prosecutor – within six months after the registration of the *notitia criminis* – should request the dismissal of the charge or, if he believes it is still possible to find a suspect, the authorization to keep investigating (Article 415, paragraph 1 CCP).

446. It is important to stress that any investigative act performed outside the time limits is unusable in the preliminary hearing (Article 406, paragraph 8 and Article 407, paragraph 3 CCP).

2. Investigation by the Public Prosecutor

447. The public prosecutor can perform a wide range of investigative acts during the preliminary investigations as described *infra*, paragraph 487.

230. G. Conso & V. Grevi, *Compendio di procedura penale* 530 (Padova 2006).

3. Investigation by the Judicial Police

448. The judicial police – after having received the *notitia criminis* and until the public prosecutor takes the lead of the investigation – can carry out on their own initiative, acts of preliminary investigation in order to ensure the collection of proof that could be useful in applying the criminal law.

In particular, the judicial police can collect 'every element useful for a reconstruction of the fact and the individuation of its author' by investigating both individuals informed about the fact and objects or traces pertinent to the offence (Article 348, paragraphs 1 and 2 CCP). The police may also preserve any leads and the state of places. See *infra*, paragraphs 488 et seq.

449. After the public prosecutor takes the lead of the investigation, the judicial police can still carry out acts:

(1) necessary to fulfil directives from the public prosecutor (Article 348, paragraph 3 CCP);
(2) specifically delegated by the public prosecutor (Article 370, paragraph 1 CCP);
(3) neither delegated nor respondent to public prosecutor's directives which are necessary in order to ascertain the perpetration of the crime or those acts that became necessary after new investigation elements arise. In such case, the public prosecutor should be promptly informed (Article 327 and Article 348, paragraph 3 CCP).

4. Investigations by the Defence Lawyer

450. Article 327*bis* CCP states that the defence lawyer has the power to carry out investigations in order to collect proof in favour of his client. In order to carry out such activity, the lawyer can use a private investigator or a technical consultant for his search purposes.

It is important to stress that the defence lawyer can carry out investigative acts not only during the preliminary investigation phase, but also before it starts, so long as the lawyer is properly retained and has a power of attorney to act on behalf of the accused.

Moreover, this right also extends to counsel for private parties, such as the victim, a civilly liable party, or a party civilly obliged for the pecuniary sanction. A civilly liable party is one who can be liable for the actions of the offender (e.g., a company civilly responsible for the acts of its employees), while a party civilly liable for pecuniary sanctions is one bound to pay the criminal fine (e.g., a company which must pay the fines related to the acts of an employee).

Whenever the defence lawyer decides to examine a potential witness about the facts, he or she has to inform the person about:

(1) his or her position and the purpose of the conversation;
(2) the kind of exam he or she wants to carry out, i.e., if he or she desires a written declaration, a documented exam, or a simple conversation;
(3) the duty of the person interviewed to declare whether he or she is under investigation or charged in the same trial or in a trial connected to the latter;
(4) the witness' right to refuse to answer;
(5) the prohibition against disclosed questions eventually made by the judicial police or by the public prosecutor and the answers given to them; and
(6) the risk of a perjury claim, if the witness gives false answers (Article 391*bis*, paragraph 3 CCP).

5. The Probatory Hearing (incidente probatorio)

451. In theory, until the beginning of the court hearing or trial, the work carried out by the parties cannot be used as evidence, since evidence is collected during the court hearing. However, under the Code, there are certain exceptions to this general principle.

452. The preliminary investigation is carried out under the public prosecutor's command and supervision and furnish elements usable by the public prosecutor to decide whether or not to prosecute; by the judge for the preliminary investigations (GIP); by the judge for the preliminary hearing (*giudice dell'udienza preliminare* or GUP) and for the special proceedings. Such elements should not be used in the trial phase by a judge who, in the accusatory system, should make his findings only on evidence gathered in a forum where there is the guarantee of debate (i.e., the trial).

453. Nevertheless, it could happen that throughout the preliminary investigation, acts are carried out which are not repeatable in the trial phase (such as inspection reports, confiscation, search, unrepeatable technical controls, telephone interceptions) and are crucial to the judge's evaluation of the case. For this reason, the law provides for the *incidente probatorio* aimed at allowing the gathering of evidence before the GIP or GUP with the guarantee of cross-examination. The evidence collected in the *incidente probatorio* is admissible at trial.

454. The evidential hearing may be requested to gather:

(1) testimony, when there are reasons to believe the person who must be questioned will not be able to testify in the trial phase because of disability or any other impediment, or that he or she could be threatened, attacked or receive money in order to refrain from testifying;
(2) examination of the investigated person about facts concerning someone else's liability;
(3) examination of persons charged in a connected proceeding;
(4) comparison between the person sub letters (a), (b), and (c) if they made incompatible statements on important circumstances;

(5) a survey or a judicial experiment on someone or something or a place at risk of unavoidable modification or a survey that could last so long that it could delay trial for more than sixty days;
(6) an urgent ascertainment;
(7) testimony of a person under 16 in a proceeding regarding offences against personality or sexual freedom. (Article 392, paragraph 1 CCP).

455. The public prosecutor or the accused may make a request to the GIP for an *incidente probatori* within the end of the preliminary investigations (Article 392, paragraph 1 CCP), while an offended or injured person can only solicit a request from the public prosecutor (Article 394 CCP).

It is worth stressing that the time limitation of the investigative phase no longer applies to the *incidente probatorio* because the Constitutional Court has stated that such limit violates the right of a person to prove his innocence. Therefore, now the *incidente probatorio* can be requested during the preliminary hearing (*infra*, paragraphs 475 et seq.) as well.[231]

456. With regards to the content of the request, it must indicate:

(1) the evidence requested, the facts proven by it, and the reasons for its importance;
(2) the person with knowledge of the facts to be proven through the evidence requested; and
(3) the matter of urgency (Article 393 CCP).

Furthermore, it is possible to proceed to an 'incidente probatorio' in some particular cases relating to sexual offences, if there is a request from the defendant or the victim.[232]

457. If the judge accepts the request for *incidente probatorio*, the probatory hearing takes place with the attendance of the public prosecutor and the investigated person's defence counsel, who may ask the judge to question the witness. The investigated person and the offended person can participate when there is a witness to be interrogated, while in other cases they can attend only a hearing if authorized by the judge (Article 401, paragraphs 1 and 2 CCP).

In such hearing, no further discussion about the validity of the request is allowed since the hearing is merely aimed at gathering admitted evidence.

It is worthwhile to point out that the evidence gathered during a probatory hearing can be used only against a person whose defence counsel attended or has been invited to attend to the probatory hearing. If the final decision is based upon evidence collected during an *incidente probatorio*, it does not have value in a civil proceeding for damages unless the damaged person has accepted it, even tacitly (Article 404 CCP).

231. Constitutional Court Decision No. 77 of 10 Mar. 1994.
232. As established by Art. 392 CCP as amended by Law No. 172 of 1 Oct. 2012.

C. *The Judge for Preliminary Investigations*

458. The pre-trial phase is conducted under the control of the judge for preliminary investigations (GIP – *giudice per le indagini preliminari*), who controls the work of the public prosecutor and guarantees the rights of the person being investigated (Article 328 CCP).

As during the preliminary phase, the judge remains external to the investigation and only intervenes when there are requests made by the parties and only in those cases provided by law.[233]

The preliminary judge has the task of adopting measures – when requested by the public prosecutor – restricting personal freedom if this proves necessary during the investigation. The GIP also decides whether it is necessary to extend these measures, following a request by the public prosecutor. In addition, at the request of the parties, the GIP decides whether to admit the taking of evidence during the pre-trial phase and presides over the proceedings.

Furthermore, the GIP decides on any requests to set the case aside made by the accused or the public prosecutor.

D. *The End of Preliminary Investigation*

459. According to Article 415*bis* CCP, before the expiry date of the preliminary investigation, the accused must be notified of the conclusion of preliminary investigation (i.e., receive a Notice of Conclusion or *avviso di conclusione delle indagini preliminari*). For the offences covered by Articles 572 and 612*bis* PC the notice must also be notified to the lawyer of the injured party.

It is important to underline that before the moment in which the accused receives the notice, the public prosecutor does not have any duty to inform or to examine him or her about the facts on which investigative acts are being carried out. However, when the investigation is going to exceed the time limit determined by law and an extension is requested from the GIP, the public prosecutor must inform the investigated person about the request (*supra*, paragraph 445).

As previously mentioned, this notice has the purpose of giving the accused an opportunity to introduce defensive arguments in an attempt to convince the prosecutor to request the GIP dismiss the case.

460. The Notice of the Conclusion must contain:

(1) a summary description of the charge;
(2) an indication of the law provisions that have allegedly been infringed; and
(3) an indication of the time and place of the crime.

The accused must be warned that, within twenty days, he or she (and the defence lawyer) has the right to:

233. Court of Cassation (Fifth Section) Decision No. 781 of 30 Jul. 1991.

(1) examine and make copy of the file of the prosecutor;
(2) exhibit defence briefs and documents;
(3) present the result of the investigations carried out by the defence counsel;
(4) ask the prosecutor for further investigations;
(5) release spontaneous statements;
(6) ask the prosecutor to be examined.

The public prosecutor also has the duty to inform the indicted that the judicial documents are deposited, and that he has the right to inspect them, to make copies, to be subjected to interrogation, and to file written submissions (Article 415*bis* CCP).

461. The end of the investigation is also the point in time in which the public prosecutor must formulate the criminal charge (if any).

462. Once the preliminary investigation is concluded, the prosecutor must decide whether to proceed or to dismiss the action. In this respect, the public prosecutor has five options:

(1) directly commit the defendant for trial, with respect to those crimes punishable by imprisonment of less than four years (i.e., direct citation – Article 550 CCP);
(2) request dismissal of the charge, if the prosecutor believes the charge is groundless (Article 408 CCP);
(3) request the defendant be committed for trial (Article 416 CCP);
(4) request a proceeding by decree (Article 459 CCP);
(5) request an immediate trial, when the evidence of the crime is manifest (Article 453 CCP).

In the first case, the public prosecutor drafts a request for trial of the defendant (*richiesta di rinvio a giudizio*); in the latter four cases, he must ask the judge for preliminary investigations (GIP) to issue the order. More specifically, should the public prosecutor decide to commit the investigated person (who is now called the defendant) for trial, he or she can directly issue such an order if the criminal offence falls under the competence of the Justice of the Peace. When the crime involves the competence of either the Tribunal or the Court of Assizes, the prosecutor sends his or her request to the preliminary judge. The GIP must decide whether or not to accept the request after listening to both parties in chambers.

463. It is important to note that both the dismissal of charge and the request for trial must be evaluated by the GIP since the law aims to reserve to an independent and impartial body the ascertainment of whether there are sufficient grounds for filing a charge and whether the dismissal of the charge would represent a violation of the prosecutor's duty, provided for by Article 112 of the Italian Constitution, to exercise the criminal action.[234]

---

234. G. Conso & V. Grevi, *Compendio di procedura penale* 532 & 533 (Padova 2006).

E. *Options for the Public Prosecutor at the End of the Preliminary Investigation*

1. Direct Citation

464. The prosecutor may use direct citation for misdemeanours or crimes punishable by imprisonment of not more than four years or by a fine, alone or in conjunction with detention.

465. Direct citation may also be used for the following offences:

(1) violence or threat to a public official (Article 336 PC);
(2) resisting a public official (Article 337 PC);
(3) aggravated insult of a magistrate during a hearing (Article 343(2) PC);
(4) aggravated breach of a seal (Article 349(2) PC);
(5) aggravated fighting (Article 588(2) PC), excluding those cases resulting in serious injury or death;
(6) aggravated theft (Article 625 PC);
(7) receiving of stolen goods (Article 648 PC).

466. If the prosecutor is seeking to prosecute a criminal action with direct citation for an offence which requires a preliminary hearing and the relative exception is made within the period specified in Article 491, paragraph 1 (e.g., preliminary questions as to jurisdiction, etc.) the court issues an order transmitting the acts to the prosecutor.

2. Dismissal of the Charge

467. At the end of the preliminary investigation, the public prosecutor can request that the judge (GIP) dismiss the charge when the *notitia criminis* is groundless (Article 408 CCP) because the evidence collected is not enough to support a charge (*dismissal of charge caused by evidencial inadequacy*).

In other words, based on the evidence collected during the investigation, it is possible to infer that the fact did not occur or does not constitute a crime; the investigated person did not commit the crime; or the evidence collected is insufficient, conflicting, or could not be used at trial.

The dismissal of charge is also requested when a condition for prosecution is lacking, the fact is not provided for by the law as a crime, the crime is extinguished, or the authors are unknown (Article 415, paragraph 1 CCP). The latter should be requested when it is certain that a crime has been carried out, but no author has been found, and it is possible to deem that no suspect could be found if the investigations would be continued.

468. Once the judge receives the request for the dismissal of charge, he or she can:

(1) approve the request through a reasoned decision and return the file to the public prosecutor (Article 409, paragraph 1 CCP);[235] or
(2) set a hearing giving notice of such to the public prosecutor, the investigated person, his defence counsel and the damaged person.[236]

In the second case, at the end of the hearing, the judge pronounces an order with which he, alternatively:

(1) approves the dismissal of charge and returns the file to the public prosecutor if, after a more careful consideration, the GIP believes that the request for the dismissal of charge is grounded (Article 409, paragraph 5 CCP);[237]
(2) indicates to the public prosecutor the further investigations that he or she has to carry out and the applicable time limit, if he believes the investigation is incomplete (Article 409, paragraph 4 CCP);[238]
(3) orders the registration of a possible author of the crime, if he believes the dismissal of charge – based upon the fact that the author is unknown – is unwarranted (Article 415, paragraph 2 CCP); or
(4) orders the public prosecutor to press the criminal charge within ten days, if he believes that from the investigation emerged enough elements to support a criminal charge (Article 417 CCP).

469. It is worth noting that the latter represents a waiver of the general principle of impartiality of the judge. It is nevertheless true that such provision guarantees, in

---

235. Article 409(1) PC:

> Except in cases where the objection referred to in Art. 410 has been lodged, if the judge grants the request for the proceedings to be discontinued, he or she shall make an order to that effect, giving reasons, and return the file to the public prosecutor's office.

236. Article 409(2) PC:

> If the judge rejects the request [to discontinue the proceedings], he or she shall fix the date of the private hearing and shall inform the public prosecutor, the accused and the injured party accordingly. The procedure shall be conducted in accordance with Art. 127. The documents shall be deposited with the registry up to the day of the hearing, and copies may be obtained by counsel.

237. Article 409(5) PC:

> Where the circumstances described in para. 4 above do not apply and the judge rejects the request to discontinue the proceedings, he or she shall issue an order instructing the public prosecutor to draw up the indictment within ten days.

238. Article 409(4) PC:

> After the hearing, if the judge considers additional investigative measures to be necessary, he or she shall issue an order to the public prosecutor detailing the measures and laying down a binding time limit for their completion.

pursuance of Article 112 of the Italian Constitution, jurisdictional supervision with respect to the public prosecutor's duty to exercise the criminal action.[239]

470. Moreover, it is important to point out that the injured person(s) has the opportunity to oppose to the request for dismissal of charge. This is the reason why the public prosecutor has the duty to notify the injured person of the request if the latter has asked the prosecutor (in the *notitia criminis* or subsequently) to be informed about requests for dismissal. In the notification, the public prosecutor informs the damaged person that within ten days after receipt, it is possible to examine the investigation results and, eventually, to file an opposition containing a motivated request to carry on the investigation and the object of the supplementary investigation and the related evidence to be collected (Article 410, paragraph 1 CCP).

Once the ten days term expires, the public prosecutor transmits the file case to the GIP, as well as the request for dismissal of charge and the opposition of the damaged person, if any. If the opposition is inadmissible and the request for dismissal of charge is grounded, the judge approves the request through a reasoned decision.[240] If, on the contrary, the opposition is admissible (i.e., it does not present any form of defect), aside from its merits, the GIP fixes the hearing at the end of which the judge pronounces one of the above-mentioned orders (see *supra*, paragraph 462 Nos (1), (2), (3), and (4)).

471. If the request to dismiss the case is accepted, the case is closed, but it can be reopened at any time if new evidence is acquired. And appeals against decision to discontinue the proceedings are to be made to the Court of Cassation solely on the grounds of nullity provided for by Article 127(5) of the Italian Constitution [in particular failure to comply with the procedural provisions concerning the holding of hearings in private].

3. Motion to Commit for Trial

472. At the end of the preliminary investigation, the public prosecutor who believes there are sufficient elements to pursue a criminal action, makes the criminal charge and requests a committal for trial. Such request is invalid if it has not been preceded by a notification of conclusion of the preliminary investigation pursuant to Article 415*bis* CCP (*supra*, paragraph 460). Moreover, the request must contain:

(1) the defendant's personal details;
(2) the criminal charge;
(3) the evidence collected;

---

239. G. Conso & V. Grevi, *Compendio di procedura penale* 537 (Padova 2006).
240. Article 410(2) PC: '*Where the objection is declared inadmissible and the accusations are unfounded, the judge shall issue an order discontinuing the proceedings and shall return the file to the public prosecutor's office.*'

(4) the request for the committal for trial decree; and
(5) the date and the public prosecutor's signature (Article 417 CCP).

When the public prosecutor files the motion to commit the defendant for trial, the GIP always has the duty to fix, by decree, the date of the preliminary hearing (the so-called *udienza preliminare*). Such decree, together with the motion of committal for trial, must be served on the defendant (Articles 416 et seq. CCP).

4. Proceeding by Decree (*Decreto penale di condanna*)

473. In proceedings for indictable offences which are properly presented and on the condition the complaining party has not opposed it, if the prosecutor believes only a pecuniary penalty should be applied – even if imposed as a substitute to a prison sentence – he may petition the GIP decide the matter by criminal decree. The order must set out the amount of the penalty. The petition must be filed within six months from the date on which the name of the indicted person is entered on the criminal registry. If the defendant appeals against the sentence, an ordinary criminal law procedure is instituted (Article 459 CCP). (See also *infra*, paragraphs 502 et seq.).

5. Request for Immediate Trial

474. When the evidence of the crime is conclusive, the prosecutor or the defendant may request that the matter go directly to trial without a preliminary hearing (Article 453 CCP). (See also *supra* paragraph 507).

Table 8 Offences for Which a Criminal Action Was Commenced – Year 2010[241]

	Direct Citation	*Proceeding by Decree*	*Abbreviated Trial*	*Motion of Committal for Trial*	*Immediate Trial*	*Plea Bargain*	*Total*
Murder	1.0	– –	1.2	63.0	34.6	0.2	**100.0**
Attempted murder	2.6	0.2	3.0	39.3	53,3	1,6	**100.0**
Manslaughter	0.6	0.1	0.2	92.5	2,2	4,4	**100.0**
Assault	92.2	1.6	0.7	34.3	1.0	0.1	**100.0**

241. *Annuario statistico italiano 2012* (Italian Statistical Yearbook 2012) Ch. 6: Justice, ISTAT, http://www3.istat.it/dati/catalogo/20121218_00/PDF/Cap6.pdf (Accessed 15 Jun. 2013).

	Direct Citation	*Procee ding by Decree*	*Abbrevi ated Trial*	*Motion of Committal for Trial*	*Immediate Trial*	*Plea Bargain*	*Total*
Personal injury	67.6	3.2	9.7	13.1	5.9	0.6	**100.0**
Involuntary injury	91.9	5.4	0.1	1.8	0.1	0.6	**100.0**
Insult	93.1	3.1	0.2	3.0	0.5	0.1	**100.0**
Threat	87.7	5.8	0.7	4.4	1.1	0.3	**100.0**
Defamation	73.3	4.1	0.1	22.0	0.3	0.2	**100.0**
Family abuse	5.2	1.1	4.2	69.0	19.5	1.0	**100.0**
Theft	44.5	12.7	30.7	7.4	3.0	1.6	**100.0**
Property damage	70.2	11.9	7.7	6.5	2.9	1.0	**100.0**
Robbery	0.9	0.1	18.0	38.9	39.7	2.4	**100.0**
Extortion	2.8	0.3	4.6	59.8	30.3	2.3	**100.0**
Kidnapping	– –	4.8	– –	54.8	38.1	2.4	**100.0**
Fraud	62.2	17.2	0.9	17.7	0.9	1.1	**100.0**
Informatics Fraud	69.5	8.6	0.3	19.7	1.2	0.6	**100.0**
Fraudulent bankruptcy	9.0	4.8	–	82.4	1.4	2.4	**100.0**
Embezzle ment	3.1	1.4	0.3	83.9	6.6	4.7	**100.0**
Bribery	0.4	– –	0.9	74.4	18.4	6.0	**100.0**
Corruption	0.3	1.2	0.9	78.1	12.2	7.3	**100.0**
Omission of an act of office	4.7	6.9	0.2	87.0	– –	0.4	**100.0**
Drug-related offences	0.6	0.4	32.8	29.4	31.6	5.2	**100.0**
Sexual violence	1.0	0.3	2.3	69.2	25.2	2.1	**100.0**
Environm ental offences	36.0	15.2	24.0	22.0	0.8	2.1	**100.0**

	Direct Citation	*Procee ding by Decree*	*Abbrevi ated Trial*	*Motion of Committal for Trial*	*Immediate Trial*	*Plea Bargain*	*Total*
Immigration offences	16.9	4.1	73.0	4.2	1.5	0.4	**100.0**
Money laundering	9.1	0.1	0.7	72.5	14.4	3.2	**100.0**
Receiving stolen property	77.8	6.2	2.8	7.6	4.0	1.5	**100.0**
Usury	1.1	0.4	– –	76.1	19.5	3.0	**100.0**
Mafia association	0.4	– –	– –	83.5	14.3	1.8	**100.0**
Criminal association	2.5	0.1	0.1	69.9	18.4	9.0	**100.0**
Total	**50.6**	**17.3**	**10.7**	**15.5**	**4.8**	**1.2**	**100.0**

F. The Preliminary Hearing

1. Generally

475. This first hearing is referred to as the *preliminary hearing*. In this respect, it should be underlined that the recent reform relating to the 'single' or 'mono judge' which unified the positions of the magistrates and the trial judges has modified the system (*supra*, paragraph 22). As a result, the preliminary hearing will continue to be used primarily when the trial will be before a panel.

476. It is worth noting that in the case of a mono judge, the law provides two different types of trial. The first one is similar to that before a panel and includes the preliminary hearing. The second is characterized by the absence of the preliminary hearing. In particular, when there is a single judge, the CCP provides that in the cases provided for by Article 550 CCP, the public prosecutor must exercise the criminal action by means of the *citazione diretta*, namely he has to send the defendant directly to the trial, without a preliminary hearing.

477. The Italian criminal law system has always been inquisitorial in character, with the investigations being carried out by the investigating magistrate who was assigned for the gathering of evidence. In many cases, the court hearing was merely a form of controlling the previous phase. This underwent a substantial change when the new Code came into force in 1989. The new Code, following some proposals for legal changes, was clearly inspired by the North American accusatorial model.

The investigating magistrate was replaced by the judge for preliminary investigation (GIP) who has the task of controlling that the investigations – which in the reformed system are carried out by the public prosecutor – are in compliance with the law. The GIP also has the task of guaranteeing the rights of the person being investigated. The evidence is not normally collected during this phase, but during the court hearings.

These basic characteristics of the Italian criminal law system have undergone significant changes, however, following the decisions of the Constitutional Court in 1992 which have already been mentioned (*supra*, paragraph 82). The greater possibility to collect probatory evidence even during the preliminary investigation phase has brought about particular changes to Italian criminal procedure. Most of its accusatorial character has given way to a mixed system which is largely criticized by some scholars as having lost its original coherent and systematic character.

478. The preliminary hearing is carried out in order to have a judge evaluate in the debate the existence of elements suitable to sustain a criminal charge. Such hearing does not take place if the defendant renounces it by filing a request for immediate trial, at least three days before the date set for the preliminary hearing, or for the abbreviated trial.

The preliminary hearing must be carried out with the necessary attendance of the public prosecutor and the defendant's legal counsel. If the latter does not attend, a substitute is appointed, except where he or she communicated to the judge that he or she was absolutely unable to attend by reason of a just impediment; in such case, the hearing should be postponed (Article 420*ter*, paragraph 5 CCP). The same happens when the defendant cannot attend the hearing.

479. The hearing starts by ascertaining the appearance of the parties before the Court and then the judge declares the discussion opened. After that, the public prosecutor lays out the evidence collected, and the defendant may issue spontaneous statements or ask to be interrogated. At this point, counsel for any civil parties may state their case, followed by the parties civilly responsible for the payment of any fines. The public prosecutor and defence counsel are allowed only one opportunity to speak on rebuttal (Article 421 CCP).

Based on the documents and evidence in the file[242] and the documents admitted by the court during the hearing, the prosecutor and the defenders then state their cases and conclusions.

480. If the judge has enough elements to make a decision, he or she declares the discussion closed, otherwise, the judge:

(1) indicates the further investigations that must be made if the one concluded is incomplete (Article 421*bis* CCP);

242. According to Art. 416(2) CCP, the file should contain the notice of the offence, records of completed investigations, and reports of acts before the judge for preliminary investigations. The file should also hold all other things relevant to the offence, unless it is necessary to keep them elsewhere.

(2) orders the gathering of the evidence deemed necessary in order to pronounce a non-suit (Article 422, paragraph 1 CCP) (*infra*, paragraph 482). It is possible to infer that the judge has an ex officio power to integrate evidence within the limits set forth by Article 422 CCP.

2. The Regulation of New Charges against the Defendant

481. From the understanding of the case up to that point, the investigation acts and the evidence collected during the preliminary hearing, it may result that the defendant is charged for:

(1) a different fact (*fatto diverso*) from the one described in the request for committal for trial, i.e., the same fact but carried out at a time or place different from the one for which the defendant prepared his strategy of defence. However, if the fact is completely different, then the defendant should be acquitted and eventually charged for the new fact (Article 423, paragraph 1 CCP);
(2) an aggravating circumstance (Article 423, paragraph 1 CCP);
(3) an additional crime connected with the one for which the defendant has been committed for trial (Article 423, paragraph 1 CCP); or
(4) a new fact (*fatto nuovo*), i.e., a new crime prosecutable ex officio and in addition to the one for which the defendant has been charged and not connected to it (Article 423, paragraph 2 CCP).

In order to guarantee the respect of the accused's right to defence and to promote procedural economy, the public prosecutor must modify the *imputazione* (criminal charge), and charge it to the defendant. In the case sub (4), the judge authorizes the charge only if the public prosecutor requests it and there is the defendant's consent (Article 423, paragraph 2 CCP).

3. The End of the Preliminary Hearing

482. At the end of the preliminary hearing, the judge may pronounce a non-suit when:

(1) a procedural condition is lacking; if the fact does not exist or is not provided by the law as a crime; if the statute of limitations for the crime has expired; or the defendant is not punishable or did not commit the fact (Article 425, paragraph 1 CCP); or
(2) the elements collected are incomplete, contradictory and in any case they are not suitable to sustain a criminal charge (Article 425, paragraph 3 CCP), and it is expectable that no further and useful evidence could be gathered in the trial phase.

The judge cannot pronounce a non-suit if he or she believes that the acquittal could be followed by the application of a security measure different from forfeiture (Article 425, paragraph 4 CCP) (*supra*, paragraphs 394 et seq.).

The pronouncement of the non-suit entails the loss of effectiveness of the security measure (Article 300, paragraph 1 CCP). If the defendant is in custody, he is immediately released once the judgment has been read.

The public prosecutor, the public prosecutor at the Court of Appeal, the defendant and the injured parties (who have been joined as civil parties) may appeal the decision to the Court of Appeal.

It is important to point out that in the Italian criminal system, a non-suit is never definitive unless it is barred by limitations.

4. Decree Committing the Defendant for Trial

483. If, at the end of the preliminary hearing, the judge believes there is sufficient evidence to sustain a criminal charge at trial, he or she issues a decree committing the defendant for trial which must contain:

(1) the defendant and the other parties' personal details;
(2) the brief indication of the evidence collected; and
(3) the purview, i.e., the committal for trial.

Such decree is read during the hearing and the reading is equivalent to the notice for those parties who attend the hearing. (Article 424, paragraph 2 CCP). Those parties who do not attend the hearing must be notified of the decree (Article 429, paragraph 4 CCP).

II. Powers, Rights and Duties in the Pre-trial Proceedings

A. *Introductory Remarks*

484. The general principle that rules the investigation is that of the dependence of the judicial police to the Judicial Authority. Therefore, generally the investigative activity must be carried out under the guidance of the public prosecutor (Article 56 CCP).

This general subordination of the judicial police to the direction of the public prosecutor poses the issue of whether or not the judicial police actually have autonomous investigative power. The question is resolved in Article 55 CCP in which the judicial police are also attributed with an autonomous power in order to carry out direct activity for the insurance of the sources of proof, both before and after the intervention of the magistrate.

Therefore, the activity of the judicial police is characterized by the principle that the investigation acts of the judicial police have an atypical nature. In other words, the judicial police have the power to carry out – on their own initiative – all of the acts of investigation deemed necessary to ascertain the crime and the identity of the offender, so long as they do not receive specific directives from the public prosecutor.

At this point, it becomes particularly important to determine the moment in which the investigations involve, or is under the direction of, the public prosecutor.

B. Transmission of Notice of Crime and Inscription on the Register of Parties under Investigation

485. The judicial police have the obligation under Article 347 CCP to refer immediately to the public prosecutor all news of offences which come into their possession, indicating the sources of the proof gathered, the activities carried out and the particulars of the subjects involved. From that moment, under Article 327 CCP, the direction of the investigation is up to the public prosecutor, which issues orders directly to the judicial police.

The public prosecutor, having received from the judicial police the notice of crime or having acquired notice of the crime in another manner, has the obligation to inscribe the crime on a special register. From the moment of inscription of particulars of the person under investigation, the terms of maximum duration of the investigation begin, as established Article 407 CCP (*supra*, paragraphs 445 et seq.). The terms differ depending on the gravity of the offences.

Such terms may be derogated, in case of particularly complex investigations, but, in any event, the term – also for more serious offences – may not exceed two years. After such terms, any investigative acts may not be used in the future by the judge for the preliminary investigation.

C. The Role of the Judge for the Preliminary Investigation

486. As mentioned above (*supra*, paragraph 458), during the investigation, a role of particular importance is given to the judge for the preliminary investigations (GIP). The GIP is not responsible for the investigative activity; this remains always exclusively the duty of the public prosecutor. Nevertheless, he has the overall task of insuring the legitimacy of the investigation and to adopt – upon request of the parties – measures of specific relief. For example, it is up to the GIP to issue – upon request of the public prosecutor – an order of protective custody.

D. Powers of the Public Prosecutor

487. The public prosecutor has the power to perform a wide range of investigative acts during the preliminary investigation phase:

(1) interrogate the investigated person (Article 364, paragraph 1 CCP);
(2) receive any spontaneous declaration made by the investigated person. In fact, in the Italian criminal system, when one individual knows that investigative acts are being carried out towards him, he has the right to go to the public prosecutor in order to make a declaration. If during such encounter, the public prosecutor charges the investigated person with the offence, the interview

has the same value of an interrogation; therefore, it must be carried out in pursuance of Articles 64, 65, and 364 CCP, i.e., giving the defendant the warning that he has the right to remain silent, communicating the proof gathered against him, and informing him that he has the right to defence counsel;

(3) examine persons informed about the facts (Article 430*bis* CCP). However, the prosecutor cannot question the witness about neither questions asked during any examinations (of the witness) performed by defence counsel nor the answers given (Article 362 CCP). It is worthwhile to stress that the person with knowledge of the facts who makes false declarations, denies the truth, or is reticent throughout the public prosecutor's questioning commits the crime of false declarations to the public prosecutor, punishable by the maximum of four years' imprisonment;

(4) examine the person charged in a connected criminal proceeding described in Article 210 CCP (Article 363 CCP);

(5) compare the statements of the investigated person with those of: (i) other people under investigation; (ii) persons informed about the facts; (iii) persons charged in a connected proceeding when such individuals have made incompatible statements on crucial points of the investigation (Article 364, paragraph 1 CCP);

(6) request – in case of necessity for the immediate continuation of the investigation – identification (*individuazione*), i.e., ask a witness to identify a person or anything perceptible by senses (Article 361 CCP);

(7) carry out searches on individuals, places or objects which could reveal the commission of the crime (Articles 244 and 364, paragraph 1 CCP);

(8) make any technical operation such as photographs and descriptions, even delegating such task to a technical consultant (Article 359 CCP);

(9) make the probatory seizure of the *corpus delicti* (Article 253, paragraph 1 CCP);

(10) ask the judge (GIP) for authorization to intercept communications. When the interception is of the utmost urgency for the investigation, the public prosecutor can proceed through a reasoned decision, which must be validated by the judge within twenty-four hours (Article 267, paragraph 2 CCP);

(11) carry out a pre-emptive seizure in case of urgency through a reasoned decision which must be transmitted to the judge within forty-eight hours to be validated.

In the exercise of such activities, the public prosecutor has coercive powers; thus, he or she can ask for the intervention of the judicial police and, if necessary, the State police (Article 378 CCP).

E. Powers of the Judicial Police

488. The powers of the judicial police, set forth in Articles 347 et seq. CCP, should be specifically considered.

489. However, first it is important to distinguish between two different kinds of investigative acts which can be carried out by the judicial police. The judicial police can perform both formal investigative acts (e.g., those specifically provided by the law) and informal activity (e.g., not provided by the CCP and not requiring authoritative powers).

490. With regard to formal acts of investigation, the judicial police may:

(1) identify the investigated person and individuals who can give information about the illicit fact, also by carrying out fingerprinting, photographs and anthropometrical verifications;
(2) bring into their offices, the investigated person or one informed about the facts who refuses to give his personal details. The detained person may be kept only for the time necessary for the identification, but for not more than twelve hours, or twenty-four hours if the assistance of a consulate or interpreter is needed. The detained person is entitled to notify a family member or domestic partner. In addition, the police must inform the public prosecutor both about the detainment – in such case, the prosecutor may release the investigated person if they believe the police have not observed the legal requirements – and about the release of the person (Article 349, paragraphs 4–6 CCP);
(3) carry out the police interrogation (*interrogatorio di polizia*) of the investigated person, on condition that he is not under arrest and his defence counsel attends the interrogation. In such case, the police must inform the investigated person that he has the right to remain silent but he is obliged to answer to the questions aimed at identifying him (Article 350, paragraphs 1–4 CCP);
(4) gain from the investigated person statements useful for the immediate furtherance of the investigation, even without being advised of the right to remain silent or the presence of defence counsel; however, the statements obtained may not be documented or used for purposes other than furtherance of investigations. (Article 350, paragraphs 5–6 CCP);
(5) receive spontaneous statements from the investigated person, i.e., statements not stimulated by questions; however, the statements are not permitted to be used at trial, except to discredit the person's subsequent testimony (Article 350, paragraph 7 CCP);
(6) receive brief information from the people informed about facts, as long as the judicial police do not ask any question about what has been said in any inquiry by defence counsel (Article 351, paragraph 1 CCP). Differently from the false declaration to the public prosecutor, in case of reticence or false declaration to the judicial police, no specific crime is provided by the law, but at the most, a conviction for libel or abetting could occur. Additionally, if from such interrogatory, evidence comes out regarding the culpability of the investigated person, the judicial police should interrupt the examination, warn the person that he could be the subject of an investigation and to appoint defence counsel (Article 63 CCP). Statements made before this moment cannot be used as evidence against the person; thus, the same happens when the police use an undercover agent to obtain evidence against someone;

(7) obtain statements from persons charged in a connected proceeding warning them about their right to remain silent except for questions aimed at identifying them (Article 351, paragraph 1 *bis* CCP);

(8) in case of an offender caught in the action or jailbreak, search his body or a place in which there is reason both to believe that objects connected to the crime are hidden and the investigated or escaped person could be located. The search record should be transmitted immediately to the *Procuratore* so that he can validate it within forty-eight hours from its receipt;

(9) carry out verifications about the state of places, objects and persons and distrain the *corpus delicti*, if there is a risk of losing evidence pertinent to the crime or its traces and the public prosecutor cannot intervene unreasonably or still has not taken the lead of investigation (Article 354 CCP). The seizure record should be transmitted within forty-eight hours to the *Procuratore*, and he or she must validate it within the next forty-eight hours or command the return of the items seized to the owner. If the police find sealed bundles, these must be transmitted to the *Procuratore della Repubblica* except in cases of urgency. In fact, when there is a matter of urgency, the judicial police should immediately inform the public prosecutor who can authorize the opening of the bundles without delay (Article 353, paragraphs 1 and 2);

(10) suspend the dispatch of letters, bundles, packs or telegrams at the post office, informing the public prosecutor, who should authorize the seizure within forty-eight hours; otherwise, the objects must be sent (Article 353, paragraph 3 CCP);

(11) carry out the pre-emptive seizure of objects pertinent to the offence when their possession could worsen or extend the consequences of the fact or its perpetration, in cases of urgency (Article 321, paragraphs 1 and 3*bis* CCP). The seizure record should be transmitted to the public prosecutor within forty-eight hours, who must ask the GIP to validate it within the subsequent forty-eight hours, under penalty of cancellation.

491. More specifically, with respect to investigation, interrogation and search, the judicial police may carry out the following.

1. Investigation of the Things and the Leads Pertinent to the Crime, Search for Witnesses

492. The general principles that relate to the investigation activity are the freedom of form and the atypicality of acts. Accordingly, the judicial police may turn to instruments not specifically covered by the Code to carry out the investigation, and therefore, for example, the police may film the material apprehension of objects that are spontaneously handed over, and so on.

When the judicial police have identified the person under investigation, they must invite that person to declare or elect a domicile for the receipt of future notifications.

Additionally, the judicial police have the power to take into their office, those persons who refuse to be identified or those persons for whom they have doubts regarding their proper identification.

Persons taken into the offices of the judicial police may be detained only for the time strictly necessary for identification, but for not more than twelve hours, or upon previous notification – also oral – to the public prosecutor, not more than twenty-four hours in cases in which identification is particularly complex.

2. Interrogation of Persons Subject to Investigations and Tests

493. With regards to the power to interrogate the persons under investigation (Article 350 CCP), it is necessary to make some distinctions:

(1) At the place and time of the fact, the judicial police officials may – also without the presence of defence counsel – assume from the person under investigation, as well as if arrested or stopped, information and useful indications for the purposes of continuing the immediate investigation. This information, if assumed without the presence of a defence attorney, cannot be documented or used in the means of proof.
(2) The judicial police officials may take a summary of the information from the person under investigation, recording the declarations, on the condition that there is advance notice to the defence attorney and if the interrogation occurs in the presence of a defence attorney in case of representation. The summary of the information cannot be carried out by the judicial police with those in the state of arrest or detention. The assumption of information must be preceded by notification that the person under investigation has the right to not respond, and the declarations he makes may be used against him.
(3) Finally, the judicial police can receive spontaneous declarations from the person under investigation, but such declarations cannot be used in debate of the matter.

With regards to the assumption of information from persons not under investigation, the judicial police have no limit.

3. Searches

494. The judicial police have the power to carry out searches both of the person and the place in the case of a flagrant crime or in case of escape, when there is reason for believing that they can find concealed on the person things or leads pertaining to the crime that could be cancelled or disposed or which things or leads are found in a determined place or that are found on the person under investigation or trying to escape (Article 352 CCP).

In this case, the judicial police transmit without delay – and in any event, not more than forty-eight hours – to the public prosecutor of the place where the location of the search is, a report of the operations carried out. If the public prosecutor, verifies that there exist the requirements that legitimate the activity of the judicial police and within forty-eight hours of the communication, he or she confirms the search.

Moreover, the judicial police have the power to carry out the verification and survey of the status of the places and the things when the public prosecutor cannot intervene at the right time or has not yet assumed direction of the investigation or there is danger that the things, leads and the places relevant to the ascertainment are at risk of destruction or modification.

III. Special Procedures

495. In addition to the normal procedures, the Italian CCP also provides for other types of criminal law procedures, the so-called alternative or special procedures.

A. Abbreviated Trial

496. The abbreviated trial (*giudizio abbreviato*) is regulated by Article 438 CCP, which states that a defendant may ask for a decision to be pronounced during the preliminary hearing on the basis of the evidence collected during the preliminary phase.

The defendant should make the request to be judged with the scheme of the abbreviated trial, orally or through a written act. Such request may be filed during the preliminary hearing (Article 438 CCP). The Court of Cassation has specified that such timeframe includes the entire trial phase; thus, the deadline for asking for an abbreviated trial is the moment in which the discussion is concluded.[243] If the judge considers it possible to adjudicate on the basis of the existing evidence, he or she pronounces the judgment. It is worthwhile to note that in case of an abbreviated trial before the judge of the preliminary hearing (GUP), this judge does not have the function of deciding on the committal for trial. On the contrary, as the judge of first degree, he must find the defendant guilty or not guilty, based on the evidence existing at that stage.

In case of abbreviated trial and direct citation (*citazione diretta*) (in case of a solo judge) (*supra*, paragraphs 464 et seq.), i.e., when there is no GIP or GUP phase, the request has to be filed with the trial judge during the hearing but before the trial is declared open (Article 452, paragraph 2 CCP).

The choice of the abbreviated trial does not require the consent of the public prosecutor and grants a reduction of the applicable punishment by one-third. The judgment issued from an abbreviated trial may be appealed either by the defendant or the public prosecutor.

Article 438, paragraph 5 CCP provides the possibility for the defendant to subordinate the request for abbreviated trial to a request to gather additional evidence. The judge will accept such request only if he deems the additional evidence necessary and if such activity would not compromise the speed of trial. It should be noted that only the defendant may make such request, while they may only ask for

243. Court of Cassation, First Section, Decision No. 755 of 14 Nov. 2002, published 11 Jan. 2003.

the admission of the evidence necessary to challenge those introduced by the defendant.[244]

B. Plea Bargaining

497. If both the defendant and the public prosecutor agree, they, may ask for a substitute sanction or a reduction of up to one-third of a pecuniary sanction, or a reduction of the detention, so long as when evaluated on the basis of the circumstances and reduced by one-third, does not exceed five years (*Patteggiamento, Applicazione di pena su richiesta*) (Article 444 CCP).[245] If the judge considers the proposed sentence appropriate, he or she applies the negotiated sentence.

Such special procedure is forbidden with regard to certain kind of offences and, with regard to the character of the defendant.

498. Plea bargaining is not allowed for those offences connected with pornography, paedophilia and sexual harassment (Articles 600*bis*–600*quinquies* and 609*bis*–609*octies* CCP), while with regard to the character of the defendant, such special procedure is forbidden for habitual offenders or professional criminals (e.g., hired assassins), and for those individuals who have criminal tendencies.

Furthermore, with respect to certain offences against public authority the request for a plea bargain is subject to the refund of the price or the profit of the offence (Article 444, paragraph 1*ter* CCP). This condition was inserted recently, when Article 444 CCP was amended by Law No. 69 of 27 May 2015 (on Anti-Corruption), introducing a new paragraph, 1*ter*. This condition applies to the following offences: Article 314 CP, embezzlement of public property by an officer; Article 317 of the CP, extortion; Article 318, corruption for the exercise of the function, Article 319 of the CP, corruption for an act contrary to official duties, Article 319*quarter* CP, inducement to give or promise undue advantages and Article 322*bis* CP; bribery of foreign public officials.

499. The advantages for the defendant are a reduction of up to one-third of the sentence, no court costs and no pre-trial security measures are applied.

500. In summary, a plea bargain may be requested provided that:

(1) the custodial punishment, taking into account all (mitigating and aggravating) applicable circumstances and reduced by one-third (for the choice of this proceeding), does not exceed five years of *arresto* or *reclusione*; and
(2) there is the consent of the public prosecutor. In the event the public prosecutor does not give his consent, the judge can accept a plea bargain when, at the end of the trial, he considers it just.

---

244. Court of Cassation, Sixth Section, Decision No. 6587 of 1 Mar. 2000, published 2 Jun. 2000.
245. The sanction limit has recently been increased from two years to the current five years by means of Law No. 134 of 12 Jun. 2003.

Even in the case all mentioned requirements are fulfilled, the judge can decide differently, being of the opinion that, on the basis of the judicial documents of the case:

(1) an acquittal judgment has to be issued; or
(2) the punishment agreed (by the public prosecutor and the defendant) is not adequate to the charges.

501. The demand of plea bargain can be filed until the end of the preliminary hearing, and if has been filed and denied in the preliminary hearing, it can be re-submitted at the opening of the trial of first degree.

The plea bargain, in particular, implies neither a confession nor an admission of hidden responsibilities. Consequently, convictions, administrative sanctions and disqualifications cannot derive from it, unless expressly provided for by law.

C. *Proceeding by Decree*

502. For less serious offences which are prosecutable ex officio, if the public prosecutor believes that only a pecuniary penalty should be applied, he or she can ask the judge for preliminary investigation (GIP) to decide the case by decree (*decreto penale di condanna*).

The judge must evaluate the admissibility of such request. If the GIP accepts the request, a decree is issued which contains the sentence. In such case, the law allows a decision to be made at the end of the preliminary investigations, without debate between the parties (*contraddittorio*). Therefore, the preliminary hearing phase is eliminated, and such abolition is allowed on the basis of an objective parameter: the applicability of a pecuniary sanction.

The proceeding by decree represents a useful instrument to reduce the overload of criminal cases.

503. The defendant who receives a conviction by decree requiring the payment of a fine or the person civilly responsible for paying the fine may oppose – either personally or through defence counsel – the decree within fifteen days from the service. The objection is to be filed with the clerk of the GIP who issued the decree or the clerk of the court or justice of the peace of the place where the person is located. (Article 461(1) CCP).

The opposition must set forth – under penalty of inadmissibility – the details and date of the decree and identify the judge who issued it. If not done previously, in the declaration, the opposing party must appoint defence counsel (Article 461(2) CCP).

In the application, the opposing party may request:

(1) payment of a fine (*oblazione*), when the offences committed are *contravvenzioni* punished only with *ammenda* or alternatively with *arresto* or *ammenda* (Article 162 and 162*bis* PC);
(2) immediate trial;
(3) abbreviated trial; or
(4) plea bargain. (Article 461(3) CCP).

504. If the opposition does not contain the requisite information, is not filed in time, or is submitted by an unauthorized person, the application is not admissible and the judge who issued the original decree, may execute it. The inadmissibility of the application may be appealed to the Court of Cassation (Article 461(4–6) CCP).

505. If the opposition is granted, an ordinary criminal law procedure is instituted. Where the opposing party has asked for an immediate trial, the court makes an order under Article 456, paragraphs 1, 3, and 5 CCP. If the opponent has asked for summary proceedings, the court fixed the hearing, giving notice at least five days to the public prosecutor, the accused, the defence lawyer and the victim. If the opponent has requested the application of a penalty under Article 444 CCP (i.e., a substitute sanction or fine), the court fixes a deadline for the public prosecutor to object, providing that the opposing party must serve the request and the decree on the prosecutor. If the prosecutor does not give consent within the prescribed period or the defendant has not made any request in the opposition application, the court makes an order for immediate trial. (Article 464(1) CCP).

506. Proceedings by decree are considered to be a special procedure of a mixed nature: it begins with a decision of the public prosecutor but it needs a manifestation of the defendant's will, even tacit, to conclude.

D. Immediate Trial

507. When there is conclusive evidence, the public prosecutor and the defendant can ask to pass immediately from the preliminary investigation phase to trial, without holding a preliminary hearing (i.e., *giudizio immediato*).

A defendant on whom a motion of committal for trial has been served can request an immediate trial when he considers his innocence evident and he desires a final acquittal verifying his innocence as soon as possible (Article 453 CCP). For this reason, the law does not provide for any reduction in penalty.

The request for immediate trial is a personal choice of the defendant; thus, the judge does not have to examine the request other than with respect of the time limit, namely three days before the date of the preliminary hearing. Once the judge has found such prerequisites, he issues the immediate trial decree in pursuance of Article 419, paragraph 6 CCP.

When a defendant chooses the immediate trial, he loses the chance to ask for an abbreviated trial or plea bargain because the law does not allow, in a short period, the defendant to cancel his decision to advance the trial stage which would lead to the end of trial before the debate.[246]

If the prosecutor considers the proof gathered against the defendant sufficient, he can ask the judge to suppress the preliminary phase (i.e., ask for an immediate trial). Nevertheless, the judge must agree in order for the public prosecutor to obtain the writ of subpoena for the immediate trial from the magistrate.

When the immediate trial is requested by the public prosecutor, the law provides for some conditions which impede the acceptance of the immediate trial.

508. The immediate trial should be refused only when:

(1) The defendant would not be able to testify to the judge about the facts on which the charge is based upon (Article 453, paragraph 1 CCP), in order to avoid that such procedure becomes inequitable.
(2) The judge deems it indispensable to maintain two related trials (Article 453, paragraph 2 CCP).[247]
(3) The request is not made by the public prosecutor within ninety days of registration of the *notitia criminis* (Article 454, paragraph 1 CCP).

E. Summary Trial

509. Summary trial (*giudizio direttissimo*) is allowed when an offender is caught red-handed (*in flagrante delicto*), or when he has confessed to the crime. The defendant appears directly before the court, although he or she has the right to apply for an abbreviated trial or a plea bargain.

There is no preliminary phase because in this case the evidence of guilt is so decisive that the search for further proof would serve no purpose. The difference from an immediate trial is that in the summary trial, the needed proof is clear, i.e., flagrancy or confession.

It is important also to distinguish between situations where the person charged has been arrested or situations where they are free. In the first case, the public prosecutor brings the defendant directly before the judge and the offence is orally and immediately charged to him (Article 450, paragraph 1 CCP). If the defendant has not been arrested, he receives a subpoena for trial (Article 450, paragraph 2 CCP).

510. The fact that the public prosecutor has the power to choose the summary trial does not prevent the judge from controlling the presence of the prerequisites

246. G. Conso & V. Grevi, *Compendio di procedura penale* 618 (Padova 2006).

247. Article 453(2) CCP: When the offence for which an immediate trial is requested is linked to other crimes which lack the conditions for an immediate trial, separate proceedings are carried out for the other crimes and against the other defendants, unless this would seriously undermine the investigation. If joinder is absolutely necessary, the ordinary proceeding prevails.

for the proceeding. For this reason, the law states that the request brief must be returned to the public prosecutor, if the request is found not to be in conformity to the requirements of law, so that the prosecutor may choose a different procedure (Article 452, paragraph 1 CCP).

F. Service of the Summons to Immediate Trial or Abbreviated Trial

511. The defendant who has been summoned to summary trial (*giudizio direttissimo*) may demand either an abbreviated trial (*giudizio abbreviato*) (Article 452, paragraph 1 CCP) or a plea bargain (Article 444 CCP).

IV. Personal Precautionary Measures

A. General Conditions of Applicability

512. Before a final conviction is issued, it is possible to restrict the freedom of the person who is the subject of the proceeding.

In order for the person to be subject to precautionary measures, there must be serious indications of guilt, no recognizable justifications for the offence, and the crime must not be barred by limitations.

Precautionary measures are available:

(1) When there are specific and binding needs related to the investigation of the offence; when there are concrete risks related to the acquisition or genuineness of the proof. The order must set forth the basis for the precautionary measures; otherwise, the order is subject to nullity. However, the refusal of the person under investigation or indictment to render declarations is not considered a risk or danger so as to support a precautionary measure.
(2) When the accused escapes or there exists a concrete and actual[248] risk of escape, and the judge maintains there could be a possible sentence of greater than two years of imprisonment.
(3) When, in light of circumstances of fact and considering the personality of the person under investigation or indictment, it is inferred – by behaviours or actual acts or previous convictions – that there is the actual risk he will commit serious crimes with the use of arms or other means of personal violence or offences of organized crime or of the same type of the pending proceeding. If the risk regards the commission of a crime of the same type of the pending proceeding,

248. Article 274, para. 1 (*b*) CCP has been recently amended by means of Law No. 47 of 16 Apr. 2015. In particular, the law requires that there is an imminent risk of escape; moreover it introduces a new provision which establishes that '*Situations of real and present danger cannot be deduced solely from the gravity of the offence's name for which [the suspect] is prosecuted.*'

the measures of protective custody are available only for those crimes for which the penalty of incarceration is not less than four years.[249]

B. *The Precautionary Measures*

513. The following precautionary measures are available:

(1) a prohibition to go abroad which prevents the accused from leaving the country without the permission of the judge;
(2) an obligation for the accused to present himself on a predetermined time and date before a specific office of the judicial police;
(3) the prohibition from access to or the obligation to stay in a specific location;
(4) house arrest and the accompanying measures whereby the judge orders the accused not to leave his home or another private lodging or clinic/place of assistance. This measure can be accompanied by the prohibition for the accused to communicate with persons other than those with whom they live or who are assisting him;
(5) protective custody in prison in which the judge issues an order instructing the judicial police to capture the accused and place him in protective custody.[250]

Along with those measures which limit personal liberty, there are also interdictive provisions which can consist of the temporary prohibition to carry out determined functions, or professional or entrepreneurial activities.

C. *Applicable Proceedings*

514. The precautionary measures are arranged upon request of the public prosecutor who presents the elements on which the request is founded.

They are adopted during the preliminary investigation by the judge for the preliminary investigations (GIP) and during the trial by the trial judge.

Not more than five days after the beginning of the implementation of the prison custody and not more than ten days from the beginning of whatever other precautionary or interdictive measure, the judge who has imposed the precautionary measure must hear from the accused to evaluate his defence and permanence, and whether the precautionary measure should be continued.

---

249. Article 274, para. 1 (*c*) CCP has been recently amended by means of Law No. 47 of 16 Apr. 2015, which establishes that '*Situations of real and present danger, even in relation to the personality of the accused, cannot be deduced solely from the gravity of the offence's name for which [the suspect] is prosecuted.*'

250. Law No. 47 of 16 Apr. 2015 introduced new rules concerning protective custody. In particular, according to Art. 275, para. 3 CCP, the judge can order to place the accused in protective custody only in case the interdictive or coercive measures appear unsuited. Moreover, the judge has to indicate the reasons for which he considers, in the actual case, the measure of house arrest unsuited (Art. 275, para. 3*bis* CCP).

The overall length of the protective custody, also considering the extension of Article 305 CCP cannot exceed the following terms:

(1) two years, when the proceeding is for a crime for which the law establishes a penalty of incarceration of not more than six years;
(2) four years, when the proceeding is for a crime for which the law establishes a penalty of incarceration of not more than twenty years, save the provisions of (a) above;
(3) six years, when the proceeding is for a crime for which the law establishes a penalty of life imprisonment or incarceration of more than twenty years.

D. *Challenging the Coercive Order*

515. Within ten days of the execution or notification of the disciplinary order that applies coercive measures, it is possible to make a request for review which is filed with a special section of the court of the main town of the district (i.e., the 'Review Court').

The grounds which sustain the review can be deposited during the hearing before the Review Court. The authority that has issued the coercive measure is advised immediately of the request and, in any case no later than the fifth day, the authority must transmit to the Review Court all of the examined acts used in the adoption of the measures and also all of the subsequent acts.

The Review Court must decide within ten days of receipt of the acts – confirming, reforming or annulling the coercive measure.

For all orders regarding precautionary measures different from the first filing, such as in the case of request of revocation, it is possible to appeal to the Review Court by a proceeding similar to that for review, but without having to indicate the terms.

Decisions or appeals of the Review Court may be appealed by both the accused and the public prosecutor to the Court of Cassation within ten days of the notification of the measures.

The motives must be set forth in the petition, save the right to indicated new motives in front of the Court of Cassation before the beginning of the discussion.

The Court of Cassation must decide within thirty days of receipt of the acts. Finally, it must be added that, where there is the assertion that the measure is in violation of the law, the accused may proceed directly to the Court of Cassation instead of going to the Review Court.

V. The Trial Phase

A. *Constitutional Principles of the Italian Process*

516. In the Italian criminal system, the trial can be considered as a result of a motion for committal for trial (*supra*, paragraph 472), immediate trial (*supra*, paragraphs 507–508) or abbreviated trial (*supra*, paragraph 496).

The trial opens a new phase which brings to a close the criminal investigation phase. It represents the principal moment of the criminal action, given the importance recognized to debate and in the light of the collection of evidence during the trial pursuant to the accusatory system adopted in the Italian criminal system. As known, the accusatory model is the opposite of the inquisitorial model: the accusatory model is based on the unilateral collection of evidence by the investigating body outside the trial and, thus, without the possibility of the parties to debate. In the accusatory system, on the contrary, the evidence gathering is carried out before a judge, during the hearing in the debate of parties.

Corollaries of such systems are:

(1) the principle of parity between the positions of prosecution and defence and the parties' right to object to the evidence. However, from a practical standpoint, the principle of parity has several exceptions, in particular, with reference to the transfer and utilization of evidence gathered by the public prosecutor (during the preliminary investigations) at trial when such evidence is qualified as unrepeatable. When such evidence is formed without the participation of the defence, there is a derogation from the principles of the 'adversary system', which have inspired the redaction of the CCP;
(2) the principle of 'orality' and 'immediacy' (*oralità-immediatezza*), in pursuance of Constitution Article 111, paragraph 4: orality must not be considered as a modality of collecting orally the evidence, but it must be deemed as a direct link between the judge and the proof (immediacy), because the one who gathers the evidence must decide the matter;[251]
(3) the principle of 'concentration' (*concentrazione*): the trial should be carried out in a sole hearing or a limited number of continuous hearings so that the final verdict is as close as possible to the reconstruction of the facts;
(4) the principle of the distinction between the functions of the judge and the prosecution in order to guarantee the judge's impartiality, which could be influenced by the construction of the crime hypothesis.

517. It is worthwhile to point out that Constitutional Law No. 2 of 23 November 1999 modified Article 111 of the Italian Constitution by introducing the 'fair trial' principle (*giusto processo*) and, in particular, the principle of 'debate in the collection of evidence' (*contraddittorio nella formazione della prova*).

Thus, there has been inserted into the cornerstone of Italian law a definition of fair trial which prior to 1999, was contained only in International Conventions, in particular the ECHR. The necessity of a fair trial, implies that the trial must grant parity between the positions of the prosecution and defence before a third party and impartial judge; the trial must have a reasonable duration; and the indicted must be informed in the shortest period and be in condition to defend himself and to examine the prosecution's witnesses who have made statements against him (Constitution Article 111).

251. G. Conso & V. Grevi, *Compendio di procedura penale* 654 (Padova 2006).

518. In order to give a general framework of the criminal procedure principles which are laid down by the Italian Constitution, in addition to Article 111, it is useful to mention:

(1) the guarantee of the 'right to defence', according to which 'defence is an inviolable right in any stage and degree of the proceeding' (Constitution Article 24);
(2) the principle of the 'natural judge', according to which the judge is predetermined by law (Constitution Article 25);
(3) the 'presumption of innocence', according to which the defendant is not considered guilty until a final conviction (Constitution Article 27);
(4) the 'compulsoriness of the prosecution of offences', according to which the public prosecutor is always obliged to prosecute any crime (Constitution Article 112); and
(5) the 'inviolability of personal freedom', according to which any form of abridgment of personal freedom (detention, inspection, search) can only be imposed on the basis of a grounded act of a judicial authority and only in the cases and with the modalities determined by law (Constitution Article 13).

519. As mentioned in paragraph 513 above, the provisions of the Italian Constitution are in line with the ECHR, and in particular with respect to Article 6 and such issues as the right to fair trial, the principle of debate and the inviolability of personal freedom (see *infra,* paragraphs 556 et seq.).

B. The Principle of Debate in the Collection of Evidence

520. The principle of debate in the collection of evidence can be considered as the most significant intervention made by means of the constitutional reform.

Such principle, nevertheless, has not been intended by the law in a restrictive sense. In particular, what is required is not the actual creation of the evidence in the debate, but that debate is guaranteed at trial on the evidential results gathered elsewhere.

In fact, given that a strict application of such principle would be difficult to fulfil, the Constitution itself provides for some exception to this rule stating '*the law regulates the cases in which the evidence collection is not carried out in the debate of parties in the hypothesis of defendant's consent, objective impossibility or proven illicit conduct*' (Constitution Article 111, paragraphs 4 and 5).

The first exception is needed to admit consensual special proceedings that otherwise would be unconstitutional because they imply a waiver of the debate and the utilization of the evidence collected during the preliminary investigations.

The second exception allows the utilization without debate of those investigative acts carried out in the course of the preliminary phase, which would not be repeatable in the trial phase (*supra*, paragraphs 451 et seq.).

Finally, the third exception is directed to save the value of those statements, even if not acquired in the debate, given by persons who suffered illicit pressures (i.e., violence or threat) to withdraw them.

521. The defendant is also entitled to the principle of debate under the ECHR (see also *infra,* paragraph 556), for example, pursuant to Article 6(3)(d), the accused is entitled to: '*examine or have examined witnesses against him and to obtain the attendance and examination of witnesses on his behalf under the same conditions as witnesses against him*'. The European Court of Human Rights has clarified that when a statement is used to find a conviction, the accused must be given an opportunity to challenge and question the witness. However, this does not mean that all pre-trial statements are inadmissible. The statements may be used so long as the rights of defence have been respected.[252] Moreover, according to the Court, not only does the term witness include victims, civil parties, experts and law enforcement officials, but it also includes co-accused.[253]

C. *The Acts of the Trial*

1. The Preliminary Acts

522. Generally speaking, the trial can be divided into three parts: (1) preliminary acts, (2) the hearing, and (3) the acts following the hearing (which includes the resolution and the final verdict). Book VII of the CCP is dedicated to the trial.

The preliminary acts phase goes from the end of the preliminary hearing (i.e., receipt of the committal for trial decree (Article 465 CCP) and runs until the start of the trial, which is generally considered to be the constituting of the parties (Article 484 CCP). During this phase, the President of the judging panel has jurisdiction. In addition to determining the hearing date, the President can acquire evidence that cannot be delayed in the same cases as the *incidente probatorio* (*supra*, paragraphs 451 et seq.), respecting the forms required by the trial.

It is also possible in such phase to pronounce an unappealable acquittal verdict if the fact cannot be prosecuted or if the crime is bared by limitations, or it is clear from the evidence, that there is no point in proceeding with the trial as the result is foreseeable. In this situation, the judge meets with the prosecutor and accused, and if they do not object, the judge issues a reasoned decision, and the accused is acquitted (Article 469 CCP). Article 469 CCP has been recently amended by means of Legislative Decree No. 28 of 16 March 2015, which introduced a new paragraph, 1*bis.* According to this provision it is also possible to pronounce an unappealable acquittal verdict if the defendant is not punishable under Article 131*bis* CP (which excludes punishment in case of weak facts[254]), provided that the injured party is heard by the judge in chambers, if appears. Within seven days from the hearing date,

252. *Isgrò v. Italy*, ECtHR judgment of 19 Feb. 1991, para. 34.
253. *Luca v. Italy*, ECtHR judgment of 7 Aug. 1996, para. 12.
254. This article – inserted by means of Article 1, para. 2, Legislative Decree No. 28 of 16 March 2015 – introduces a new legal institution: exclusion of punishment in case of particular tenuity of the fact. In particular, according to this provision the defendant cannot be punished if the maximum penalty for the crime does not exceed five years of imprisonment and the judge considers the committed actions not socially dangerous as the offence is not serious (considering the particular tenuity of the fact) and the defendant's behaviour is not habitual.

the parties can file their lists of witnesses, consultants and experts, indicating the matter on which they are to be questioned. (Article 468 CCP). This provision is aimed at avoiding that the parties attempt to introduce surprise evidence; hence, such lists have a 'discovery' function and are not filed in order to obtain the admittance of the evidence by the judge. If requested by one or both of the parties, the President of the judging panel may also summon witness as long as they are not forbidden by the law or trial economy (Article 468 paragraph 2 CCP).

It is also possible, pursuant to the right to cross-examination, to file a list of rebuttal witnesses outside the seven-day term (Article 468, paragraph 4 CCP).

2. The Hearing

523. The provisions related to the hearing are about the modality of its development, which must be pursuant to the principles of openness and efficiency. In accordance with the first principle, the judge can authorize – with the parties' consent – the filming or photographing of the hearing so long as there would not be prejudice to the regular development of the hearing.

Notwithstanding the principle of openness, particular importance is given to the privacy of the parties, witnesses and minors with regard to telephone tapping or testimony with regard to the particular object of it (Article 472, paragraphs 2 and 4 CCP).

524. Before starting the debate, the judge confirms the parties are present (Article 484 CCP).

With regard to the attendance of the defendant, Article 9 Law No. 67 of 28 April 2014 introduced considerable changes, abolishing the legal concept of 'contumacy' or contempt.[255] In particular, according to the amended Article 420*bis* CCP, if the defendant renounces expressly to attend the hearing, if it is presumed that the defendant has knowledge of the proceedings or if the defendant voluntarily avoided informing himself about the proceedings, the judge will not declare the contumacy, but he will declare the 'absence' of the defendant. The hearing will then go forward without the attendance of the defendant. If the defendant remains untraceable (after trying in vain to serve a notice), the judge issues a decision to stay. During the suspension, the judge can gather evidence which collection cannot be delayed. At the expiration of the first year, and each following years, the judge orders new searches

255. Previously the law gave particular relevance to contumacy in order to guarantee the defendant's right of defence. In particular, if, after careful review, it was believed the defendant's absence at the hearing was unintentional, e.g., because the notification failed or he or she had a just impediment, the defendant was not be held in contempt. If the judge declared the defendant in contempt, the hearing went forward without the attendance of the defendant, who was represented by the defence counsel, but he maintained the right to receive the notification concerning the final verdict so that he or she could eventually appeal it. Different from contempt was absence, which occurred when the defendant expressly declared that he or she did not plan on attending the hearing. In such case, the guarantees recognized in case of contempt did not apply, and the law considered the defendant as present.

of the defendant. As long as the absence lasts the statute of limitations period is suspended. On the contrary, if the search is a success, the judge fixes a new hearing and the proceedings start again. The defendant can make the request to be judged with the scheme of the abbreviated trial (*giudizio abbreviato*) or may demand a plea bargain (*patteggiamento*) (Article 420*quinquies* CCP).

a. The Preliminary Questions

525. After ascertaining the parties' attendance (see Article 484 CCP) and before opening the debate, the judge must resolve any preliminary issues. These are issues or questions that must be addressed in a pre-emptive way because they concern the institution of debate.

Preliminary questions generally fall into one of two groups. The first concerns the judge's competence, the validity of the acts and the attendance of private parties other than the defendant. The second group is related to the content of the file and the joinder or severance of proceedings.

The discussion on the preliminary questions must be fast and synthetic, and the decision must be made in the form of an order. If the preliminary issues are not timely considered, they are considered waived (Article 491 CCP).

b. The Opening Statements and Requests for Evidence

526. The opening statements represent an important and fundamental moment because the judge – at the beginning of the trial phase – knows nothing about the results of the preliminary investigations except for the criminal charge and the limited number of acts already included in the trial dossier. Such importance is underlined by the fact that the dismissal of the charge is not motivated, but it simply contains an indication of the means of proof and the facts to which they refer (Article 429 CCP).

Thus, the subject of the discussion is established by the parties *in limine litis* (i.e., at the start of the proceeding). In such phase, the judge does not have an active role, but he is limited to receiving the public prosecutor and defence counsel's initiatives.

527. First the public prosecutor, then defence counsel and counsel for any private parties identify the facts they intend to prove and the evidence they wish to be admitted (Article 493, paragraph 1 CCP).

The parties can also file written statements – especially in the substantial proceedings – to serve as memory aids for the judge (Article 121 CCP). It is important to note that such statements may not be a way of informing the judge about matters that the law does not allow him to know directly (e.g., the acts contained in the public prosecutor's dossier).[256]

528. The admission of evidence takes place at the end of the opening statements, and the judge decides by written order on the parties' requests. The general rules are established by Article 190 CCP and recalled by Article 495 CCP.

256. G. Conso & V. Grevi, *Compendio Di Procedura Penale* 687 (Padova 2006).

Article 190 CCP states that evidence is admitted only upon the parties' request and in exceptional cases, ex officio. It also provides that the judge must decide on such requests immediately and expressly; thus, he can neither suspend his judgment nor simply imply the reasoning for his decision.

529. With regard to the waiver of evidence already admitted following a party's request, Article 495, paragraph 4*bis* CCP solves the debate regarding whether the party has such freedom to waive or the principle of the trial acquisition applies. Once evidence is admitted by the judge, it becomes usable by all parties and cannot be waived only by the party who requested it. The mentioned provision states that such waiver is possible as long as there is the other parties' consent.

530. The judgment on the admission of evidence must be carried out on the basis of Articles 187 and 190 CCP.

531. The parties are also given the possibility to file requests for evidence not included in the list filed before the trial (Article 493, paragraph 2 CCP), if the party demonstrates such omission was not culpable. Article 493, paragraph 3 CCP also provides that the parties can arrange for selected acts contained in the public prosecutor's dossier and the results of the defence counsel's investigations be included in the court file. Once such acquisition is made, by reading the act, the latter becomes directly usable for the final decision.

c. The Regulation of Evidence in the Trial Phase

532. Article 496 CCP defines the order of evidence, establishing that first evidence requested by the public prosecutor is gathered and then the evidence sought by other parties.

533. Articles 497 and 498 CCP provide rules regarding the direct examination of witnesses (the so-called *esame diretto*) in the trial by stating that once the party who requested the examination concludes his questioning, the other parties can cross-examine the witness (the so-called *controesame*). With regard to the examination modalities, Article 499 CCP provides that the questions must refer to specific facts without giving the witness the opportunity to discourse about his experience. The question must be pertinent, in pursuance of Article 194, paragraph 1 CCP, which requires that the examination must regard the facts which constitute the object of the proof (see *infra,* §4, Part III, A).

534. In the course of the examination, questions which could damage the sincerity of the answers (Article 499, paragraph 2 CCP) and leading questions, i.e., those tending to suggest the answer (Article 499, paragraph 3 CCP) are prohibited.

The latter are forbidden only in the direct examination and during cross-examination, which has more leeway as it is the means of testing the witness' credibility.[257] In any event, the examination must be done in a respectful manner, and it is up to the president to insure this is done (Article 499, paragraph 4 CCP).

During the examination, the president also intervenes in order to guarantee the pertinence of questions, the genuineness of the answers, the fairness of the examination, and the correctness of objections, ordering, if necessary, the exhibition of the minutes of trial which contain the statements used for the objections (Article 499, paragraph 6 CCP).

535. A particular regulation is provided for cross-examination. It states that the examination must be carried out directly by the public prosecutor and defence counsel. The president has power of direction and surveillance.

After the witnesses' examination, follow the expert witnesses and the examination of technical consultants. Thereafter, private parties who have made an express request or gave their consent are examined in pursuance of Article 502 CCP.

The defendant can choose whether or not to be examined. It is worthwhile to point out that Constitutional Court Decision No. 361 of 1998 states that the defendant cannot refuse to be examined when he is questioned about another person's liability, so that in the event he is not present for examination, the judge can order his forced presence. Nevertheless, the defendant maintains the right to remain silent.

It also must be noted that in the Italian criminal system, differently from other countries, the defendant may say whatever he feels fit for his defence and may lie, since no examination under oath is provided for by the Italian Criminal Procedure System.

536. With regard to examination of the defendant on his own facts, the CCP states that he can always refuse to be examined, but in such case previous statements given to the public prosecutor, judicial police, GIP or GUP can be read (Article 513, paragraph 1 CCP).

537. Also during the examination on his facts, the defendant maintains the right to refuse to answer, and in such case, the CCP does not provide for the reading of previous statements.

Alternatively to the examination, the defendant can always release spontaneous statements in every stage and degree of the proceeding (Article 494 CCP).

d. The Powers of the Judge in the Gathering of Evidence

538. The judge can, on his own initiative, indicate new evidence themes or expand existing examinations (Article 506, paragraph 1 CCP).

The president can also ask questions to the witnesses after the parties' examination and cross-examination is completed (Article 506, paragraph 2 CCP).

Once the gathering of evidence is finished, the college, where necessary, can order the acquisition of new means of proof (Article 507 CCP). In an accusatory

257. G. Conso & V. Grevi, *Compendio Di Procedura Penale* 714 (Padova 2006).

system, such power of the judge should be considered as an integration of the parties' initiatives. In fact, an intervention by the judge could benefit the public prosecutor who did not gather enough evidence, but the united sections of the Court of Cassation have clarified that the power of the judge exists even when there has been no previous collection of evidence.[258]

Thus, the function of the judge cannot be considered as merely additional, but it finds a limit in the fact that the relevance of the proof results from the trial dossier. In this case, Article 151 the 'implementing provisions' of the CCP states that the examination must be started by the president in order to verify whether the evidence, by reason of its content, should be attributed to the prosecution or to the defence and to establish consequently who has to carry out the examination and the counter-examination.

e. Modifications of the Criminal Charge

539. One of the most important principles applicable to the trial phase is that there must be a correspondence between the criminal charge and the sentence. In other words, the judge could not decide on a fact which was not communicated to the defendant because the latter must be in condition to prepare adequately his strategy of defence. If there is no such correspondence, the judge must decline to decide and return the acts to the public prosecutor so that he can formulate a new criminal charge (Article 521, paragraph 2 CCP). In such hypothesis, the proceeding starts again from the beginning.

But it is also possible to modify the criminal charge contained in the committal for trial decree (issued in pursuance of Article 429 CCP, see *supra*, in §2, Part I, C, d) in the course of the trial phase, in particular during the collection of evidence. It is possible to infer that the criminal charge is perfectible in order to guarantee the continuation of the trial without the necessity of returning to the preliminary phase, so long as the fact is in substance the same already charged.[259]

540. According to Article 516 CCP, only the public prosecutor has the power to ask the president to modify the charge and notify the defendant or serve him if the defendant is absent (Article 520 CCP).

When the supplementary charges enlarge the scope of the matters to be discussed in the trial, the public prosecutor must personally notify the defendant. Additional charges are limited to connected crimes (by reason of *concorso formale* or continuation), or when an aggravating circumstance emerges during the trial (Article 517 CCP).

A different regulation is adopted with regard to the case in which the fact resulting from the trial phase is completely different from the one contained in the criminal charge. The CCP, in order to distinguish such hypothesis from the case of the supplementary charge, uses the words 'different fact' and 'new fact'. The first one can coexist with the original charge, while the second one is incompatible with it.

258. Decision of the United Criminal Sections of the Court of Cassation No. 11227 of 1992.
259. G. Conso & V. Grevi, *Compendio Di Procedura Penale* 722 (Padova 2006).

According to Article 518, paragraph 2 CCP, the new fact can be charged to the defendant by the public prosecutor with the authorization of the president only if the defendant gives his consent and provided there would be no prejudice to the trial velocity. If no charge is made to the defendant for the new fact, the new crime can be prosecuted separately.

In every case, when a modification of the criminal charge is made during the trial phase, the defendant can ask for a new defence term (i.e., a term for preparing a defence), and new means of proof may be admitted (Article 519, paragraph 2 CCP).

When the criminal charge needs to be modified in one of the cases provided by Articles 516, 517 and 518 CCP, the judge must give the file case back to the public prosecutor, who will have to formulate the criminal charge again. The same regulation also applies when the judge deems the fact judged in the decision different from the one contained in the criminal charge, and no modification has been made by the public prosecutor or when the criminal charge has been modified incorrectly (Article 521, paragraphs 2 and 3 CCP). Such power of the judge could be considered contrary to the accusatory system. Nevertheless, it is necessary if one considers that otherwise the judge would be obliged to pronounce an acquittal for the old fact and the sentence, once final, would preclude a new trial on the correct charge because of the *ne bis in idem* (i.e., 'not twice for the same') principle.[260]

3. The Acts Following the Hearing

a. The Final Discussion and the Final Verdict

541. Article 523 CCP provides the modalities for the discussion. In particular, it states that once the evidence gathering is over, the public prosecutor and, then (in this order) the civil party, the person civilly liable, the person obliged for the payment of the pecuniary sanction, and the defendant's legal counsel formulate their pleadings. The discussion is directed by the judge (or president in case of a panel), who must prevent repetitions and useless digressions (Article 523, paragraph 3 CCP).

The public prosecutor and the other parties' counsel can reply to the adversarial statements just once, and in every case, the defendant and his counsel are entitled to be the last to speak (Article 523, paragraph 5 CCP). The discussion cannot be interrupted to gather new evidence, unless it is deemed absolutely necessary, and if such eventuality occurs, the judge acts in pursuance of Article 507 CCP.

Once the discussion is completed, the resolution of the judge must immediately follow in pursuance of Article 525 CCP – which also fixes the principle of the immutability or continuity of the court – according to which only judges who took part in the inquiry in court are competent to reach and pronounce the judgment.

The final judgment containing the conviction of the accused is made up of two parts: the so-called *dispositivo* (the actual decision of the court) and the reasons for the decision.

According to Article 544 CCP, immediately after the resolution the president draws up and signs the *dispositivo*.

---

260. G. Conso & V. Grevi, *Compendio Di Procedura Penale* 727 (Padova 2006).

542. With regard to the reasons of the judgment, it is important to stress that they can be given immediately where the case is not complicated. When an immediate verdict is not possible, the court must state its reasons within fifteen days from the pronouncing of the sentence (Article 544, paragraph 2 CCP) and within ninety days in cases of particular complexity due to the number of parties or to the number or seriousness of charges (Article 544, paragraph 3 CCP).

b. The Sentence: Content and Requisites

i. Acquittal

543. Article 546 CCP describes the verdict requisites including the indication of the parties' pleadings, the evidence on which the decision is based, and the reasons why the judge did not deem reliable the contrary evidence. The absence of the reasoning the incompleteness of the *dispositivo* and the absence of signature cause the invalidity of the sentence (Article 546, paragraph 3 CCP).

544. With regard to the content of the sentence, the CCP disciplines, first of all, an acquittal on the merits (Article 530 CCP), i.e., when:

(1) the fact does not exist;
(2) the defendant did not commit the fact;
(3) the fact does not represent a crime;
(4) the fact is not provided by the law as a crime; or
(5) the crime has been carried out by a non-chargeable or non-punishable person. The judge must pronounce an acquittal verdict also when special circumstances justify the defendant's conduct or excuse him (*causa di giustificazione*) (*supra*, paragraphs 203 et seq.). The basis for the acquittal must be expressly specified in the *dispositivo.*

In particular, the broadest acquittals are those which occur when the fact does not exist or the defendant did not commit the fact. In effect, both of these bases entirely deny the historical background of the accusation.[261] An acquittal sentence issued on such basis is consequently unappealable by the defendant (Article 593, paragraph 2 CCP).

The fact does not represent a crime when the fact has been actually carried out by the defendant but one element of the offence is missing or there were grounds of justification.

On the contrary, the conclusion that the fact has been carried out by a non-chargeable or non-punishable person – presupposes the commission of a crime and its ascertainment.

A fact is not provided by the law as a crime when the criminal charge does not correspond to any criminal provision (e.g., an *abolitio criminis* – abolition of the crime – has occurred).

261. G. Conso & V. Grevi, *Compendio Di Procedura Penale* 729 (Padova 2006).

The judge must pronounce an acquittal verdict also where the evidence is missing, insufficient or contradictory (Article 530, paragraph 2 CCP). In particular, the first two hypotheses involve a lapse of evidence, while the third situation regards the case when both prosecution and defence have evidence; however, neither party's evidence prevails over the other, in application of the *presumptio innocentiae* principle (Article 27 of the Constitution).

545. The CCP also regulates acquittals deriving from non-prosecutability (the so-called *improcedibilità*) of the action, i.e., when the criminal action should not have been started or carried on, or from the extinction of the crime. Both cases lead to a non-suit sentence (Articles 529 and 531 CCP). However, an acquittal on the merits must be pronounced when it results from the evidence of the case (Article 129, paragraph 2 CCP).

ii. Conviction

546. Article 533 CCP regulates the conviction, which must be issued when it has been proven that the defendant is guilty of the fact charged beyond any reasonable doubt.

In the conviction, the judge is also to award the damages (if any) that must be paid to the civil party (Article 538, paragraph 2 CCP).

§3. The Legal Position of the Accused and the Civil Party

I. Introductory Remarks

547. One of the most important foundations of Italian Criminal Procedure is that a criminal offence always constitutes a violation of the public order and in many cases, an infringement of someone's rights. This means that an offence not only creates a public claim against the offender with a view to his punishment, but also causes a private claim against him with a view to compensation for the losses arising from the offence.

This fundamental distinction leads first of all to questions about the relationship between these two claims. In order to answer to these questions, it is important to depart from the proposition that the public claim and the institution of criminal proceedings are independent from the private claim, as explicitly stated by Article 75 CCP.

In fact, this article states that the civil claim remains before the civil court when it is not transferred into the criminal proceeding when the plaintiff has failed to establish himself timely as a civil party in the criminal action (Article 75, paragraph 2 CCP) (see *infra*, paragraph 559). It is inferable that the civil claim and the criminal proceeding can proceed in perfect autonomy.[262]

Moreover, the prosecution can start an inquiry when no loss has been suffered or no victim formulates a claim for the compensation of a loss. Conversely, a victim

262. G. Conso & V. Grevi, *Compendio di procedura penale* 121 (Padova 2006).

has the right to bring his case before a civil court even if the prosecution takes no action against the potential offender.

However, Article 75 CCP also contains a provision, which expresses a close connection between the two claims. In fact, it states that if a private claim is filed separately before a civil jurisdiction, after its filing in the criminal proceeding or after a first degree verdict has been issued, the civil action will be suspended as long as no final decision has been made with regard to the previously opened criminal proceeding (Article 75, paragraph 3 CCP).

A link between the two claims is also inferable from the provision contained in the first paragraph of Article 75 CCP, which states that '*the claim filed before a civil court can be transferred before the criminal court until a final civil verdict is obtained, even if it is appealable. The exercise of such faculty entails the renunciation to the civil trial*'.

It is worthwhile to take into account that in recent years the legal position of the suspect/accused and of the plaintiff/civil party has received an increasing amount of attention. As far as the suspect/accused is concerned, this attention is predominantly the result of the growing case law of the European Court of Human Rights (see *infra*, paragraph 559).

II. The Legal Position of the Accused

548. In order to explain the rights of the accused at trial, a starting point is represented by the ECHR of 4 November 1950) as amended by the fourteenth protocol.

In fact, for all purposes, this safeguard is part of the Italian Legal System in that no national law can conflict with its provisions. (The ECHR has been signed by all members of the Council of Europe and has been adopted by Italy.)[263] The ECHR provides that persons have the right to an independent and impartial trial in an impartial tribunal and the right to life, liberty, safety and property (Articles 1, 2, 5, and 6 ECHR).

The ECHR also states that the accused has the right to a public trial, with some exceptions, within an adequate period of time, to be informed of the nature and content of the accusation, to cross-examine witnesses for the prosecution, to subpoena witnesses for the defence, the right to counsel, and the right to be presumed innocent. The Italian Constitution also provides for general principles such as the inviolable rights to liberty and counsel, and the equality of all citizens before the law.[264]

A. *The Provisions in the CCP*

549. Principles similar to those found in the Italian Constitution and the ECHR can also be found in many sections of the PC and Code of Penal Procedure. For

263. The Fourteenth Protocol of the ECHR was ratified in Italy by Law No. 280 of 15 Dec. 2005.
264. Constitution, Arts 3, 13 and 24; Arts 5 and 6 ECHR.

instance, the accused has the right to be fully informed of the charge and the existing evidence against him or her, and to be informed of the source of the evidence, such as the identity of the claimant(s), unless this would be detrimental to the investigation. The accused also has the right to remain silent and is considered not guilty until a final sentence has been pronounced. Uncertainty about the guilt of the accused due to insufficient or contradictory evidence can result in a judgment of full acquittal. The accused also has the right to be present at trial, to confront opposing witnesses, and to have all witnesses cross-examined by the defence attorney.[265]

550. In addition, the accused has the right to be tried by a judicial panel or by a single judge, depending on the type of court, according to territorial jurisdiction where the crime has been committed. The accused cannot be removed from the 'natural judge', meaning, from the judge who is competent to try the case, under law. The accused may not be tried twice for the same crime and has the right to be tried in a fair trial, that is, by an independent and impartial tribunal.[266]

551. With regard to the assistance to the accused, he has the right to select and employ a defence attorney in order to get legal assistance and to produce evidence in his or her defence at any stage of judicial proceedings, including the arrest and investigation stage. If the accused does not designate a defence attorney, a counsel is appointed by the court. This applies to all offences of all types of severity. The law states that indigents must be provided with counsel. The local association provides a roster of available attorneys who are legally bound to provide defence counsel. A bar association exists in each district; therefore, many rosters of attorneys are available. If eligible, the accused can select and employ a defence attorney at State expense, under law. Eligibility is determined on the basis of personal or family income (*supra*, paragraph 67).[267]

B. The Freedoms of the Citizens in the European Convention of Human Rights

552. The ECHR contains several significant provisions with respect to the legal position of the suspect and the accused.

553. The first of these is found in Article 3 which sets forth that no one shall be subjected to torture or to inhuman or degrading treatment or punishment. As found in the 1978 case *Ireland v. United Kingdom*,[268] the European Court of Human Rights held that this right also exists in pre-trial proceedings, and in particular, with respect to a suspect or detainee's deprivation of liberty by the police.

The provision of Article 3 is expressed in unqualified and absolute terms and, contrary to many other rights and freedoms guaranteed by the ECHR, there are no

265. Articles 65, 474, 486, 498 and 530 CCP; Constitution Art. 27.
266. Article 649 CCP and Constitution, Arts 25 and 27.
267. Articles 97 and 190 CCP; Constitution Art. 24, para. 3; Official Gazette of 30 Jul. 1990.
268. *Ireland v. the United Kingdom*, ECtHR judgment of 18 Jan. 1978.

exceptions to the prohibition,[269,270] including even in the most difficult situations like the fight against terrorism[271] or organized crime.[272] Consequently, prohibition of torture or of inhuman or degrading treatment 'enshrines one of the fundamental values of the democratic societies making up the Council of Europe'.[273] However, it must be noted that not all ill treatment is reviewable under Article 3: the treatment must attain a certain level of severity,[274] which is determined by the Member State on a case-by-case basis.[275] In making this determination, '*all the circumstances of the case [must be considered], such as the duration of the treatment, its physical or mental effects and, in some cases, the sex, age and state of health of the victim*'.[276]

554. The right to liberty and security of person is established in Article 5 of the ECHR. Specifically, under paragraph 1 of Article 5:

> (1) Everyone has the right to liberty and security of person. No one shall be deprived of his liberty save in the following cases and in accordance with a procedure prescribed by law:
> (a) the lawful detention of a person after conviction by a competent court;
> (b) the lawful arrest or detention of a person for non-compliance with the lawful order of a court or in order to secure the fulfilment of any obligation prescribed by law;
> (c) the lawful arrest or detention of a person effected for the purpose of bringing him before the competent legal authority on reasonable suspicion of having committed an offence or when it is reasonably considered necessary to prevent his committing an offence or fleeing after having done so.

555. The third important provision regarding the legal position of the suspect and the accused is Article 8, which gives every person the right to respect for his

269. *Ireland v. the United Kingdom*, ECtHR judgment of 18 Jan. 1978, para. 163:

> The Convention prohibits in absolute terms torture and inhuman and degrading treatment or punishment, irrespective of the victim's conduct. Unlike most of the substantive clauses of the Convention and of Protocols Nos. 1 and 4, Article 3 makes no provision for exceptions and, under Article 15(2), there can be no derogation therefore even in the event of a public emergency threatening the life of the nation.

270. C. Ovey, *Prohibition of refoulement: the Meaning of Article 3 ECHR*, 2, www.ecre.org/elenahr/art3.pdf.
271. See *Chahal v. United Kingdom*, ECtHR judgment of 15 Nov. 1996 and *Aksoy v. Turkey*, ECtHR judgment of 18 Dec. 1996.
272. See *Martinez Sala et al. v. Spain*, ECtHR judgment of 2 Nov. 2004.
273. *Soering v. United Kingdom*, ECtHR judgment of 7 Jul. 1989.
274. Harris, O'Boyle & Warbrick, *Law of European Convention on Human Rights* 56 (Butterworths, 1995).
275. M. Addo & N. Grief, *Is There a Policy behind the Decisions and Judgments Relating to Article 3 of the ECHR?* Eur. L. Rev. 188 (1995).
276. *Ireland v. the United Kingdom*, ECtHR judgment of 18 Jan. 1978.

private and family life, his home and his correspondence. Public authorities – including judicial and enforcement – cannot infringe on these rights except when it:

> *[i]s in accordance with the law and is necessary in a democratic society in the interests of national security, public safety or the economic well-being of the country, for the prevention of disorder or crime, for the protection of health or morals, or for the protection of the rights and freedoms of others.*

C. *The Rights of the Defence in the European Convention of Human Rights*

556. For a defendant, Article 6 of the ECHR is the source of significant rights:

(1) In the determination of his civil rights and obligations or of any criminal charge against him, everyone is entitled to a fair and public hearing within a reasonable time by an independent and impartial tribunal established by law. Judgment shall be pronounced publicly by the press, and public may be excluded from all or part of the trial in the interest of morals, public order or national security in a democratic society, where the interests of juveniles or the protection of the private life of the parties so require, or the extent strictly necessary in the opinion of the court in special circumstances where publicity would prejudice the interests of justice.
(2) Everyone charged with a criminal offence shall be presumed innocent until proved guilty according to law (*presumptio innocentiae*).
(3) Everyone charged with a criminal offence has the following minimum rights:
   (a) to be informed promptly, in a language which he understands and in detail, of the nature and cause of the accusation against him;
   (b) to have adequate time and the facilities for the preparation of his defence;
   (c) to defend himself in person or through legal assistance of his own choosing or, if he has not sufficient means to pay for legal assistance, to be given it free when the interests of justice so require;
   (d) to examine or have examined witnesses against him and to obtain the attendance and examination of witnesses on his behalf under the same conditions as witnesses against him;
   (e) to have the free assistance of an interpreter if he cannot understand or speak the language used in court.

557. Under Article 6(1), the accused is entitled to a fair trial within *a reasonable amount of time*. With respect to the length of judicial proceedings, over the past thirty years, Italy has been the subject of more complaints than almost any other Member State. In fact, in 2009, there were 2,183 cases against Italy concerning the excessive length of judicial proceedings. In response to this situation, the European Committee of Ministers issued Interim Resolution CM/ResDH (2009) 42 regarding Execution of the judgments of the European Court of Human Rights concerning the excessive length of judicial proceedings in Italy. While this interim resolution commended Italy's progress in certain areas, the resolution also commented on the continuing problem and issued a series of recommendations for alleviating the situation.

558. Other cases against Italy before the European Court of Human Rights include those concerning such issues as the unfairness of criminal proceedings where the applicants were sentenced *in absentia* to several years' imprisonment;[277] the monitoring or limiting of prisoners' correspondence and rights in mafia-related cases[278] and the right to interrogate witnesses. However, the Court has also held that the right to a fair trial under Article 6 does not guarantee a right to take part in an appeal hearing, if the applicant has participated in earlier hearings and the proceedings were of an adversarial nature.[279,280]

III. The Legal Position of a Civil Party

559. The 1988 CCP encourages civil claims to be brought before the Civil Court in order to avoid delaying the criminal proceeding with further matters to be judged. In spite of this, the Italian criminal system provides a wide range of guarantees for the civil party, as such party is considered quite a legitimate opposition to the defendant.[281]

Among the potential parties to a criminal proceeding, are those civil parties whose participation is justified by the fact that they suffered losses for a particular

277. *Sejdovic v. Italy*, ECtHR Grand Chamber judgment of 3 Jan. 2006; *Kollcaku v. Italy*, ECtHR judgment 2 Aug. 2007; *Pititto v. Italy*, ECtHR judgment of 6 Dec. 2007; *Zunic v. Italy*, ECtHR judgment of 21 Dec. 2006. In these cases, the ECtHR found there had been denial of justice, first, because it had not been shown that the applicants had been fugitives from justice or had declined to appear or to defend themselves, and second, having been informed of the judgments against them, the defendants had not been able to go before a court to determine the validity of the accusations against them. In Art. 175 CCP (as amended by Legislative Decree No. 17 of 21 Feb. 2005) sets forth, the parameters of the remedy referred to as *istanza di rimessione in termini* (application for suspension of the time limit for appeal against sentence). Under this provision, a judgment pronounced *in absentia* may be reopened upon request of the accused, and thus it is possible to appeal against judgments rendered *in absentia* at first-instance even if the normal deadlines have expired. However, there are two exceptions to this rule: where the accused has had 'effective knowledge' of the proceedings against him or of the judgment, and when he or she has wilfully decided not to appear or to appeal.
278. These cases concern the special prison regime provided by Art. 41*bis* of Law No. 354 of 26 Jul. 1975 (as amended by Law No. 279 of 2002) relating to prisoners convicted of mafia-related offences. See *Messina Antonio No. 2 v. Italy*, ECtHR judgment of 28 Sep. 2000; *Ganci v. Italy*, ECtHR judgment of 30 Oct. 2003; *Musumeci Carmelo v. Italy*, ECtHR judgment of 11 Jan. 2005; *Bifulco v. Italy*, ECtHR judgment of 8 Feb. 2005; *Gallico v. Italy*, ECtHR judgment of 28 Jun. 2005; *Argenti v. Italy*, ECtHR judgment of 10 Nov. 2005; *Salvatore v. Italy*, ECtHR judgment of 6 Dec. 2005; *Viola v. Italy*, ECtHR judgment of 29 Jun. 2006; *Asciutto v. Italy*, ECtHR judgment of 27 Nov. 2007; *Papalia v. Italy*, ECtHR judgment of 4 Dec. 2007 and *Enea v. Italy*, ECtHR judgment of 17 Nov. 2009.
279. See *Hermi v. Italy,* ECtHR Grand Chamber judgment of 18 Oct. 2006.
280. See also *Bracci v. Italy*, ECtHR judgment of 13 Oct. 2005 and *Majadallah v. Italy*, ECtHR judgment of 19 Oct. 2006.
281. G. Di Chiara, *Parte Civile*, in *Digesto delle discipline penalistiche* 244, 245 (Torino 1995).

offence, so the attendance is aimed at obtaining restitution or the recovering of damages (Article 185 PC). The Code explicitly states that not only is the direct victim a civil party, but also successors, legal persons and companies. However, it is important to distinguish between a victim/offended party and a damaged party, although they are often the same. For example, in the case of a homicide, the person killed would be considered the victim, while surviving family members might be considered damaged parties, if they were directly affected by the act. It is also imperative to note that for certain crimes, such negligent disaster under 434 PC, there are no victims, only damaged parties.

Under Italian law, an application to join the proceedings as a civil party may only be made once the accused has been committed for trial. Prior to this point, the injured parties have very limited powers to participate in the preliminary investigation. For example, if a prosecutor were to request a technical examination which could not be repeated under Article 360 CCP, the injured party is limited to requesting the public prosecutor apply to the judge for the immediate production of evidence. Only if the application is granted, may the injured party request the investigating judge question the experts.

Once a civil party is admitted, they are entitled to a determination of their rights within a reasonable time.[282]

If the accused is not committed for trial, the injured party no longer has recourse in the criminal courts, but must pursue his claim in a civil tribunal. Moreover, if the injured party's legitimate interests were protected during the preliminary investigation (i.e., the investigative activities were independently and properly carried out and the injured party had sufficient access to the procedures).[283]

A. General Observations

560. Legitimatio ad causam is the identification of those subjects who may be a civil party.

Article 74 CCP states that a civil action can be filed by a subject, hence also a collective body, who seeks the recovery of suffered damages (both patrimonial and non-patrimonial) or who wants to obtain restitution. In particular, such claims concern all disadvantages that arise from injuries resulting from the wrongful act, i.e., the criminal offence concerned. It is not a prerequisite of the constitution of a civil

282. ECHR Art. 3(1). See also *Calvelli and Ciglio v. Italy,* ECtHR Grand Chamber judgment of 17 Jan. 2002.

283. See *Giuliani and Gaggio v. Italy*, ECtHR Grand Chamber judgment of 24 Mar. 2011. *Giuliani* involved the death of the applicants' son and brother during the G8 summit held in Genoa from 19 Jul. 2001. The victim was killed by the *Carabinieri* during an outbreak of violence. Criminal proceedings were brought against the two *Carabinieri* officers most closely involved. Based on the preliminary investigation, the investigating judge discontinued the proceedings, and the applicants filed a claim before the European Court of Human Rights. The Grand Chamber found there had been no violations of the ECHR, and in particular Art. 2 (right to life); Art. 3 (prohibition against inhuman or degrading treatment); Art. 6 (right to a fair hearing); Art. 13 (right to an effective remedy); or Art. 38 (adversarial examination of the case).

party to be the victim. For example, a creditor could be a civil party when his debtor died as a consequence of the behaviour of the accused person.[284]

The civil party, as well as parties civilly liable and parties obliged for any pecuniary sanctions, need defence counsel with a special power of attorney. Additionally, the civil party must file a statement setting forth the reasons justifying his claims (*fumus boni iuris*) (Article 78 CCP).

However, Article 79 sets a statute of limitations for the constitution of civil parties. The initial term coincides with the preliminary hearing (given that Article 79 is quite generic, it is implied that such term starts with the exercise of the criminal action)[285] while the term concludes with the fulfilment of the Court's ascertainment of the parties at trial; thus, the civil action must be filed before the discussion of the preliminary questions.

Another question relates to the persons against whom one may constitute oneself a civil party. A civil party cannot only take action against principals and accomplices, but also against those who are legally liable to them in a given case.

In fact, Article 185 PC individuates the subjects obliged to pay damages arising from a certain offence with *the author and the persons who, in pursuance of civil laws, are responsible to him* (person civilly liable, the so-called *responsabile civile*) (Article 185, paragraph 2 PC). For example, a company might be civilly liable for the criminal actions of its employee.

561. The civil law sets out those who are considered liable when a crime is committed by another subject, by reason of their relationship (e.g., Article 2048 of the Italian Civil Code concerning parental liability; Article 2054 of the Italian Civil Code concerning the liability of the vehicle owner for damages caused by the driver).

562. Italian law also provides for another case in which someone may be called in the course of a criminal trial in order to fulfil the pecuniary sanctions against the guilty (person civilly obliged for the payment of the pecuniary sanction, the so-called *civilmente obbligato per la pena pecuniaria*) when the latter is insolvent (Article 89 CCP). For example, a company might also be liable for any pecuniary penalties stemming from criminal actions of its employee.

563. In the CCP, the legal position of a plaintiff as a civil party is not supported by a complex system of principles in relation to his rights, freedoms and duties: criminal procedure has always been focused on the suspect and the accused.

B. The Role of the Private Party in the Preliminary Phase and in the Trial Phase

564. During the preliminary investigation – thus prior to the preliminary hearing – the victim has certain rights. According to Article 90 CCP, '*the victim shall*

284. For this example, see F. Cordero, *Procedura Penale* 270, 271 (Milano 2006).
285. See G. Riccio & G. Spangher, *La Procedura Penale* 116 (Napoli 2002).

exercise the rights and powers expressly afforded to them by law and may furthermore, at any stage of the proceedings, submit pleadings and, except in cassation proceedings, request the inclusion of evidence'. The victim may:

(1) appoint a legal representative for the exercise of the rights and powers afforded to them (Article 101 CCP);
(2) appoint experts when the public prosecutor orders examinations or any other technical operation calling for a specific competence and the prosecutor may not refuse to cooperate (Article 359, paragraph 1, CCP). Moreover, where the examination concerns persons, objects or places in a State subject to alteration, the public prosecutor shall inform the accused, the injured party and the lawyers without delay of the date, time and place designated for the briefing of the experts and of the possibility of appointing experts (Article 360(1) CCP). And, any lawyers or experts appointed shall have the right to attend the briefing of the experts, participate in the examinations, make observations and express reservations (Article 360, paragraph 1 CCP);
(3) request the public prosecutor to apply for the immediate production of evidence under Article 392 CCP.[286] If the public prosecutor refuses the request, he or she shall give reasons for the decision and serve it on the injured party. (Article 394 CCP); and
(4) object to dismissal of the proceedings (Article 409 CCP).

565. With respect to all private parties (i.e., not only the victims, but civilly liable parties and parties civilly liable for the payment of sanctions), as the introduction of a civil claim in the criminal proceeding brings the necessity of proving further matters and since the civil party carries the burden of proof with regard to his claims, the civil party has a broad 'right to proof'. In fact, the civil party can appoint a technical consultant (Article 225 CCP), file acts and documents during the preliminary hearing and before the trial starts (Article 421, paragraph 3 CCP), ask for the admission of documents, witnesses, technical consultants or the questioning of person charged in connected proceedings, ask for the admission, during the phase of the preliminary acts to the trial, of evidence that cannot be delayed (Article 467 CCP), to discuss the admission of the evidence requested by other parties (Article 495, paragraphs 1 and 4 CCP), ask to be examined and, when the request of the civil party examination is filed by another party, to give his consent to such request (Article 503 CCP).

And with regard to attendance at trial, the civil party has the right to:

(1) an attorney with a special power of attorney and in case one is indigent, to obtain the legal aid (Article 98 CCP);
(2) receive the notification of the committal for trial decree, the hearing postponement decree (Article 465 CCP), and acts of appeal (Article 601 CCP);
(3) the *vocatio in iudicium* regularity, i.e., the renovation of void notifications;

286. Article 392(1) CCP: In the course of the preliminary investigation, the public prosecutor and the accused may apply to the judge for the immediate production of evidence.

(4) knowledge of the brief case, before the preliminary hearing starts, thus the civil party has the opportunity to be informed about the investigative acts carried out and the evidence gathered;
(5) ask for seizure in order to obtain guarantees for his claim;
(6) interject in the trial phase. In fact, the civil party can participate in the preliminary question debate (Article 491, paragraph 3 CCP); indicate the facts that he wishes to prove and ask for the admission of evidence (Article 495 CCP) and debate other parties' requests. In the final debate, before the pronunciation of the sentence, the civil party must file a submission which indicates the amount of damages, if damages are being requested (Article 523, paragraph 2 CCP);
(7) appeal against any sentences adverse to his position as far as it concerns the civil claims, while for those criminal statements contained in the sentence, the civil party can urge the public prosecutor to appeal, by filing him a reasoned request (Article 572, paragraph 2 CCP).

§4. THE RULES OF EVIDENCE

I. General Introduction

566. As already explained above, in the Italian criminal system the investigative stage and the trial stage are separated (see *supra*, paragraph 444).

This implies that the preliminary investigations and the preliminary hearing just serve to prepare the trial phase. In fact, the evidence gathered by the judicial police and by the public prosecutor during the preliminary investigations are aimed at giving the latter the instruments to evaluate whether to exercise the criminal action or not, while the evidence collected during the preliminary hearing by the GUP allows the judge to evaluate whether the prosecutor's motion of committal for trial is grounded and the criminal charge is serious.[287]

For this reason, the regulation of evidence during the trial phase is of a crucial importance, because it is on this evidence that an eventual conviction will be based (except for the *incidente probatorio* cases).

Thus, given the importance of the evidence, the entire third book of the 1988 CCP has been dedicated to it.

567. Before the creation of the new CCP, the previous code, which dated back to 1930, was the expression of the authoritarianism of the political regime of that period. In particular, it highlighted the inquisitorial character of the Italian criminal system by giving greater emphasis to the pre-trial phase and almost completely abolishing the participation of the defence counsel in this phase.

With the creation of the new code, the inquisitorial model has been abandoned and the criminal procedure system is now based on the accusatorial model. Therefore, the 1988 Code assigned the trial hearings a central (and, at least in theory, a sole) role of obtaining evidence, thus excluding this activity from the pre-trial investigative phase.

---

287. G. Conso & V. Grevi, *Compendio di procedura penale* 561 (Padova 2006).

This is the reason why the rules of evidence have a central role in the Italian criminal system. Additionally, the rules of evidence assist in the purpose of a trial, specifically to achieve a factual reconstruction as plausible as possible.[288]

II. General Principles

568. The beginning of the third book of the CCP sets forth the general principles of evidence (Articles 187–193 CCP).

569. First, it should be pointed out that not every fact can be proven in a criminal proceeding; thus, the starting point is represented by the individuation of the 'object of proof', i.e., the facts that need to be proven in order to ascertain the truth. Such elements are commonly defined as *thema probandum* (object in dispute) and are expressly provided for by Article 187 CCP, which states that they are those related to:

(1) the criminal charge;
(2) the defendant's punishability;
(3) the determination of the sanction or of the security measure (Article 187, paragraph 1 CCP);
(4) the questions resulting from the constitution of the civil party (Article 187, paragraph 3 CCP); and
(5) the facts from which depend the application of the provisions regulating the trial (Article 187, paragraph 2 CCP).

570. Once the *thema probandum* has been identified, the second point to analyse is the distinction between the 'direct proof' and the 'indirect proof', depending on whether or not the evidence refers immediately to the *thema probandum*. Thus, direct proof is that which concerns directly the fact that must be proven, while the indirect proof concerns another fact from which the judge may trace the fact that must be proven through inductive reasoning.[289] The latter are commonly defined as 'circumstantial evidence' (the so-called *prove indiziarie*), and they are given by clues (the so-called *indizi*) which can be defined as an element that gives just elements instituting the *fumus commissi delicti* and which are capable of becoming real proof.

571. Another distinction may be made between 'critical evidence' (or non-representative evidence) and 'historical evidence' (or representative evidence) depending on whether the fact to be proved is described or immediately reproduced before the judge or, on the contrary, the judge must make a mental inference.

---

288. G. Ubertis, *Prova in generale*, in *Digesto delle discipline penalistiche* 301 (Torino 1995).
289. G. Conso & V. Grevi, *Compendio di procedura penale* 301 (Padova 2006).

A. The Rules of Evidence in the CCP

572. The CCP provides for a wide range of means of proof. It is important to note the distinction made by the Italian system between the means of proof (the so-called *mezzi di prova*) (Articles 194–243 CCP) and the means for researching the proof (*mezzi di ricerca della prova*) (Articles 244–271 CCP).

573. The means of proof (testimony, examination of the parties, confrontations, recognitions, judicial experiments, assessments and documents) offer the judge evidence elements directly utilizable in making his decision, as these means are created during the trial. The means for researching the proof (inspection, search, seizure, phone tapping) do not represent a source of the proof, but a means for acquiring elements which could have relevance for the case.

Hence, the CCP expressly defines and identifies different types of evidence, and this elaboration leads to one important question on which the Italian scholars are currently divided, i.e., whether or not atypical proofs (namely those not provided by the PC) are admissible. On the one hand, some writers believe that the criterion of the freedom of evidence is applied; on the other hand, the opposite trend denies the peremptoriness of the evidence list drawn up by the CCP admitting also atypical means of proof.

The solution adopted by the CCP can be defined as intermediate of such extreme trends. In fact, the CCP considers the peremptoriness list too strict and assigns the judge the task of evaluating, on a case-by-case basis, the admissibility of evidence, as long as the proof is suitable to give knowledge of the facts, and the evidence does not compromise the person's moral freedom. Although such solution is to be preferred, one may be puzzled about the absence of any provision regulating the powers of the judge in the acquisition of the atypical means of proof.[290] In fact, Article 189 CCP states that once the judge has considered the evidence admissible, he has the further task of actually defining the way the proof must be gathered, after having conferred with the parties.

574. The limit of moral freedom is of a crucial importance. In fact, in accordance with Article 189 CCP, no evidence may be gathered whenever it could manipulate one's mind. More specifically, '*it is forbidden to use, even if there is the consent of the person, systems of evidence gathering which may influence one's self-determination capacity or twist one's capacity to remember or evaluate the fact*'.

Hence, the decision of the judge is not based on the type of evidence alone, but the judge must decide whether unspecified evidence may represent a threat to the moral liberty of the person.

290. G. Ubertis, *Prova in generale*, in *Digesto delle discipline penalistiche* 327 (Torino 1995). See also E. Zappalà, *Il principio di tassatività dei mezzi di prova nel processo penale* 98 (Milano 1982) and following; G. Guarneri, *Tassatività dei mezzi di prova*, Riv. Dir. Pen. 787–789 (1980).

B. The Admission of the Evidence

575. In ruling on the admission of evidence, the judge is bound by two limits. First of all, the CCP establishes everything that is both *relevant and not superfluous* to the decisions to be made by the judge can be used as evidence. Moreover, the evidence must not be forbidden by the law (Article 190, paragraph 1 CCP).

In order to verify the relevance of evidence, the judge must consider whether it is pertinent to the *thema probandum* defined in Article 187 (*supra*, paragraph 569); while to establish the non-superfluity of evidence, the judge should consider its utility in the decision-making process.

The judge will decide whether these two requisites have been met before making an order admitting the evidence. As already mentioned, the evidence, in fact, is provided by the parties, and the role of the judge is to ascertain whether it can be admitted on the basis of the two above-mentioned criteria. With the adopting of the accusatorial system, the principle of acquiring evidence ex officio no longer exists. This principle represented the main criterion under the previous Code, which was inquisitorial in character. Although the judge can acquire the evidence ex officio, this is an exception to the rule. Article 507 CCP establishes that ex officio attainment can be resorted to only when the acquisition of the evidence has been terminated (i.e., the evidence proposed by the parties) and only if this is absolutely essential.

Such principles are to be considered as general; thus, they can be applied not only in the trial phase, but also in the preliminary hearing and in the *incidente probatorio.*

576. Any proof that is unlawfully acquired, i.e., in violation of the laws, cannot be used. Such proof has no value at all, cannot become valid, and can be ascertained as invalid by the judge (Article 191 CCP). The laws to which such sanction refers are those concerning both the admission and the gathering of evidence.

It is important to point out that evidence of non-usability can be found also ex officio at any stage of the proceeding (Article 191, paragraph 2 CCP).

Non-usable evidence includes statements made by defendants in connected cases or co-defendants at a trial, which can never be used as evidence, but must be confirmed by other evidence (Article 192 CCP).

C. The Presumptio Innocentiae Rule

577. One of the most fundamental rules in Italian evidentiary law is that an accused person is presumed innocent. This rule has several important consequences.

578. The first one is that the accused is never obliged to prove his innocence, but the defendant has the 'right to proof' (in pursuance of Article 6 of the ECHR and Constitution Article 111, paragraph 3), i.e., the right to obtain the admission of the evidence in his defence against the facts proven through the evidence gathered by the prosecution. The second important consequence is that the accused has the privilege against self-incrimination; thus, no one can compel him to cooperate in an active way in his own condemnation. The third consequence is the right to remain silent. The fourth is that if there is uncertainty about the proof of his guilt, the accused should be given the benefit of the doubt (*in dubio pro reo*). The fifth and final consequence is that the accused is free to organize his defence as he sees fit.

579. The *presumptio innocentiae* rule goes together with a second basic principle, notably that the prosecution is obliged to prove the case against the accused person beyond any reasonable doubt. That is to say, the prosecution service has to prove the existence of all the elements which make up the criminal offence in question.

D. The Judge's Freedom to Decide on the Evidence

580. With regard to the evaluation of proof collected at trial, in Italy the judge is free to rule on the means of proof as long as he clarifies explicitly the grounds for his decision (Article 192 CCP). Such specification serves the purpose of avoiding an arbitrary use of the judge's discretion.

It should be noted that the judge's evaluation concerns only that evidence which has been already legally admitted and gathered, in pursuance of Article 187 CCP.

581. As far as the evaluation of the evidence is concerned, the Italian Code of Civil Procedure reiterates the traditional principle of Italian law, i.e., the judge is free to evaluate, although he or she is obliged to justify his decision. In this respect, it should be recalled that failure to provide written reasoning for a decision is one of the main bases for appeals to the Court of Cassation.

582. In addition to the limits concerning the rationality of the reasoning of the decision, the principle of the freedom of the judge to make a decision is also limited by other legal factors.

III. The Means of Proof

A. Testimony

583. As mentioned above (*supra*, paragraph 573), testimony (*testimonianza*) is a means of proof which offers the judge evidence immediately utilizable for decision purposes. In such case, the evidence is formed directly before the judge and it is not made prior to trial.

584. Testimony is regulated in Articles 194–207 CCP. Article 194 CCP sets out the subject and the limits of the testimony, stating that the witness is to be examined on facts that are within the *thema probandum* and cannot give testimony about the defendant's morality unless his statements refer to specific facts from which it may be possible to make inferences about the defendant's personality and social dangerousness (Article 194, paragraph 1 CCP). The examination can also concern the relationship between the witness and the other parties and circumstances which may be useful in order to evaluate the reliability of the witness. The declaration about the offended person's personality is admitted only when the crime must be evaluated in the light of the offended person's behaviour (Article 194, paragraph 2 CCP). Finally, the witness must be examined on well-defined facts, and he can neither testify on rumours nor express his personal opinions, unless it is impossible to separate them by the fact (Article 194, paragraph 2 CCP).

585. It is worthwhile to consider the difference from indirect testimony, i.e., when the witness refers to other persons' statements. In such case, the judge should – by the request of a party or even ex officio – order the issuer of the statement be called to testify, otherwise the testimony is not usable at trial, unless the examination of the informer is impossible due to death, mental insanity or it is impossible to trace the informer (Article 195, paragraphs 1–3 CCP). Consequently, the CCP prevents the use of testimony given by a person who refuses to declare his source of information. Such provision recalls the one regarding the prohibition to use information coming from confidential informers whose identity the police did not want or could not reveal (Article 203 CCP).

586. Everyone has the capability to testify (Article 196, paragraph 1 CCP), but the CCP provides for some cases of incompatibility, namely the defendant and the co-defendant, persons charged in a connected proceeding, persons civilly liable for damages or the payment of the pecuniary sanction, the judge or the public prosecutor of the criminal proceeding, and the attorney who carried out investigating acts (see Articles 197 and 197*bis* CCP).

587. With regard to the duties of the witness, Article 198 CCP states that he is obliged to appear before the judge and answer truthfully the questions addressed to him. Nevertheless, the witness cannot be obliged to answer questions from which criminal liability may arise (guarantee against self-incrimination).

B. Examination of the Parties

588. Article 208 CCP states that the defendant, civil parties who are not to be heard as witnesses, and persons civilly liable for damages or the payment of the pecuniary sanction can be examined when they make a specific request or they consent (i.e., *esame delle parti*). Thus, the carrying out of such means of proof is conditioned to the parties' will. Once consent is given, the person loses his right to silence, and if the party refuses to answer, such fact is mentioned in the hearing minutes (Article 209, paragraph 2 CCP). Nevertheless, the guarantee against self-incrimination provided by Article 198, paragraph 2 CCP applies.

C. Confrontations, Recognitions and Judicial Experiments

589. Confrontations (*confronti*) are allowed only as to persons already examined or questioned when there is a conflict between their statements with regard to important facts and circumstances (Article 211 CCP). During trial, the judge asks the persons submitted to the confrontation, whether they confirm or would like to modify their statements and invites them to challenge other parties' statements (Article 212, paragraph 2 CCP).

Recognitions (*ricognizioni*) can concern people or objects. Here, the person or the object that must be recognized is placed side by side with at least two other similar persons or objects. If there is reason to believe that the person to be recognized may intimidate the other person, the judge may order that such activity is carried out in a manner which prevents the person being recognized from seeing the recognizer (Article 214, paragraph 2 CCP).

590. With regard to judicial experiments (*esperimenti giudiziali*), these are aimed at verifying whether a fact may have occurred in a certain way by reproducing the situation and by repeating the relevant modalities (Article 218, paragraphs 1–2 CCP).

D. Expert Evaluation

591. The expert evaluation (*perizia*) is allowed when it is deemed necessary to carry out investigative acts or to obtain data or evaluations which require specific artistic, technical or scientific skills (Article 220, paragraph 1 CCP). Once such necessity occurs, the judge is obliged to admit, even ex officio, the expert evaluation.

Such means of proof is forbidden when it is aimed at establishing criminal habitualness or professionalism, criminal inclination, the defendant's personality, and in general his psychic qualities not depending on pathologies (Article 220, paragraph 2 CCP). The court appoints the expert from those enrolled on the appropriate registers or those having the relevant expertise. If the opinion is declared invalid, a new expert is appointed. When the case is particularly complex and opinions on different areas, the court may appoint more than one expert (Article 221 PC).

Once appointed by the court, the expert must take an oath to carry out his duties according to law. The expert then prepares his written report which must be submitted to the court within the established deadline that can be not more than ninety days. If the case is particularly complex, the time period may be extended for thirty days at a time; however, in any event, the term may not exceed six months (Article 227 CCP).

592. Experts must be differentiated from technical consultants (*consulenti tecnici*), who are appointed by the parties or the public prosecutor. Private parties who are indigent are entitled to technical consultants at the State's expense.

The parties may each appoint up to two technical consultants, who work with the expert and may submit to the court reports containing their comments and observations on the matter. Technical consultants may also participate in court-appointed expert's examination and propose additional investigations.

If the technical consultant is nominated after the investigation, they may review the report of the court-appointed expert, and ask the court to examine the person, place or things which was the subject of the investigation. However, the appointment of technical consultants and the conduct of their business cannot delay the execution of the report and the completion of other proceedings (Article 230 CCP).

E. Documental Evidence

593. The starting point in addressing documental evidence (*prova documentale*) is the fundamental distinction between judiciary deeds and other documents. The former are those acts created within the trial and they represent what happened during it, such as the hearing minutes, while the latter, to which the documental evidence regulations apply, are those created outside the proceeding and that the parties wish to introduce.

594. The CCP considers as a document a wide range of items including writings or any other document which represents facts, persons or objects by means of photography, cinematography, phonography or any other instrument (Article 234, paragraph 1 CCP).

595. As already seen with regards to testimony, also in case of documental evidence, the law prohibits the gathering of documents which contain rumours or concern the parties' (also witnesses', experts', and technical consultants' morality (Article 234, paragraph 3 CCP). However, an exception to this rule is given in Article 236 CCP which states that documents concerning the defendant or the offended person's personality (e.g., criminal records, social service or security offices documents or sentences) can be gathered when the fact must be evaluated in the light of such parties' behaviour or moral aptitude (Article 236, paragraph 1 CCP). The law always allows the gathering of documents and electronic data held abroad, including those which are not available to the public, with the consent, in the latter case, of the lawful owner (Article 234*bis* CCP, recently introduced by means of Article 2 Legislative Decree No. 7 of 18 February 2015).[291]

596. Anonymous documents cannot be accepted except where they represent the *corpus delicti* or they come from the defendant (Article 240 CCP). In fact, documents constituting the *corpus delicti* or coming from the defendant must always be admitted (Articles 235 and 237 CCP).

291. Converted into Law No. 43 of 17 Apr. 2015.

IV. Obtaining the Means of Proof

A. *Inspections and Searches*

597. The CCP starts the description of the means for the proof by covering two unrepeatable instruments: inspections and searches.

598. Inspection (*ispezioni*, from the Latin *inspicere*) is aimed at ascertaining the traces or other effects of the crime on persons, places and objects, including computer and telecommunication systems (Article 244 CCP). However, searches (*perquisizione* from the Latin *perspicere*) seek to find the *corpus delicti* (i.e., proof that a crime has occurred) or other items pertinent to the crime in order to have a basis for arresting a suspect (Article 247 CCP). In practice, there is a very fine line between inspections and searches.

599. The CCP dedicates different disciplines for the inspection of persons (Article 245 CCP) and to the inspection of places and objects (Article 246 CCP).

In particular, it provides certain guarantees in both cases. With regard to the first, the Code states that during the personal inspection, the tested person has the right to be assisted by a person he trusts. Moreover, the personal inspection must be carried out respecting the person's dignity and decency (Article 245, paragraph 2 CCP). In the case of inspection of places and objects, the person who is in possession of them must receive an order regarding the inspection.

600. Many guarantees are recognized also in the cases of searches (*perquisizioni*), which must be ordered by means of a reasoned decision (Article 247, paragraph 2 CCP). Additionally, the CCP states that it is possible to make searches also on persons who are present or who arrive in the place where the search is underway when the judge believes that they may hide the *corpus delicti* or other items pertinent to the crime (Article 250 CCP). The law also provides for specific time limits when the search is performed on a person's domicile (Article 251 CCP). When there is reason to believe that data, information, or software related to the offence is contained on a computer or computer system, even if protected by a password or other security measure, the search must be performed in a manner and using the technical measure necessary so as to ensure the preservation of the original data and to prevent tampering (Article 247, paragraph 1*bis* CCP)

601. What is found by means of the search may be subject to seizure (Article 252 CCP).

B. *Seizure*

602. First, it is worth distinguishing seizure (*sequestro*) as a means of gathering proof from seizure with security purposes.

The seizure regulated in the third book regards only the *corpus delicti* or other items pertinent to the crime which are deemed necessary in order to ascertain the fact (Article 253, paragraph 1 CCP). Subsequently, the same article provides a definition of *corpus delicti* (see *supra,* paragraph 598) stating that it is those objects on which or by means of which the crime has been carried out and the objects which are the product, profit or price of the crime (Article 253, paragraph 2 CCP).

The CCP is very detailed with respect to certain situations such as the seizure of correspondence and electronic communications (Article 254 CCP) and seizure involving telecommunications and Internet service providers (Article 254*bis* CCP) and banks (Article 255 CCP).

603. Once the seizure decree is issued, the interested person can also ask for its re-examination (Article 257 CCP).

604. It is important to point out that the seizure expires when there are no longer reasons justifying it (Article 262, paragraph 1 CCP), or the case is no longer subject to impugnation (Article 262, paragraph 4 CCP), and the person(s) holding the rights to the item may request the judge order restitution of the items, unless forfeiture must be ordered. In the case of seized monies, if no claim is made within five years after the sentence is no longer subject to appeal, then the money becomes the property of the State (Article 262, paragraph 3*bis* CCP, as inserted by Article 2(612) of Law No. 244 of 24 December 2007).

605. With specific regards to the seizure of assets of organized crime, Italy has developed a complex confiscation system. The Italian system is the result of numerous legislative interventions taking place over the last fifty years. More precisely, with the law No. 1423 of 27 December 1956 the legislator introduced preventive measures of imprisonment of dangerous people for safety and public morality. Subsequently, was enacted Law No. 575 of 31 May 1965, concerning *Provisions against Mafia*, which introduced an explicit reference to members of associations based on the mafia structure and imposed the application of preventive measures to the individuals, and their properties, suspected of belonging to mafia, camorra organizations, or to other local illegal associations. More recently, the Italian legislation against mafia-type associations was codified by Legislative Decree No. 159 of 6 September 2011 in the '*Code of Anti-Mafia Laws and Preventative Measures as well as New Provisions in Anti-Mafia Documentation, in Accordance with Articles 1 and 2 of Law No. 136 of August 13, 2010*' (so-called Anti-Mafia Code). By means of these provisions Italy improved its strategy in order to fight deeply organized crime and to attack its financial bases.

As part of its anti-mafia efforts,[292] Italy has created the National Agency for the Administration and the Destination of Assets Seized and Confiscated from Organized Crime *(L'Agenzia Nazionale per l'amministrazione e la destinazione dei beni sequestrati e confiscati alla criminalità organizzata).*[293] The Agency was

---

292. According to Europol, Italy is one of five hubs of organized crime in Europe and home to such criminal networks as the *Camorra, Ndrangheta* and *Sacra Corona Unit.* See http://www.europarl.europa.eu/document/activities/cont/ 201210/20121015ATT53636/20121015ATT53636EN.pdf (Accessed in June 2015).
293. www.benisequestraticonfiscati.it (Accessed in June 2015).

established by Decree Law No. 4 of 4 February 2010, converted into Law No. 50 of 31 March 2010; today the Agency's tasks are defined in the so-called Anti-Mafia Code. Primarily based in Reggio Calabria, with offices in Rome, Naples, Palermo, and Milan, the Agency is a stand-alone legal entity with organizational and financial autonomy and placed under the supervision of the Minister of the Interior.

Among other things, the Agency is responsible for managing the seizure and confiscating of assets resulting from organized crime as allowed by the Italian Antimafia law (Law No. 575 of 31 May 1965, now incorporated into the Anti-Mafia Code),[294] as well as the eventual allocating and use of any confiscated property. In particular, the Anti-Mafia Code provides for the seizure and confiscation of assets for which no legitimate provenance has been demonstrated, and which are found to be at the direct or indirect disposal of someone suspected of belonging to a Mafia-style organization. These measures, aimed at deterring persons deemed socially dangerous from committing crimes, are, therefore, applied independently of the existence of a previous crime.

C. Phone Tapping and Interceptions

606. Phone tapping and interception (*intercettazioni telefoniche*) regulations must be studied in light of Article 15 of the Italian Constitution which states the general principle of freedom and secrecy of communications. The latter are defined as inviolable, and they may be infringed only by means of a motivated act issued by a judge with the guarantees provided by the law.

Such means of proof can only be admitted with regard to certain specific offences specifically listed in Article 266 CCP which refers to the most serious crimes, such as those concerning drugs, weapons, contraband and usury.

607. The public prosecutor must file the interception request before the judge for the preliminary hearing (GUP), who authorizes it by means of a reasoned decision only where there are serious clues about the commission of a crime, and the interception is definitely necessary to carry on the investigation (Article 267, paragraph 1 CCP).

The public prosecutor can also act on his own initiative, issuing himself the interception decree in case of urgency, provided that he informs the judge within the next twenty-four hours. The latter must validate the public prosecutor's decree within forty-eight hours starting from the time the decree has been issued. If the decree is not validated by the judge, the interception operations must be immediately stopped and the results achieved to that point are not usable in the proceeding (Article 267, paragraph 2 CCP).

With regard to the execution of interception operations, the CCP states that they must be carried out by using equipments installed at the public prosecutor's office (*Procura della Repubblica*), and there must be a complete transcription of the conversation intercepted (Article 267, paragraphs 3 and 8 CCP).

---

294. Law No. 575 of 31 May 1965, as amended by Legislative Decree No. 159 of 6 Sep. 2011.

Part III. Execution of Sanctions

Chapter 1. Sources of Penitentiary Law and Nature of Regulations

608. The organization of the Italian penitentiary system is described *supra*, paragraphs 56–59. Additionally, it should be reiterated that the sources of penitentiary law find their basis in Article 27 of the Constitution, according to which punishment cannot consist in treatment contrary to human dignity and must aim at rehabilitating the condemned.

The discipline of the Italian penitentiary system is, therefore, in line with those international conventions on the topic.

The principle just enunciated inspires the ordinary discipline of the prison regime, which is contained, first of all, in Articles 648 et seq. of the CCP.

One of the fundamental aspects of these provisions is that all of the enforcement phases of the penalty are carried out under the jurisdiction of the enforcement (or Surveillance) judge and the Surveillance Court, which are described in point 6b of section II of the general introduction above.

It is worth underlining that the mentioned provisions prevent the implementation of the penalty from being carried out merely in an administrative environment, without the control of an independent judge. Consequently, even the detainee condemned to a final sentence has the possibility to go before a court to ask for enforcement of their rights and first, the right to a treatment which corresponds to the principles set forth in Article 27 of the Constitution.

609. Furthermore, the discipline of the penitentiary system is contained in Law No. 354 of 26 July 1975, in which Article 1 explicitly recalls the tenor of Article 27 of the Constitution, which sets forth the principles on which the prison system must be based.

The penitentiary treatment must conform to the humanity of and must insure respect of the dignity of the person.

The treatment must be characterized by absolute impartiality, without discrimination with respect to nationality, race and economic or social conditions, political opinions or religious beliefs.

In the institutions, there must be maintained order and the discipline. There must be put into place a re-educative treatment that prepares, also by means of contact with the outside world, the prisoners and the internees for reinsertion into society.

610. Along with the ordinary disposition, particular attention should be given to those regulations – which ascribe penitentiary system rules and those measures which deprive or limit liberty – approved by Presidential Decree No. 230 of 30 June 2000.

The first disposition of the regulations establishes that the treatment of the detainees must sustain their humane, cultural and professional interests, and promote the modification of their conditions and personal attitude, as well as family and social relations that impede a constructive participation in society.

Chapter 2. The Prison System

§1. Aspects of Living Conditions

611. The general principle is that the detainees and the internees are assured a balanced life. Nevertheless, the principle of balance may be derogated from, also significantly, in the presence of particularly dangerous situations.

First, there is provided a particular surveillance regime for a period of not more than six months, extendable from time to time every three months, for those who compromise the security of the penal institutions, or behave in a violent or threatening manner with the other detainees.

The particular surveillance regime – established by the penitentiary administration and subject to review by the Surveillance Court – implies a system of restricting the rights of the detained, that however may not regard food, literature, the practice of rites, the stay in the open for at least two hours a day, visits with defence counsel, and those with close family.

612. An ulterior regime – detention in an *elevato indice di vigilanza* (EIV) or high surveillance unit – is provided, for motives of public order and security, for those subjects who have committed particularly dangerous crimes and, in particular, for those who participate in terrorist or mafia associations (Article 41*bis* of Law No. 354 of 26 July 1975). (See also *supra,* paragraph 558.) The regime in which Article 41*bis* of Law No. 354 of 26 July 1975 is applied by decree of the Minister of Justice and subject to claims to the Surveillance Court.

In these cases, it is possible to suspend the rules that govern prison treatment, with the reduction, among others things of the possibility to have visits with family and the conditions in which the visits can be carried out, as well as with the reduction of rapport with other detainees, communication with the outside world, and stay in the open. The harshness of the prison regime provided for the participants of terrorist and mafia associations poses a conflict of that regime with the principles of Article 27 of the Constitution.

613. In addition, when confined, the prisoner must be given a reasonable amount of space,[295,296] and the situation must be suitable in light of the prisoner's physical

---

295. See *Torreggiani and Others v. Italy* (Nos 43517/09, 46882/09, 55400/09, 57875/09, 61535/09, 35315/10 and 37818/10), ECtHR judgment of 8 Jan. 2013, http://hudoc.echr.coe.int/sites/eng/pages/search.aspx?i=001-115860#{'itemid':[' 001-115860']} (Accessed 15 Jun. 2013). The Court awarded the seven applicants a total of EUR 100,000 and gave Italy one year to resolve its problem of prison overcrowding and to implement a procedure for providing redress to victims after finding the petitioners' rights under Art. 3 (prohibition of torture and inhumane or degrading treatment) of the European Convention on Human Rights because they were being given only 3 square metres of personal space. On 27 Jun. 2013, the Grand Chamber rejected Italy's appeal against the January provisional sentence.).

296. See *Sulejmanovic v. Italy,* ECtHR judgment of 26 Jul. 2009. In *Sulejmanovic*, for over two and a half months, the applicant had to share a 16.2 square metres cell at the Rebibbia prison in Rome with five other detainees (thus the space available to each detainee was only 2.7 square metres. The Court found the applicant had been subjected to inhuman or degrading treatment by being forced to live in an excessively confined space, much smaller that the minimum cell size (7 square metres)

condition[297] so as to not cause the offender to suffer inhuman and degrading treatment in violation of Article 3 of the ECHR.

Inmates with dependent children are housed in sections which can accommodate for children up to 3 years of age. As of 31 December 2013, there were forty detainees with dependent children, almost all with one child, and seventeen pregnant detainees. There were seventeen nurseries operating as of this date.[298]

In terms of prisoner protest, the most common form is hunger strike (7,851 cases in 2013), followed by refusal of food and therapies (1,548 cases) and damage to objects (736 cases).

§2. Visits, Correspondence, Telephone Calls, Information and Media

614. The detainees and the internees are allowed to have visits and correspond with spouse and other persons, also to prepare judicial acts. The visits are carried out in a location under the visual, but not the auditory, control of prison personnel, with particular favour given to visits with family.

615. The penitentiary administration must make available to the detainees and the internees the stationary supplies necessary for correspondence.

616. It is also possible to authorize telephone privileges with family, and in particular cases, with third parties.

617. With regard to correspondence, overall it can be exchanged without limitation. Nevertheless, for investigative or security reasons, the Surveillance Magistrate may restrict a detainee's correspondence for a period of not more than six months, extendable every three months for an additional three-month period. Among these limitations, a particular mention should be made to the so-called *visto*

---

recommended by the European Committee for the Prevention of Torture and Inhuman or Degrading Treatment or Punishment. The Court further noted this measurement was just a guideline, and that it could not provide the exact and definitive measure of the personal space which should be granted to each detainee pursuant to the Convention, as this depends on several factors, such as the length of the deprivation of liberty, the possibilities of access to outside exercise or the mental and physical conditions of the detainee.

297. See *Scoppola v. Italy*, ECtHR judgment of 10 Jun. 2008. *Scoppola* concerned degrading treatment suffered by the applicant, a life prisoner, due to the conditions of his of detention, which were not appropriate to his state of health. The applicant, who was confined to a wheelchair and suffered from several diseases, requested to be transferred to a more suitable prison. Based on the medical evidence, the Rome court responsible for the execution of sentences granted the applicant detention at home, but because applicant did not have lodging adapted to his needs, the decision was set aside. In December 2006, the competent bodies of the Ministry of Justice ordered the applicant's transfer to a prison with appropriate facilities for disabled inmates; however, the transfer did not take place until eight months later. The European Court found Italy in violation of Art. 3 of the ECHR the state by failing to transfer the applicant timely to a better equipped facility.

298. *Anno 2013: I detenuti nelle carceri italiane* (Year 2013: Inmates in Italian Prisons), Statistical Report by *Ministero della Giustizia Dipartimento Amministrazione Penitenziaria* (Ministry of Justice, Department of Prison Administration), http://www.istat.it/it/archivio/153369 (Accessed June 2015).

di controllo, in which the correspondence must be under the control of the judicial authority or by delegation of the same to the control of the director of the penal institution.

618. Finally, the detainees are authorized to receive newspapers, periodicals and books freely sold on the market, as well as to make use of other means of information.

619. For what concerns instruction, it is provided that in the penal institutions, the cultural and professional formation is addressed by the organization of obligatory education classes and professional training courses, according to the orientation in force and with the aid of methods adequate to the conditions of the subject.

§3. Prison Labour, Practice of Religious Rites, and Cultural, Recreational, and Sporting Activities

620. In the penal institutions, there is the preference that the detainees be assigned to work, and that they participate in professional formation courses.

Work is obligatory, may not have a disturbing character and must be remunerated. The remuneration is established with relation to the quality and quantity of the work, and, in any case, cannot be less than two-thirds of the economic treatment provided by the collective labour contracts. To this end, it is provided that a special commission should be instituted, which establishes the economic treatment of the detainees.

However, as of 2013, only 23.3% of the inmates have the opportunity to work. Forty years ago, when the cost of labour was lower, the rate was approximately 50%. What is more, there are significant regional differences. For instance, in Veneto approximately half of the detainees work outside the Prison Administration.[299]

621. The detainees must be insured free liberty to profess their religious faith and to participate in rites.

In the institutions, the celebration of Catholic rites is assured, and in every one there is attached at least a chapel.

For those practising a religion other than Catholicism, they have the right to receive, upon request, the assistance of a cleric of their respective religion and to participate in its rites.

622. Finally, the institutions must encourage and organize cultural, sportive and recreational activities, and any other activity to promote the re-education of the personality of the detainees.

---

299. *Anno 2013: I detenuti nelle carceri italiane* (Year 2013: Inmates in Italian Prisons), Statistical Report by *Ministero della Giustizia Dipartimento Amministrazione Penitenziaria* (Ministry of Justice, Department of Prison Administration), http://www.istat.it/it/archivio/153369 (Accessed in June 2015).

In 2012/2013, there were 991 scholastic classes offered. A total of 24.7% of the prison population frequented these courses. Also, 318 vocational courses were offered during this time.[300]

§4. Leave from Prison

623. The penitentiary regulations provide four types of leave from the penal institution.

The first hypothesis is that of a labour assignment outside the institute, which may be arranged after the expiration of at least one-third of the penalty and, however, not more than five years on measure of the penitentiary administration, subject to the approval of the Surveillance Magistrate.

The second hypothesis is to allow admission of the detainee to the outside in order to assist with their children who are less than 10 years in age. This is a measure which benefits primarily the mother, and if she is dead or this is impossible, the father. The Surveillance Magistrate may also authorize temporary leave in the case of imminent life threat of cohabitating family members and on exception for particularly serious events.

624. Denial of an application for leave may be appealed, as stated before, to the Surveillance Court.

625. To those prisoners that have maintained regular behaviour and are not considered dangerous to society, the Surveillance Magistrate, having heard from the director of the institute, may grant periods of leave not more than every fourteen days to allow the cultivation of affective or cultural interests or work. The duration of the leave may not exceed forty-five days in one year of expiation.

§5. Disciplinary Measures

626. In the prison environment, the detainees are subject to a disciplinary regime, in order to stimulate a sense of responsibility and self-control.

In the same prospective, there is also provided a system of remuneration that provides for the granting of benefits in the prison life, such as the admission to a fixed work and fixed assignment.

627. The disciplinary system is based on the principle of legality and, as a consequence, the detainees may not be punished for a fact that is not expressly covered

300. *Anno 2013: I detenuti nelle carceri italiane* (Year 2013: Inmates in Italian Prisons), Statistical Report by *Ministero della Giustizia Dipartimento Amministrazione Penitenziaria* (Ministry of Justice, Department of Prison Administration) http://www.istat.it/it/archivio/153369 (Accessed in June 2015).

as an infraction in the penitentiary rules. The sanctions must be inflicted with motivated action or through a previous challenge, with the possibility of the detainee to express their justification.

628. The disciplinary sanctions range from the isolation during a stay in open air to the exclusion of activities. Lighter violations are decided by the director of the penal institution and, in the case of serious violations, by a disciplinary committee.

However, use of physical force against the detainees is never allowed, except when indispensable to prevent or impede acts of violence, to impede escape attempts, or to overcome resistance also passive, to the execution of given orders.

Chapter 3. Forms of Alternative Execution of the Prison Sentence

629. To relieve the congestion of the penal institutions, which as a rule are overcrowded, and for the purpose of promoting the rehabilitation of those prisoners with a definitive sentence, Italian law provides certain measures alternative to detention.

First, if the prison term inflicted does not exceed three years or the penalty still to serve is inferior to three years, it is possible to assign the convict to probation with social services for a period equal to the penalty still to serve. The trial implies that social services control the conduct of the subject, help to overcome the difficulty of adapting to life in society, and refer periodically to the Surveillance Magistrate on the behaviour of the subject.

If the results of the trial period are positive, the prison sentence and every penal effect are extinguished.

630. As explained *supra,* paragraph 364, another alternative measure to incarceration is house arrest (*detenzione domiciliare*). This alternative is available to those over 70 years of age, regardless of the duration of the prison sentence, so long as the conviction does not refer to particularly dangerous crimes or there are no subjective situations, such as the offender being a habitual offender or professional criminal (contract killer), that indicate a particular danger.

For those who are under 70 years of age, house arrest may be available for a penalty of not more than four years, also if it constitutes a residual part of a greater penalty, when there are particular health or family conditions.

House arrest is revoked by the Surveillance Court when the behaviour of the subject appears incompatible with the prosecution of the measure.

631. Particular measures alternative to detention are also provided for those affected by AIDS or serious immune deficiencies. See *supra,* paragraphs 368–369.

632. The regime of semi-liberty is also an alternative to incarceration and involves allowing the convicted person to spend part of the day outside the institution to participate in work or education activities, or endeavours useful for reinsertion into society.

633. The regime of semi-liberty may be granted only after the expiation of the minimum prison penalty, variable in relation to the type of crime, and only if there are conditions for a gradual reinsertion of the subject into society. See *supra,* paragraph 365.

Chapter 4. Early and Conditional Release

634. While the hypotheses examined to this point constitute an alternative form of expiation of conviction, the focus now turns to early and conditional release.

635. When the person condemned to imprisonment has proven rehabilitation through participation in re-education, he is granted recognition for this participation; and for the purpose of a more effective reinsertion into society, there is a subtraction of forty-five days for every single semester of the penalty. To this end, the period passed in the state of protective custody or house arrest is also taken into consideration. Therefore, the detainee is released in advance with respect to the expiration of the penalty, calculating the sum of the various subtractions which have matured over time.

636. The conditional release, however, consists of an anticipated suspension of the expiration of the penalty, subject to revocation in case of illegal conduct.

In particular, a person condemned to imprisonment, who during the term of execution of the penalty, has maintained suitable behaviour may be eligible for conditional liberty, if he has served at least thirty months and at least half of the penalty inflicted, so long as the remainder of the penalty is not more than five years.

The convict condemned to life imprisonment may be eligible for conditional liberty when he has served at least twenty-six years of the penalty.

Chapter 5. Revision of Sentences

§1. Sentences Subject to Revision and Cases of Revision

637. With regard to the sentences no longer susceptible to impugnation, i.e., the subject of a final judgment, under certain conditions, it is possible to request a revision of the sentence.

Revision is allowable only with respect to sentences of conviction or bargained sentences. The fact that the penalty has already been carried out or is extinct is not an impediment to revision.

638. According to Article 630 CCP, revision may be requested:

(1) if the facts on which the sentence or the penal decree of conviction are founded cannot be reconciled with those established in another irrevocable criminal sentence issued by an ordinary or special judge;
(2) if the sentence or conviction has considered an offence charged to the accused as a result of a subsequently revoked civil or administrative sentence which involved one of the prejudicial questions provided in Article 3 CCP[301] or Article 479 CCP;[302]
(3) if after the conviction, new proof is discovered or arises that – alone or with that which has already been evaluated – demonstrates the convicted needs to be acquitted under the law of Article 631 CCP;
(4) if it is demonstrated that the conviction was pronounced as a consequence of a falsity in the acts or in the justice or another fact provided by the law on the crime.

For revision to be possible, the law requires the elements demonstrate, if ascertained, that the conviction should be absolved.

---

301. Article 3 CCP states:

> (1) When the decision depends on the resolution of a dispute regarding family status or citizenship, if the matter is serious and a civil action is already in progress, the court may stay the trial until the judgment on the matter is issued; (2) The suspension involves a matter being appealed to the Court of Cassation; (3) The suspension of the process does not prevent the adoption of urgent measures urgent; and (4) The civil court's irrevocable decision which has considered a question of family status or citizenship has a res judicata effect on the criminal proceedings.

302. Article 479 provides:

> (1) Subject to the provisions of Art. 3, where the decision on the existence of the crime depends on the resolution of a particularly complex civil or administrative dispute, which is already in process, the court may suspend the trial until the pending matter is resolved so long as the law does not place restrictions on the proof of the issue in controversy. (2) The suspension is prepared by order, against which can be appealed to the Supreme Court. The appeal does not have suspensive effect. (3) If the civil or administrative proceedings are not concluded within one year, the court, also ex officio, may revoke the suspension order.

However, it should be noticed that recently, the Italian Constitutional Court declared Article 630 CCP unconstitutional, insofar as the article does not provide for revision of a sentence or decision in order to achieve the reopening of the case where this is necessary, pursuant to Article 46, paragraph 1 of the ECHR in order to comply with a final ruling of the European Court of Human Rights.[303]

§2. Legitimate Subjects and the Form of the Request

639. The request for revision of conviction may be sought by the convicted or one of his close relatives, or, if the convicted is deceased, his heirs or next of kin, or the Prosecutor General of the Court of Appeal in the district in which the sentence of conviction was pronounced (Article 632 CCP).

The revision request is proposed personally or by means of a special power of attorney. It must contain specific indications of the reasons of the justifying evidence and must be presented, together with the required acts and documents, in the clerk's office of the competent Court of Appeal (Article 633 CCP).

§3. Procedure, Suspension of the Execution and Granting of the Request

640. If there are no indications of inadmissibility, the President of the Court of Appeal issues a decree of citation for a hearing *in camera di consiglio*. The proceeding is carried out under the ordinary applicable rules and limited to the reasons invocated in the revision request.

At any time, the Court of Appeal can arrange by order the suspension of the execution of the penalty, eventually ordering alternative coercive measures such as the obligation of presentation to the judicial police, the prohibition from or the obligation to stay in a place and house arrest.

If the revision request is granted, the judge may revoke the sentence or conviction and pronounce the acquittal indicating the cause for the disposition.

The judge cannot pronounce the acquittal exclusively on the basis of a different valuation of the proof assumed in the preceding trial.

When a request for revision is outside the provisions of Articles 629 and 630 CCP, does not comply with Articles 631, 632, 633, and 641, the Court of Appeals may order the individual who brought the request to pay a fine of EUR 258–EUR 2065. The order is served on the person making the request, who may appeal to the Court of Cassation, which then refers the issue to another Court of Appeal (Article 634 CCP).

303. Constitutional Court Decision No. 113 of 4 Apr. 2011.

Selected Bibliography

§1. LEGISLATION

ITALIAN PENAL CODE, Royal Decree No. 1398 of 19 October 1930.
ITALIAN CIVIL CODE, Royal Decree No. 262 of 16 March 1942.
CONSTITUTION OF THE ITALIAN REPUBLIC, entered in force on 1 January 1948.
ITALIAN CODE OF CRIMINAL PROCEDURE, Presidential Decree No. 447 of 22 September 1988.

§2. CASES

Constitutional Court Decision, No. 190 of 1970.
Constitutional Court Decision, No. 146 of 19 June 1975.
Court of Cassation Decision of 29 April 1977, in *Mass. Dec. Pen.*, 1977, No. 135.724 and 135.725.
Decision of the European Court of Human Rights, *Ireland v. United Kingdom* 5310/71 [1978] (18 January 1978).
Court of Cassation (Second Section) Decision No. 7362 of 2 February 1978 (deposited 10 June 1978) in *Cass. Pen. Mass. Ann.*, 1140.
Constitutional Court Decision No. 177 of 1980, in *Giur. Cost.*, 1980, I, 1548.
Court of Cassation Decision of 10 June 1982, in *Mass. Pen.*, 1983, 882.
Court of Cassation Decision of 19 November 1982, Kitzeler, CED 157312.
Court of Cassation Decision of 9 February 1987, Graziani, CED 175260, in *Foro It.*, 1987, II, 409.
Constitutional Court Decision No. 364 of 24 March 1988 in *Giur. It.*, 1988, I, 1, 1076.
Court of Cassation Decision of 1 June 1989 (In re: *Caveduri*), CED 183083, *Giust. Pen.*, 1991, II, 214.
Court of Cassation Decision of 27 April 1989 (In re: *Calvano*).
Court of Cassation Decision of 27 September 1989, Fera, CED 182915.
Court of Cassation Decision of 23 March 1990 (In re: *Lavia*).
Constitutional Court Decision No. 88 of 1991.
Court of Cassation Decision of 20 December 1989, Pistoia, CED 184044, in *Riv. Pen.*, 1991, 197.
Court of Cassation Decision of 30 April 1990, in *Riv. Pen.*, 1991, 162.

Court of Cassation (Fifth Section) Decision No. 781 of 30 July 1991 (deposited 27 August 1991).
Court of Cassation Decision, United Sections, 18th June 1991 (deposited 24 July 1991.
Court of Cassation Decision of 6 December 1990, in *Foro it.*, 1992, II, 36.
Court of Cassation Decision of 28 February 1992 (In re: *Scialpi*).
Court of Cassation (sitting in united session) Decision No. 11227 of 1992.
Constitutional Court Decision No. 111 of 1993.
Court of Cassation Decision of 22 October 1993 (In re: *Galatolo*).
Court of Cassation Decision of 27 February 1993, in *Riv. Pen.*, 1994, 52.
Constitutional Court Decision No. 77 of 10 March 1994.
Constitutional Court Decision No. 241 of 1994.
Court of Cassation (First Section) Decision of 4 May 1994 (deposited 27 May 1994).
Court of Cassation Decision of 27 February 1995 (In re: *Gherrino*) in *Cass. Pen.* 1997, 56.
Court of Cassation Decision No. 4636 of 27 April 1995.
Court of Cassation Decision of 8 March 1995.
Court of Cassation Decision of 17 March 1995 (In re: *Papagni*).
Court of Cassation Decision of 8 November 1995 (In re: *Piccolo*).
Court of Cassation Decision of 30 July 1996, in *Giur. It.*, 1997, II, 584.
Court of Cassation (Second Section) Decision No. 2655 of 8 April 1997 (deposited 2 September 1997).
Court of Cassation Decision of 1 April 1998.
Court of Cassation Decision of 7 June 2000, in *Riv. Pen.*, 2000, 1140.
Court of Cassation (Sixth Section) Decision No. 6587 of 1 March 2000 (deposited 2 June 2000).
Court of Cassation Decision of 5 December 2003, CED 228424.
Court of Cassation (First Section) Decision No. 755 of 14 November 2002 (deposited 11 January 2003).
Court of Cassation (sitting in united session) Decision No. 9163 of 8 March 2005.
Court of Cassation Decision No. 16761 of 3 May 2010.

§3. Journals

Delogu, T. 'La responsabilità penale dell'agente provocatore'. *STSA* (1938): 19, 34.
Guarneri, G. 'Tassatività dei mezzi di prova'. *Riv. Dir. Pen.* (1980): 787–789.
Fiandaca, G. 'Principio di colpevolezza e ignoranza scusabile della legge penale: "prima lettura" della sentenza n. 364/88'. *Foro it.*, I (1988): 1385.
Morselli, E. 'Il tentativo'. *Giust. Pen.*, II (1988): 40.
Petrone, M. 'Reato abituale'. *Nuov. Dig. It.*, XIV (1967): 941.

§4. BOOKS

Antolisei, F. *Manuale di diritto penale. Parte generale*. Milano, 2006.

Battaglini, G. & Grifo. 'Imputabilità'. *Nov. Dig. Ital.*, VIII (1962): 451.

Califano. *L'agente provocatore*. Milano, 1956.

Caraccioli, I. *Il tentativo nei delitti omissivi*. Milano, 1975.

Conso, G. & V. Grevi. *Compendio di procedura penale*. Padova, 2006.

Cordero, F. *Procedura Penale*. Milano, 2006.

Crespi, A. 'Imputabilità (diritto penale)'. In *Enciclopedia del diritto*, XX. Milano, 1970.

Di Amato, A. *Diritto Penale dell'Impresa*. 6th edn. Milano, 2006.

Di Amato, A. Italian Law on Business Crime. London, 2001.

Di Amato, A. *Trattato di Diritto Penale dell'Imprese*. Padova, 1991–2007.

Di Chiara, G. entry 'Parte Civile'. *Digesto delle discipline penalistiche*. Torino, 1995.

Fiandaca, G. & E. Musco. *Diritto penale parte generale*. 3rd edn. Bologna, 1995.

Gallo, M. *Lineamenti di una teoria sul concorso di persone nel reato*. Milano, 1957.

Garofoli, R. *Manuale di diritto penale, Parte generale*. 3rd edn. Milano, 2006.

Latagliata, A.R. *I principi del concorso di persone nel reato*. Napoli, 1964.

Maezger, E. *Diritto Penale*. Padova, 1935.

Magliaro, A. *Principi di diritto penale. Parte generale*. Milano, 1998.

Mantovani, F. *Diritto penale*. Padova, 2007.

Marinucci, G. & E. Dolcini. *Manuale di diritto penale. Parte generale*. Milano, 2006.

Petrocelli, G. *Il delitto tentato*. Padova: Studi, 1966.

Riccio, G. & G. Spangher. *La Procedura Penale*. Napoli, 2002.

Romano, M. & G. Grasso. *Commentario sistematico del codice penale*, II. Milano, 2005.

Ubertis, G. 'Prova in generale'. In *Digesto delle discipline penalistiche*. Torino, 1995.

Vannini, O. *Il problema giuridico del tentativo*. Milano, 1950.

Zappalà, E. *Il principio di tassatività dei mezzi di prova nel processo penale*. Milano, 1982.

Selected Bibliography

Index

The numbers here refer to paragraph numbers.

Index

Index

Index

www.ingramcontent.com/pod-product-compliance
Lightning Source LLC
Chambersburg PA
CBHW071437230926
51846CB00001B/264
* 9 7 8 9 0 4 1 1 6 9 4 4 0 *